Intermediality

THE EDGE: CRITICAL STUDIES IN EDUCATIONAL THEORY

Series Editors   Joe L. Kincheloe, Peter McLaren, and Shirley Steinberg

Intermediality: The Teachers' Handbook of Critical Media Literacy
edited by Ladislaus M. Semali and Ann Watts Pailliotet

Power/Knowledge/Pedagogy: The Meaning of Democratic Education in Unsettling Times
edited by Dennis Carlson and Michael W. Apple

The Misteaching of Academic Discourses: The Politics of Language in the Classroom
Lilia I. Bartolomé

Teachers as Cultural Workers: Letters to Those Who Dare to Teach
Paulo Freire

Revolutionary Multiculturalism: Pedagogies of Dissent for the New Millennium
Peter McLaren

Kinderculture: The Corporate Construction of Childhood
edited by Shirley Steinberg and Joe L. Kincheloe

Pedagogy and the Politics of Hope: Theory, Culture, and Schooling (A Critical Reader)
Henry A. Giroux

Literacies of Power: What Americans Are Not Allowed to Know
Donaldo Macedo

FORTHCOMING

Discourse Wars in Gotham-West: A Latino Immigrant Urban Tale of Resistance and Agency
Marc Pruyn

Everyday Knowledge and Uncommon Truths: Women of the Academy
edited by Linda K. Christian-Smith and Kristine S. Kellor

Presence of Mind: Education and the Politics of Deception
Pepi Leistyna

Education and the American Future
Stanley Aronowitz

Intermediality

The Teachers' Handbook
of Critical Media Literacy

edited by

Ladislaus M. Semali
Pennsylvania State University

Ann Watts Pailliotet
Whitman College

Westview Press
A Member of the Perseus Books Group

The Edge: Critical Studies in Educational Theory

Copyright © 1999 by Westview Press, A Member of the Perseus Books Group

Published in 1999 in the United States of America by Westview Press, 5500 Central Avenue, Boulder, Colorado 80301-2877, and in the United Kingdom by Westview Press, 12 Hid's Copse Road, Cumnor Hill, Oxford OX2 9JJ

Library of Congress Cataloging-in-Publication Data
Intermediality : the teachers' handbook of critical media literacy /
  Ladislaus M. Semali, Ann Watts Pailliotet, editors.
    p.   cm. — (The edge, critical studies in educational theory)
  Includes bibliographical references and index.
  ISBN 0-8133-3479-9 (hc.). — ISBN 0-8133-3480-2 (pbk.)
    1. Media literacy.   2. Critical thinking—Study and teaching.
  I. Semali, Ladislaus, 1946–   . II. Pailliotet, Ann Watts.
  III. Series.
  P96.M4I58   1999
  302.23—dc21   98-35451
                                                                            CIP

The paper used in this publication meets the requirements of the American National Standard for Permanence of Paper for Printed Library Materials Z39.48-1984.

10   9   8   7   6   5   4   3   2   1

Contents

Series Editors' Foreword   vii

1   Introduction: What Is Intermediality and
    Why Study It in U.S. Classrooms?
    Ladislaus M. Semali and Ann Watts Pailliotet   1

2   Deep Viewing: Intermediality in Preservice
    Teacher Education, *Ann Watts Pailliotet*   31

3   Intermediality in the Classroom: Learners
    Constructing Meaning Through Deep Viewing,
    Sherry L. Macaul, Jackie K. Giles, and Rita K. Rodenberg   53

4   Preservice Teachers' Collages of Multicultural Education,
    Ramón A. Serrano and Jamie Myers   75

5   A Late-'60s Leftie's Lessons in Media Literacy:
    A Collaborative Learning Group Project for a
    Mass Communication Course, *Arnold S. Wolfe*   97

6   The Power and Possibilities of Video Technology
    and Intermediality, *Victoria J. Risko*   129

7   A Feminist Critique of Media Representation,
    Donna E. Alvermann   141

8   Critical Media Literacy as an English Language
    Content Course in Japan,
    Carolyn Layzer and Judy Sharkey   155

9   Critical Viewing as Response to Intermediality:
    Implications for Media Literacy, *Ladislaus M. Semali*   183

10 Intermediality, Hypermedia, and Critical Media Literacy,
    Roberta F. Hammett   207

11 Afterword, *Douglas Kellner*   223

About the Editors and Contributors   229
Index   233

Series Editors' Foreword

As Western societies have raced into an electronic era, into an informa-tion-saturated hyper-reality, schools have been slow to recognize the so-cial and educational implications of such a historical sea change. Oper-ating with this understanding, Ladislaus Semali and Ann Watts Pailliotet and their authors present *Intermediality*. The power of media and the hermeneutics of media texts have too long been ignored by a teacher education that has relegated them to the domain of entertainment. Of-ten in my own career as a teacher educator, I have been met with com-bative responses to my call to add media literacy to the professional cur-riculum; "Why must you insist on trivializing our serious work?" my critics have asked. Semali and Watts Pailliotet adeptly respond to such myopia by delineating a justification for such analysis and offering ped-agogical models for how it might be accomplished. They understand that the mediascape and its omnipresence in the lives of students de-mands a reconceptualization of literacy that expands the concept to in-clude facility with the communicative arts.

The facility includes the ability to read and make meaning of language arts as well as the visual representations of drama, art, film, video, and television. In this assertion, we find Semali and Watts Pailliotet's defini-tion of intermediality: the ability to work with diverse symbol systems in an active way where meanings are both received and produced. From the authors' perspective, such a process cannot be separated from ques-tions of knowledge production, power, subjectivity, and justice. Thus, in-termediality is ever alert to the complex ways power wielders deploy media symbol systems to win consent to their political agendas at the end of the millennium. Indeed, as Semali argues, such power-driven media work to construct hierarchies of individual worth around the axes of race, class, gender, and sexuality.

In this context, the authors use intermediality to explore the connec-tions between students' personal experiences and their everyday en-counters with electronic media. Thus, intermedial pedagogy is not an isolated school experience but a holistic encounter with the ways con-temporary media mold all of us in all phases of our lives. Such a peda-gogical process, the authors contend, involves the difficult task of help-ing students connect particular media images to the sociopolitical context in which they are produced and received. This dynamic is a key component in the effort to understand the profound importance of what Semali and Watts Pailliotet and their authors have accomplished in this volume. Teacher educators, teachers, and other readers will profit from a specific understanding of this feature of intermediality.

Teachers and students who cannot make this text-context connection will gain little from intermediality or medial literacy of any variety. Recognizing this aspect of the literacy process, Semali and Watts Pailliotet write of individuals without a worldview or a sense of themselves as part of the larger culture. This disconnectedness, unfortunately, seems to be a pervasive aspect of the postmodern condition—an aspect that consistently undermines critical educational goals and political activism. In light of such an understanding, the authors induce their readers to think about intermediality and the production of identity. Students unsure of who they are may find an avenue to self-reflection via the media studies outlined here. As media-savvy knowledge producers, students and teachers find it difficult to avoid confronting the social, political, pedagogical, economic, and cultural forces that shape their lives.

In this context, individuals step back from the world as they have been conditioned to see it. In the process, they uncover power-driven representations, linguistic codes, cultural signs, and embedded ideologies—a central dynamic in the critical process of remaking their lives and renaming their worlds. In a mutating, globally expanding technocapitalism that seeks to use media to colonize everything from outer space to inner consciousness, questions of intermediality become more important than ever before. Thus, consciousness, cognition, and pedagogy cannot be separated from the media context outlined here. As Doug Kellner argues, consciousness is not deterministically constructed by media and other sociohistorical power formations; at the same time individuals do not construct their consciousness autonomously, unencumbered by the forces of power.

Semali and Watts Pailliotet's concern is to bring to the surface the ways that media operate to construct consciousness. The schemas of power that guide a culture are rarely part of an individual's conscious mind. It was this realization that Antonio Gramsci had in mind when he argued from Mussolini's prisons that criticalism involves the ability to criticize the ideological frames individuals use to make sense of the world. The authors are dedicated to making sure that teachers and students understand the ways these ideological frames are constructed through the pleasures of media in contemporary society in ways that elicit identification with extant institutions.

Watts Pailliotet's concept of *deep viewing* specifies the classroom practices of intermediality. Insisting on reflection and action in the classroom, deep viewing carefully lays out various strategies that can be used to accomplish the critical, socially contextualized, power-conscious understanding of media texts. Teachers will be delighted with Watts Pailliotet's detailed description of the process and the types of questions students and teachers might ask in their textual encounters. In essence what Watts Pailliotet offers is a hermeneutical process for media analysis—an invaluable modus operandi for teachers struggling to develop a media pedagogy. Familiarity with deep viewing in the larger context of intermediality does not breed contempt but grants teacher and students the ability to construct their own consciousness and transform the society in which they operate. Thus, Semali and Watts Pailliotet and their authors have written an empowering book that promises to change the field of media literacy.

Joe L. Kincheloe and Shirley Steinberg

References

McMahon, B. & Quin, R. (1990). *Monitoring standards in education.* Western Australia: Ministry of Education.
McMahon, B. & Quin, R. (1993). Knowledge power and pleasure: Direction in media education. *Telemedium, 39* (1–2), 18–22.

1 Introduction: What Is Intermediality and Why Study It in U.S. Classrooms?

Ladislaus M. Semali
Ann Watts Pailliotet

This book grew out of reflections emerging from conversations among teachers attending the 1996 National Reading Conference (NRC) Media Literacy Study Group. At this meeting, these educators posed many questions: Given the rise of mass media and technology in contemporary social and educational contexts in the United States, how might our conceptualizations of literacy change? What counts as the text of literacy? What theories best help us understand evolving definitions, texts, and practices? What research is needed to understand individuals, texts, classrooms, and society? What are the implications of new conceptualizations of literacy and conditions for instruction and learning? *Intermediality* is a response to these concerns and needs, specifically responding to questions about relations among knowledge, power, identity, and politics, in connection with issues of justice, equality, freedom, and community.

The term *intermediality* arose from the authors' ongoing discussions during the conception and writing of this book. As critical educators, researchers, and authors of this volume, we are deeply concerned with meanings of many sign systems, including language. The concept of intermediality has intrinsic value for advancing our thinking on the use of multiple texts, especially those represented on videos, the Internet, and CD-ROM materials, to develop dynamic learning environments. Our main task in this volume is to demonstrate how intermediality can stimulate thinking in a manner in which multiple texts can be used to create classrooms where community is valued and developed, where students are encouraged to learn privately and collaboratively, where multiple viewpoints are heard and respected, where both the teachers and students generate issues and problems they think are important to pursue. Stimulating students' learning in the study of multiple texts provides a dynamic way for helping students understand the complexity and multiple uses of information they are learning. As will be illustrated in this volume, intermediality provides a methodology to read printed and visual representations of meaningful ideas and the influence of multimedia on learning, pedagogy, and social practices in educational communities.

Even as we use the term intermediality in this volume, we realize that educational terms such as this have potential to construct and replicate power relations, often reducing teachers' capacities to understand or act (Goodman, 1992). We know, however, that all definitions have shifting denotative and connotative meanings (Barthes, 1957). All understandings of language are, by nature, incomplete (Benveniste, 1986). On the one hand, many educational definitions are broad but vague. They allow people to reach consensus on an abstract, intellectual level, but may fail to provide means for personal interpretation and pragmatic, observable actions or results. On the other hand, narrow, specific, rigidly defined terms often are elitist, exclusive, overly prescriptive, dogmatic, or irrelevant to individuals in actual classrooms (Mosenthal, 1993). Moreover, much educational language "has failed to offer a meaningful alternative vision . . . of organization, curriculum . . . and actual practice" (Goodman, 1992, pp. 273–6) because it fails to connect theory to real-life conditions, people, and actions in classrooms. The authors of the various chapters of *Intermediality* document the thinking and practice of progressive educators, attempting to eliminate inequalities of learning and instruction that have made their way into classrooms based on social class. We provide a basis for a more inclusive or multicultural education that is sensitive to a wide array of antisexist, antiracist, and antihomophobic classroom-based curricula and policy initiatives.

Guiding Principles and Theoretical Bases for Intermediality and Critical Media Literacy

The following dictionary entries offer partial views of intermediality. In the next section, we articulate the principles and premises that guide our intermedial thinking and critical media literacy practices.

Inter: "between . . . among . . . within . . . combining form meaning . . . with or on each other . . . together," (Guralnik & Friend, 1964, p. 761); "mutual . . . reciprocal . . . international . . . interdependent" (Pritchard, 1994, p. 437).

Media/medium: "something intermediate . . . middle state or degree . . . an intervening state through which a force acts or an effect is produced . . . any means, agency or instrumentality . . . environment . . . any material used for expression or delineation" (Guralnik & Friend, 1964, p. 914);"a position, condition or course of action midway between extremes . . . an agency by which something is accomplished, conveyed or transferred . . . a means of mass communication . . . the communications industry or profession. . . . means of expression as determined by the materials or creative methods involved . . . an environment in which something functions and thrives" (Pritchard, 1994, p. 519).

Mediacy: "of or in the middle . . . neither beginning nor end . . . intermediate" (Guralnik & Friend, 1964, p. 913).

Mediate: "to be in an intermediate position or location . . . to be an intermediary or conciliator between persons or sides. . . . to be a medium for bringing about (a result), conveying (an object), communicating (information) . . . dependent on acting . . . connected through some intervening agency . . . related indirectly. . . . friendly intervention . . . by consent or invitation" (Guralnik & Friend, 1964, p. 913); " To resolve or seek to resolve differences by working with all . . . parties" (Pritchard, 1994, p. 519).

Debates about educational terms and definitions are indeed important and will likely continue in the future, but these issues are not the focus of our book. Instead, we offer educators diverse, real-life images of intermediality. Through case studies, we illustrate how critical media literacy's theoretical concepts mediate actual classroom practices. This text is neither an abstract treatise nor simply a how-to handbook of intellectually ungrounded instructional activities. In the following chapters, the authors present varied portraits of teachers and students employing scholarly reflection and pedagogical action to transform themselves and their lives. Our goal is to show how critical scholars and educators construct dynamic middle grounds, embracing relations among theory and practice. It is our hope that in-service educators, preservice teachers, scholars, and researchers who read this book will critically question the authors' ideas, examine their practices, and reflect on their results, in order to create their own relevant, dynamic intermedial definitions and outcomes in schools and society.

Intermedial theories: "to resolve or seek to resolve differences by working with all . . . parties . . . " "with or on each other . . . " "together," . . .

"mutual . . . reciprocal . . . international . . . interdependent" (Guralnik & Friend, 1964).

Over the years, both of us have read widely and taught in many contexts. We've discovered that scholars in disparate fields—literacy, media studies, critical theory, semiotics, discourse analysis, social sciences, reader response, and composition—have many mutual and reciprocal views. Our own personal theories about teaching and education have arisen "between," "among," "within," "with or on each other," as we've identified, synthesized, and implemented interdependent ideas from diverse academic disciplines. Intermediality, at its core, arises through these connections. For us, critical media literacy is the bridge among ideas, disciplines, people, texts, processes, and contexts, educational purposes and outcomes, theory and praxis.

Intermedial texts: to be a medium for bringing about (a result), conveying (an object), communicating (information) . . . combining form meaning . . . any material used for expression or delineation.

We define texts broadly. Intermediality requires expertise in understanding and generating not only print media but also visual (Considine & Haley, 1992; Lester, 1995), oral (Goody, 1978), popular (Bianculli,1992; Witkin, 1994), and electronic sources (Reinking, 1995); student-generated texts (Bissex, 1980); life experiences (McCaleb, 1994); cultural/social events (Barthes, 1957); and combinations of media (Flood, Heath, & Lapp 1997).

All texts share common elements, including conventions, genres, and structures (Burton, 1990; Frye, 1957; Lusted, 1991); metaphors (Lakoff & Johnson, 1980); signs, symbols, and signification (Barthes, 1957; Bopry, 1994; Saint-Martin, 1990); images (Barthes, 1971; Pettersson, 1992); discourse patterns (Goffman, 1981; Moffett, 1968); levels of meaning (Herber & Herber, 1993; Himley, 1991; Messaris, 1994; Kervin, 1985); rules or grammars (Gumpert & Cathcart, 1985); and rhetorical devices (Lusted, 1991; Ohlgren & Berk, 1977).

Texts are not value-neutral, unchanging, "objective" artifacts; they convey shifting meanings and reflect cultural ideologies (Althusser, 1986; Derrida, 1986; Fiske, 1989). For us, texts are bringing about (a result), conveying (an object), communicating (information); combining form meaning; any material used for expression or delineation. Educators can (and must) teach students varied processes to access, construct, connect, and analyze texts in order to understand and evaluate tacit and explicit meanings.

In an attempt to establish a more comprehensive term that includes all textual analysis, *information literacy* has emerged in recent years as an all-encompassing ability to process all texts that transmit information of any kind. Information literacy is applied to the skills involved in deciphering or sifting through the layers of information. According to the U.S. Department of Labor Secretary's Commission on Achieving Necessary Skills (SCANS), information literacy is necessary for preparing students for the 21st century. Many different educational groups in this country echo this call and recognize the importance of information literacy. For example, in 1991, the Association of Supervision and Curriculum Development (ASCD) adopted goals of information literacy as follows: Information literacy equips individuals to take advantage of the opportunities inherent in the global information society. Information literacy should be a part of every student's educational experience. ASCD urges schools, colleges, and universities to integrate information literacy programs into learning programs for all students (American Association of School Librarians, 1996). Also, this imperative has been emphasized by the National Forum on Information Literacy (NFIL). NFIL challenges teachers to open up classrooms for intermedial enterprises. To become effective information users, students must have frequent opportunities to handle all kinds of information. By integrating information literacy as part of every subject across the curriculum, students will be able to locate, interpret, analyze, synthesize, evaluate, and communicate information. Also, they will have unlimited access to multiple resources in the classroom, the library media center, and beyond the school walls.

Intermedial processes: dependent on acting . . . a position, condition, or course of action midway between extremes . . . an agency by which something is accomplished, conveyed, or transferred . . . means of expression as determined by the materials or creative methods involved . . . of or in the middle . . . neither beginning nor end.

The rise of mass media and technology in society and schools has led to new understandings of what literacy and learning entail (Bianculli, 1992; Foster, 1979; Levinson, 1994; Papert, 1980). Flood and Lapp (1995) propose a "broader conceptualization in which literacy is defined as the ability to function competently in the 'communicative arts,' which include the language arts as well as the visual arts of drama, art, film, video, and television" (p. 1). Others posit we have entered a "post typographic world" (McLuhan, 1962; Reinking, 1995) in which new languages are arising through new media environments (Altheide & Snow, 1986; Edwards, 1991; Carpenter, 1960). In particular, there has been growing awareness and analysis of visual languages in recent scholarship (e.g., Flood & Lapp, 1995; Goodman, 1992; Lester, 1995; Messaris, 1994; Saint-Martin, 1990). In response to changing media environments and languages, educators must develop new ways of teaching, learning, and understanding literacy processes (Kellner, 1995)

We believe that modern literacy is intermedial; that is, requires the ability to critically read and write with and across varied symbol systems (Barthes, 1974; Fiske, 1989). By reading, we don't just mean passively receiving information or decoding print; by writing we mean generating texts through a myriad of media forms.

All texts are constructions—that is, they involve active, varied transactions of meaning making. Rather than receiving information in a conduit, linear fashion, people interact with ("read") and mediate texts ("write") to develop understandings (Barthes, 1974; Britton, 1985; Evans, 1987; Rosenblatt, 1978; McLuhan & Fiore, 1967; Smith, 1984). These transactions have neither beginning nor end clearly defined. They involve complex, multiple, simultaneous, and recursive processes (Bissex, 1980; Elbow, 1985; Flower, 1989; McLuhan & Fiore, 1967). Readers/writers/ audiences employ many senses (Barthes, 1974; Perl, 1980; Pike, Compain, & Mumper, 1997), intellectual processes (Britton, 1985; Calkins, 1983; McLuhan, 1964; Ong, 1986; Messaris, 1994), and emotions (Brand, 1987; Lester, 1995; McLuhan, 1964) to access, construct, and interpret textual languages.

Texts, as well as processes for understanding and constructing them, are connected. Readers/writers/audiences do not create meanings in isolation. Instead, they draw from experiences of other texts, connecting past and present understandings (Bakhtin, 1988; Cooper, 1986; Goody, 1978). Since all texts share common elements, processes developed in one form of communication support others. Reading, writing, speaking, listening, thinking, acting, *and* viewing are synergistic, interdependent, and interactive processes (Flood & Lapp, 1995; Neuman, 1991; Sinatra, 1986; Watts Pailliotet, 1997). Teachers need to teach students to express themselves through many processes and media. We accomplish this by assisting students to identify their mental, sensory, and emotional positions; to develop new methods and stances; and then to choose appropriate courses of action when engaging with texts. Intermedial processes, then, are intimately connected—as are the contexts in which they occur.

Contexts: an environment in which something functions and thrives . . . between, among, within . . . any means, agency, or instrumentality.

Intermediality implies connectedness among texts; textual processes; and, thus, also contexts. Media systems permeate our lives (Kellner, 1995). High school graduates spend more time watching television than in classrooms (Lutz, 1989) and engage with mass media during most of their leisure time (Buckingham, 1993). Additionally, what we see and do outside schools has tremendous impact on what occurs within classrooms in terms of values, beliefs, and actions. For example, the symbolic forms in mass media greatly influence the ways teachers and students understand schooling and the educational roles they assume (Farber, Provenzo, & Holm, 1994; Spring, 1992; Weber & Mitchell, 1995). Furthermore, literacy development occurs across home, classroom, and community environments (Heath, 1983; Pope, 1993; Schmidt, 1993). Emig (1983) details how writers are connected to and through many social experiences as they construct texts. She calls these communication environments a "web of meaning." Other theorists also evoke the web to describe how communications environments are connected (e.g., Ball-Rokeach & DeFleur, 1986; Flower, 1989; McLuhan & Fiore, 1967; Papert, 1980; Vygotsky, 1978). This image shows that reading and writing texts doesn't just occur within the confines of classrooms.

Our students are already accomplished communicators who engage with many texts in and out of school. In, among, and between these varied environments, they construct webs of meaning—personal connections among their unique and collective social experiences. If we want our students to function and thrive in modern communicational environments, we must help them develop the means to critically read, write, and connect aspects of their lives. In particular, as intermedial educators, we are concerned with visual symbol systems, since they permeate our contemporary lives (Lester, 1995; Lutz, 1989; Messaris, 1994). Therefore, teaching must encompass many media to connect learning environments; "educational theory [and practice] must engage with the popular as the background that informs students' engagement with any pedagogical encounter" (Sholle & Denski, 1993, p. 307). Critical media literacy enables students and teachers to bridge existing learning contexts and build new ones.

Curricula: connected through some intervening agency . . . related indirectly. . . . friendly intervention . . . by consent or invitation.

Leveranz and Tyner (1996) recommend "positioning media arts, instead of traditional language arts, at the heart of all disciplines in the curriculum. In this way, reading and writing is still about pencils and books, but it is also about the symbolic and visual languages of film, video, computers and popular culture texts" (p. 10). Like Maxine Greene (1988), we envision a "coming together" of disciplines (p. 79). We see critical media literacy as the linchpin of instruction that connects learning contexts and curricula.

Intermedial ideas and critical media literacy practices support and extend many instructional frameworks and curricula. These include whole language (Fehlman, 1996), multicultural curricula (Sinatra, 1986; Considine & Haley, 1992), values education (Lickona, 1991), inquiry learning (Schmidt, 1997), interdisciplinary approaches (Considine, 1987; Schnitzer, 1990), skills-based reading and writing (Moline, 1995; Cheyney, 1992), cooperative learning (Considine & Haley, 1992), (Watts Pailliotet, 1998), content area reading and learning (Watts Pailliotet, 1997), and constructivism (Hyerle, 1996; Evans, 1987) as well as critical thinking and viewing (Considine, Haley, & Lacy, 1994; Semali, 1994).

There are many arguments for connecting curricula through critical media literacy: creating a literate, knowledgeable populace; developing critical consumers; preparing future workers; and involving participants in a just democratic process. Critical analysis of diverse media, coupled with generation of new texts, promotes student empowerment, interest, active learning, and multicultural awareness (Considine & Haley, 1992; Sinatra, 1990). When students are able to relate personal, academic, and varied social experiences, their motivation and learning may increase (Reutzel & Cooter, 1992). Perhaps most important, educators who intervene in the cycle of isolated learning experiences may empower students, inviting them into what Frank Smith calls "the literacy club" (Smith, 1984), establishing lifelong patterns of positive learning, thinking, and acting.

Purposes and outcomes: Theory into praxis: an agency by which something is accomplished, conveyed, or transferred. . . . an intervening state through which a force acts or an effect is produced.

We began this chapter by explaining how theory and practice are interdependent intermedial elements. As critical educators, we know that theory and reflection inform and interact with our own and others' beliefs and actions (Britzman, 1991; Goodman, 1992; Schön, 1983, 1987).

Our purposes and desired outcomes in intermedial instruction are grounded in the notion of praxis, "self-creative activity through which men and women . . . change (shape) the historical human world and themselves" (Sholle & Denski, 1993, p. 300). In an intermedial framework, it is not enough to simply decode or understand existing texts. Students and teachers must transform their newfound critical understandings into agency, positive acts and effects in themselves and others. This might transpire through generation of new texts and knowledge, developing ways of thinking and acting, or working toward alterations of unjust social conditions.

One classroom example of praxis at the elementary level might involve inquiry learning about a community condition, combined with direct action. Students would engage in an interdisciplinary unit about the local environment, examining varied media to gain information. They would then create public service announcements, research reports, web sites, newsletters, and action plans to address issues. A secondary classroom application involves critical analysis of content and point of view represented in social studies, mass media, or English/language arts texts. After identifying missing information, students could employ community interviews, oral histories, original documents, and mass media or artistic resources to build broader pictures of events or texts. They might write their own books or create a newspaper, a web site, a mural, or a dramatic presentation to convey their new understandings. In college, preservice teachers can also apply intermedial principles and critical media literacy to achieve praxis. Using readings, observations, personal interviews, artifacts in their own lives, videos, list serve discussions, and written reflections, they may access, articulate, examine, and adapt their beliefs about teaching, making professional changes, and formulating plans for future growth.

Connecting Analytical Skills to Social Context

The notion of intermedial instruction is grounded in connecting analytical skills to social or daily contexts. Because impending multimedia technologies and the literacies they bring to classrooms will soon become part of the fabric of contemporary life, whether we like or not, teachers must take frontline positions and learn to adopt new methods and practices necessary for multimedia environments (Witkin, 1994). Our intention in this volume is to broaden the lens for reading all texts and describe opportunities for teachers to enrich the possibilities of communication with students—thus bridging the gaps between home and school.

High school students in the present-day United States recognize the significance of technology to their lives—even if their teachers do not—and come to school expecting to see technology integrated into education. What may have seemed far-fetched remarks by Marshall McLuhan in the 1960s may now have come to face our generation of high school students. McLuhan (1978) wrote, "In the 19th century, the knowledge inside the classroom was higher than the knowledge outside. Today it is reversed. The child knows that, in going to school, he is in a sense interrupting his education" (p. 54). McLuhan warned that schools may be irrelevant and boring for students if they do not open up their curriculum and instruction to include today's technologies and media with the accompanying learning styles individuals bring to classrooms. A high school that does not heed to the current technological imperative will be out of touch with its students and runs the risk of making their education appear irrelevant to them. As educators, we know we must harness the power of emerging technologies like the Internet, but we have a lot of catching up to do. Now that TV is more than broadcast and cable, merging with the telephone and the computer, it is becoming even more pervasive and more powerful. Even before we have fully comprehended the nature of this force being ushered in by the information age, the scope of its effects, or the economics of its multibillion-dollar outreach, a tidal wave of new technologies has hit us, delivering even more information. Unavoidably, with such delivery comes a new set of ethical, moral, and social consequences that now present dilemmas in new terms. Despite these challenges and transformations, surprisingly little academic research has been undertaken around the study of media, culture, and education and how they have come to shape the agendas of literacy research and practice in U.S. classrooms (Reinking, 1995).

As readily acknowledged by media educators, the exercise of connecting home and school environment has been the most important and yet the most challenging task before teachers. Many media educators already suspect that this challenge has hindered the media literacy movement from reaching many teachers in U.S. classrooms. For example, Barbara Dobbs (1988) surmises that some early media literacy curricula "died a slow death because they were not global in their approach. The visual literacy skills that were taught in those isolated classes were not transferred to other curricula and more importantly, were not transferred to students' world outside the classroom" (p. 12). This lack of articulation of the social context prompted McMahon and Quin (1990, 1993) to undertake a systemwide study in their home state in Australia, called *Monitoring Standards in Education*. They rightly argue that the time has come for evaluation of the aims, content, and strategies of media literacy. They insist that unless students are given the skills to apply their classroom analysis skills to the world in which they live, there is the danger that this knowledge will remain in the classroom and will not achieve the aim of producing media-literate, empowered students. The results of McMahon and Quin's study indicate that although students are adept in deconstructing a given image and competent in textual analysis, they are often unable to make the conceptual leap between the text and its context. McMahon and Quin point out that students' problems with linking textual analysis to wider issues of representations, on one level, is perhaps a question of maturity. This may well be true, because students do not have a worldview or a sense of themselves as part of a wider society. For some students, society is something "out there" that they will deal with outside the school classroom after three o'clock or when they graduate from high school. In their eyes, that time is a long way from now. For others, the time for critical examinations may occur after they graduate from college.

McMahon and Quin identified the first problem of current media literacy instruction: failing to furnish students with the skills to apply their analysis skills to a wider social context. Some of the strategies outlined by McMahon and Quin include broadening the students' worldview, and our notion of intermediality coincides with their aim. They view texts as polysemous, that is, informed by various preexistent discourses. This is another way of looking at multiple texts, multilayered visuals, and multiliteracies. McMahon and Quin also suggest that media literacy strategies include inquiry, reflection, and action. They suggest that teachers encourage students to (1) ask different questions about the issue; (2) analyze the institutions that produce the prevailing views; and (3) seek alternative images that may provide a different view, such as those found in radical texts. One important point they make, which we find relevant to intermedial classrooms, is that reading oppositional texts and the language of criticism allow students and teachers to move beyond commonsense readings of daily life narratives. If teachers continue to ask the same questions on social issues, they will simply recycle prevailing views.

McMahon and Quin list "alternative questions" that could be asked around any social issue raised by the text (literature or related visuals): (1) Through whose eyes or perspective do we get the information? (2) What assumptions are being made in the view presented? (3) What representations are there of the group concerned? (4) Whose voices are not being heard? (5) If a key piece of information were changed, how would the meaning change? (6) Why has this group been singled out for depiction in this manner? Who gains from this representation? (7) What would be the effect if the various depictions were reversed? These questions form the basis of intermediality. Through questioning, reflection, and action, students get to know their social context, evaluate it, and plan action to make changes. This volume offers a way of both thinking about and negotiating through praxis the relationship among classroom teaching; the production of knowledge; the larger institutional structures of the school; and the social and material relations of the wider community, society, and the nation-state.

Technology and the Social Context

Intermediality is specially written for prospective and practicing teachers. It will illustrate that conceptions of situations from one's experiences, problems, and goals help shape individuals' agendas, desires, and actions. In addition, the rise of mass media and technology in U.S. society and schools has led to new ways of looking at the world and how we construct meaning. Our worldviews are shaped and influenced by the technology we use in our schools and homes—computers, bank teller machines, fax modems, digital television, cable, and a variety of gadgets that continue to enter our lives subsequent to the invention of the microchip. These technologies have also impacted the way we communicate and how we receive information.

When we talk about a worldview, we mean the *values hierarchy* created by media presentations to form a mythic reality that people buy into over a period of time. For example, the construction of a worldview may be a result of news reports about a country, an ethnic or racial group of people, or idea. In the United States, for instance, media presentations have often been influenced by world events as well as domestic social and political agendas, such as the Vietnam war, the Persian Gulf war, the wave of church burnings in the South, the Oklahoma bombing, and the O. J. Simpson criminal and civil trials in Los Angeles. In sum, a worldview is based on fictional or nonfictional stories with certain fundamental assumptions about how the world operates.

Often, audiences are not aware of the devices or conventions used in the telling of these stories. The way these stories are told and the person who is doing the telling play an important role in formulating the motive of the telling as well as making the story entertaining and at the same time believable. As noted by Victoria Risko in this volume, developments such as digital imaging of videos and the use of computer graphics in the morphing of images make deceptions much easier and faster to accomplish and much harder to detect. We have arrived at a time when most of the images that we see in our daily lives, and that shape our worldview, will have been digitally recorded, transmitted, and processed in a manner beyond recognition—with a blurring of the lines between the original and the stereotype image. Unfortunately, these ways of telling explain the coded genres of situation comedies, soaps, action adventures, and so on that define the system of commercial television in the United States. Therefore, we no longer can deny the fact that some of these conventions continually used in telling mythic stories allow bias, overt manipulation of the characterization or plot, stereotyping, jokes, and comedic entertainment to "creep in" to the story being told. By the same token, a particular worldview is portrayed as a value, a better way of being or doing; superior culture; morally good; or, simply put, the norm. The worldview represented in a story is often influenced by the attitude and background of its teller, its interviewers, writers, photographers, and editors. The danger presented by mythic realities such as those found in popular films and television shows is that audiences sometimes make decisions or judgments on the basis of these myths. The conventions used in advancing the plot or resolving the conflict seem so believable and yet oversimplified. Complex problems are trivialized or made to look ridiculously easy. Lifetime enemies are shown to resolve their differences with a handshake, and romantic encounters end up in sexual intercourse without courtship, love, or even considering the consequences of the sexual act.

Intermediality challenges teachers and students to examine critically their worldviews and acknowledge the fact that the ways representations of race, gender, class, age, or sexual orientation are constructed will be as important as the ideas and meaning they project, since they offer positions for us through which we recognize images as similar or different from ourselves and those around us. The recent "crisis" in the White House is a perfect example. In an instant, the whole world was engulfed in an avalanche of news about an alleged sex scandal involving President Clinton. The commercial media capitalized on this event and seductively served up to the nation a bittersweet relish of titillating news tidbits without much substance to the allegations. The long-awaited meeting in Washington between the brokers of the stalled Middle East peace process, which President Clinton was trying to jump-start (a matter of life and death for Benjamin Netanyahu's Israel and Yassar Arafat's occupied territories), was deemed not newsworthy enough to merit the place of lead story any more; it was shuffled to third and fourth place for days. The pope's visit to Cuba was also put aside, even though this event dominated the news media at the time.

Instead, the commercial media, with their web of instant communication, engulfed Washington and much of the nation in a spectacle by injecting into the airwaves allegations of a sex scandal involving the President of the United States and a young woman, Monica Lewinsky. These allegations spread like wildfire, permeating newscasts, talk shows, radio broadcasts, web sites, newspaper front pages, and street talk. Historians admit that sex scandals are not new in the White House, and yet the media would not allow any other news information to pass through their gates as this spectacle dominated lead stories and subsequent commentary. Sex sells, so goes the cliché. Media corporations made millions of advertising dollars as they capitalized on this newsbreak, which amounted to "much ado about nothing." Largely fueled by accounts from unidentified sources, reported snippets of news, speculation, innuendoes, and suggestions that the law was broken by the President's obstructing justice as he tried to deny the affair, there was little substance to the allegations.

Additionally, the line between "hard" journalism and entertainment blurred. Many of the same players, interviews, and innuendoes were reported and repeated between network newscasts and infotainment shows like *Entertainment Tonight* and *Hard Copy*. It was hard to discern fact from entertainment, narrative from reporting, reality from perception, fact from fiction. Both seemed like soap operas. Soap opera or not, what we know about this alleged scandal and the manner in which it has come to influence the words we speak and the world of media we live in probably would not have been possible in the Kennedy, Johnson, or Nixon eras. Today, the instant dissemination of news has been made possible by the sophistication of the technology and the media at hand. These technologies have forced on us new literacies; new definitions; and a new worldview about sex, power, and gossip. We have become instant neighbors with Australians, Europeans, and Chinese. Now, we can share with these distant people across the air waves and satellites our neighborhood gossip.

This blurring of traditional boundaries between school and home, fact and fiction, narrative and live reporting are confusing to some educators, to say the least. As the media from which we obtain information and stories become the main source of our daily input, the lines between truth, fiction, and history become blended. The key concept of media literacy—that media are constructions—becomes a landmark to help us keep our perspective and sort out media events as news stories unfold in front of our eyes. It is important therefore that teachers and students keep in mind that these media constructions build our reality—what we know, how we came to know it, and the attitudes or assumptions we make about the given reality. For this reason, and because all texts are constructions, we need to bring a critical stance to all texts that inform our worldview.

Toward a Critical Media Literacy

Although some teachers feel empowered by recent technological developments, others are disconcerted and daunted by what the technologies have done to learning in U.S. classrooms. The greatest challenge facing teachers in the classroom is that kids can surf the Internet all day without being bored; they can watch television while doing homework; and they can read programs such as Power Rangers, Sailor Moon, and Reboot in a manner that teachers have no patience for (Rushkoff, 1996). The realities of these technologies are perhaps what Postman (1993) envisaged when he sounded an alarmist forewarning to educators. Technologies, Postman argued, are much more than electronic envelopes for delivering the old curriculum in a marginally new way. "New technologies," he added, "alter our interests, symbols and nature of community. They represent a new curriculum requiring new competencies and a new definition of what constitutes learning as well as how and when it takes place" (p. 20). The new competencies alluded to by Postman include teaching about emerging technologies, namely those of the mass media and the Internet. Given the proliferation of media and their impact on curriculum and instruction, teachers cannot ignore them any more; nor can they afford to heed mediaphobes and technophobes whose rhetoric tends to cloud over reason with alarmist and panicky literature about the evils of the media and new technology (Bianculli, 1992).

Fiske (1987), Fiske and Hartley (1989), Worth and Gross (1981), and others counteract Postman's alarmist, protectionist rhetoric when they advocate developing viewers' competencies for interpreting "codes and modes"—conventions of symbol systems in various kinds of media. They look to both aesthetic and social characteristics of mass media as significant areas for educating viewers. This is what has come to be known as *critical media literacy*. Growing out of the burgeoning cultural studies literature, the core issue of media literacy is that reality—our worldview—is socially constructed significantly by media. The many strategies for media literacy are drawn from critical theory as studied by the Frankfurt school and later interpreted and expanded by cultural theorists to include a critique of social-cultural practices and the industries that produce them. Giroux and McLaren (1989) explain the rationale of cultural studies as a paradigm that "develops a discourse that accentuates the organic connections between cultural workers and everyday life on the one hand and schooling and reconstruction of democratic public culture on the other" (p. 21). In other words, cultural studies provides the brick and mortar on which to build the analysis of the media. In this perspective, media are no longer viewed as windows of the world or objective representations of our world, but rather as subjective and sometimes loaded with social biases regarding race, class, sexual orientation, gender, and ethnic differences (Giroux, 1991).

Like Giroux (1988), we envision teachers at all levels of education as "transformative intellectuals," who combine "inquiry," "reflection," and "action" in the interest of empowering students with the skills and knowledge needed "to address injustices" (p. xxxiv). We are also "concerned with empowering students so that [they] can read the world critically and change it when necessary" (p. xxxiv). As Goodman (1992) notes, however, "without providing vivid images of 'transformative individuals' at work in educational settings, it is difficult to understand the potential impact this vision has for schools and society" (p. 279). Educators "need a theoretical language that is informed by and rooted in images of real . . . people involved in tangible actions that take place in believable settings" (p. 281). Furthermore, "critical scholars need to . . . directly and explicitly address the question of *how* . . . (based on observations . . . or as a result of reflecting upon one's own practices) individuals or groups of people can potentially act within educational settings to advance their ideals" (p. 281).

Traditional educators have ignored the critique of schooling, social conditions, and ideological contexts for so long that it is not natural for teachers to incorporate such contexts in readings or classroom discussions. The kinds of inquiry advocated and described in this book stand apart from the objective and depoliticized analysis employed by both liberal and conservative educators who have adopted the viewer response and active viewer approaches in their classrooms without taking a critical stance. Therefore, when we talk about inquiry, we refer to a holistic and interconnected process in which teachers question and reflect and act on what they have learned to change their social conditions. On the one hand, questioning does not mean only seeking answers. Rather, it means a pursuit of deeper meaning by asking questions that generate more questions about all texts and contexts students read, including the institutions that produce them. On the other hand, reflection is neither separate from inquiry nor something that can be neatly packaged as a set of techniques for teachers to use. Reflection provides teachers and students with space to step back and analyze and apply meanings from texts to the social contexts they live in. When Dewey (1933) discussed the concept of reflection in his book *How We Think,* he urged educators to divorce their actions from routine, impulse, tradition, and authority. By confronting what is often taken for granted as a matter of routine, definitions of reality and traditional conventions are questioned. According to Dewey, as long as we continue to follow routine and not critique our actions or perceptions, we are likely to fall into the trap of perceiving reality as unproblematic and therefore immune to critique. Such a situation may well serve as an obstacle to recognizing valuable alternative viewpoints.

By this, we mean to remind teachers that there is more than one way to frame the problem. Zeichner and Liston (1996, p. 9) list five key features of a reflective teacher. A teacher who is a reflective practitioner (1) examines, frames, and attempts to solve dilemmas of classroom practice; (2) is aware of and questions the assumptions and values he or she brings to teaching; (3) is attentive to the institutional and cultural contexts in which he or she teaches; (4) takes part in curriculum development and is involved in school change efforts; and (5) takes responsibility for his or her own professional development. In short, a reflective practitioner is one who is committed to transform the social conditions of the school and society. Zeichner and Liston sum up reflective teaching as a reflexive process that entails a "recognition, examination, and rumination over the implications of one's beliefs, experiences, attitudes, knowledge, and values as well as opportunities and constraints provided by the social conditions a teacher works in" (p. 33). Even though these key features may not by any means be conclusive, they offer some insights to teachers who wish to take a critical stance in their teaching. We must reiterate, however, that inquiry, reflection, and action do not consist of a series of steps or procedures to be used by teachers. Rather this is a holistic way of meeting and responding to problems, a way of being a teacher (Zeichner & Liston, 1996, p. 9).

Teachers of Intermedial Classrooms

In these modern times, being a teacher of intermedial classrooms demands of educators that they take a critical reading of all texts and engage a critical pedagogy in curriculum and instruction. Even though critical literacy has been practiced in the academy for the past 20 years, the debate rages on about what it means to take a critical stance and how such a project can be implemented across the curriculum. Grounded in the Freirean notions of emancipatory education, critical literacy has emerged as perhaps the most talked about alternative pedagogy. Critical literacy stands in contrast to the practice of teaching the classics and a canon of acceptable literary works, far removed from the students' experiences, to be memorized for exams. As a pedagogical tool, critical literacy draws its practice from "constructivist" approaches of teaching and learning, social theory studies of popular culture, and goals of social justice. It draws from many media forms; literature; the role of the state in struggles over race, class, and gender relations; national and international economic structures; and the cultural politics of imperialism, postcolonialism, and poststructuralism (see Giroux & Simon, 1989; Kellner, 1995; McLaren, Hammer, Sholle, & Reilly, 1995). These works of critical pedagogy are particularly useful in critical inquiry, which is the driving engine to any critical literacy. In addition, they reassert the stance that discursive critical consciousness is necessary to critical education and to democratic public life.

By embracing a critical project, the authors of *Intermediality* reaffirm what critical theorists, like Calhoun (1995), explicitly define as

- a critical engagement with the theorist's contemporary social world, recognizing that the existing state of affairs does not exhaust all possibilities, and offering positive implications for social action;

- a critical account of the historical and cultural conditions (both social and personal) on which the theorist's own intellectual activity depends;
- a continuous critical re-examination of the constitutive categories and conceptual frameworks of the theorist's understanding, including the historical construction of those frameworks; and
- a critical confrontation with other works of social explanation that not only establishes their good and bad points but shows the reasons behind their blind spots and misunderstandings, and demonstrates the capacity to incorporate their insights on stronger foundations. (p. 35)

As discussed by critical theorists in many publications that have surfaced since the debates of the Frankfurt school on critical theory, all four of these forms of critique would seem to us to depend on some manner of historical understanding and analysis. Calhoun (1995) calls for "denaturalizing" the human world, recognizing it as a product of human action and thus implicitly as the product of some actions among a larger range of possibilities.

The theories, research, and teaching practices discussed in *Intermediality* expose unexplored learning spaces for students and usher in new ways of defining literacy and pedagogy. We aim to (1) develop a critical awareness of the constructed nature of representation in both print and visual media; (2) provide knowledge about the social, cultural, economic, and political contexts in which media messages are produced by a variety of different institutions with specific objectives; and (3) encourage renewed interest in learning about the ways in which individuals construct meaning from messages—that is, about the processes of selecting, interpreting, and acting on messages in various contexts. Media literacy expands the notion of critical literacy, which includes taking a critical stance to all media texts. For teachers and students, the classroom becomes a media literacy learning environment, where the learning process is not disconnected from the institutions that create knowledge and information or from the legal, cultural, political, and economic contexts that surround texts students read, whether from books, films, or the Internet. Therefore, for a teacher of an intermedial classroom, a critical media literacy project is driven by the interest to abolish social injustice and the attempt to show how repressive interests are hidden by supposedly neutral formulations of science; it's a critique of hegemonic ideology. In this book, we hope to describe how to create educational contexts where media literacy will be considered both viable and valid.

Building on Experiences

In this volume, we wish to respond to the questions posed by educators meeting at the National Reading Conference (NRC) in the recent past: How can instruction be adapted in response to the changing literacy landscape, and how can teachers and students exploit electronic forms of reading and writing to enhance teaching and learning? Since the media literacy movement was founded in North America in 1978, there has been an earnest effort to introduce media education in the classroom. Between 1978 and 1995, many workshops and institutes were held in various cities to explore the languages of media and how to teach them to students in elementary and secondary schools. During this period, *Telemedium*, a journal of media literacy, was established at the University of Wisconsin, Madison, and it has been churning out scholarly articles about theory and practice. This publication has also been useful to teachers through its offerings of lists of resource materials, including textbooks, web site addresses, and new educational films and video programs. These materials have added to the momentum already experienced in the national media literacy movement (Duncan, 1997).

Our examination of textbooks produced in the United States during the past 15 years reveals that few authors have taken time or space to focus on the theory *and* practice of critical media literacy. The largest number of these books focus on theory and have been heavily influenced by scholars who critique the mass media. Over 20 books have been published describing the language of media, particularly popular media (see, e.g., the list generated by Duncan, 1997, p. 20). Few of these books have been written by education specialists. For the most part, the authors are media critics or cultural theorists, not public school educators.

Our findings show that there is another divide. Some teachers of English simply transfer over literature response techniques to visual analysis methods advocated by media educators. As noted by Duncan (1993), there is a tension between those educators who focus on *content* (what is taught) and those who are preoccupied by *form* (how media literacy is taught). In these books, there is evident a range of considerable disagreement among theorists. Each author, however, acknowledges the need for teaching about media and acknowledges there is some benefit to be realized by students who engage in some type of media analysis. Also, the definition of media literacy seems to have come a long way, and there is some consensus about how to define media literacy following the Aspen Conference (Davis, 1992).

But many teachers complain that the least attention has been paid to practice. As many have observed, simply watching television does not lead to better media analysis skills (McMahon & Quin, 1993). The skills must be learned. These books also have dodged the practical questions of integrating media across the curriculum. Many offer frameworks that support teaching about media but are short of methods illustrating how to do it. Even though they discuss the need for developing critical thinking and critical viewing, the authors do not seem to agree in practice on what "critical" means. For example, in their book *Imagine That: Developing Critical Thinking and Critical Viewing Through Children's Literature*, Considine et al. (1994) provide many opportunities for student activities and strategies: writing and drawing tasks, making verbal connections, and developing manual and emotional experiences. Although many of these strategies are interesting and instructionally sound, they are not explicitly anchored in critical or educational theories and thus leave many important questions unanswered. Both veteran and prospective teachers are left to wonder how to implement these suggestions on Monday morning and might well ask, how might teachers take up a critical stance in their daily teaching? How might teachers' reflective and teaching practices develop a critical stance to generate a critical authoring, reading, and viewing of texts? How can teachers enable students to navigate the seas of multiple texts, especially those represented in multimedia formats currently flooding their learning environments through the Internet, videos, CD-ROMs, and so on, at a time when literacy education is no longer confined to paper-and-pencil technologies? How does the current climate of cultural conservatism present specific challenges to critical education? How can reader/viewer response analysis stimulate and help students to develop critical reading, critical viewing, critical listening, and critical thinking for lifelong learning? How does a critical pedagogy of representation as envisaged in a media literacy project fit the lessons teachers will take up on Monday morning in a language arts or social studies class? How do they fit with the requirements of academic standards and assessment prerogatives?

These are difficult questions for teachers, especially when we consider most of them operate in school districts where the curriculum is already full. There is no room to add on another stand-alone course in media literacy, yet some of the books we examined have suggested or implied that teachers should do just that. Others have indicated that language arts and social studies are the best place for teachers to begin integrating media literacy. Our analysis of North American textbooks reveals, however, the reason praxis has been so difficult to illustrate or model has to do with teachers' attitudes about application. The dilemma is the social context.

Key Concepts of Intermediality

Many of the concepts described in *Intermediality* were drawn from classroom practice of educators at various educational institutions. Presented as case studies, these classroom experiences provide important examples of theory and practice in the context of real-life, intermedial classrooms. Chapters 2, 3, 4, 5, and 7 present five case studies of intermediality. The chapters portray a variety of strategies, using examples as individual works from classroom practice. For example, in Chapter 2, Ann Watts Pailliotet introduces the concept of *deep viewing*, which combines a heuristic framework and semiotic codes for understanding all texts. The method of deep viewing is distinguished from other methods of textual analysis by an insistence on inquiry, reflection, and action. When applying this method, students are encouraged to relate the texts they read or view to their own experiences, expectations, feelings, and knowledge.

In Chapter 3, Sherry Macaul, in collaboration with Jackie Giles and Rita Rodenberg, takes Watts Pailliotet's deep viewing method and applies it to viewing a video, reading a printed text, and browsing a web site. Working with elementary/middle level students, the Macaul team explored learners' perceptions, interpretations, critiques, and sign systems as they applied to deep viewing to (de)construct meaning. The tasks given to students made evident the association and application of interactivity among various media from one's background knowledge and experience as well as in the commercial or advertisement (visual and auditory representations such as voice, music, graphic or digital images, animations, morphing, etc.) to construct meaning ("built on meaning by viewer").

Ramón Serrano and Jamie Myers, in Chapter 4, combine transactional theory and semiotic analysis to engage students in a response-oriented classroom. They compare the attitudes and questioning procedures of preservice teachers in an exercise of reading collages of multiculturalism. A combination of reading text and reading visuals introduces the concept of *multiliteracies*. By this concept, we mean to emphasize that print literacy is only one way by which meanings are signified and represent only one experience. It is in this context that we concur and applaud Flood, Heath, and Lapp's (1997) *Handbook of Research on Teaching the Communicative and Visual Arts*. The authors propose a "broader conceptualization of literacy." They focus on the multiple ways in which learners gain access to knowledge and skills. The central thesis of Flood et al.'s handbook is that by broadening our uses of varied media, formats, and genres, a greater number of students will be motivated to see themselves as learners. In this view, the new and emerging methods of literacy in the information age encompass everything from novels to theatrical performances, comic books, video games, music, graphics, sound effects, smells, and animation. Although these multiple texts have been used widely by television shows and multimedia products, the authors argue that they often represent unexplored resources in U.S. classrooms. A good illustration of what we mean is found in Chapter 5, written by Arnold Wolfe. In this chapter, the lessons of media literacy are made explicit. That is to say, intermediality extends the range of the term literacy to encompass contemporary multiliteracies in their various modes, including music.

Mediacy is another key term in intermedial classrooms. By mediacy, we mean the ability to comprehend and create such visual texts as illustrations, charts, graphs, electronic displays, electronic books, photographs, film, and video. In Chapter 6, Victoria Risko explores this notion of mediacy with video technology in a multimedia forum in which CD-ROM and hypermedia are quickly becoming part of the classroom quotidian terms. The multimedia forum has expanded the notion of reading, writing, and authorship in ways we could not have imagined before. What has dawned on many teachers is that literacy will no longer remain the ways we have known it. New technologies have altered literacy permanently; it is no longer about teaching how to read and write the printed text. Clearly, computer technology has fundamentally changed how we organize, analyze, and convey information and receive entertainment. Vice President Gore's program of wiring all schools in the United States is going to revolutionize how our children do schooling, how they access libraries, how they communicate with each other and their teachers through e-mail, how their work gets assessed, and how they access the wealth of knowledge now resident in and available through the Internet.

The authors of these case studies enable students to give full recognition to those language systems that are primarily visual and audio as well as recognizing the multiple ways of knowing that are becoming prevalent in U.S. classrooms. Other concepts evoked by the notion of intermediality in this volume include critical viewing, process, and texts. In Chapters 7, 8, 9, and 10, the authors discuss implications of intermediality in classrooms. Donna Alvermann takes up in Chapter 7 the important issues of critical pedagogy of representation focusing on gendered texts. She argues that gender is not a fixed property but rather an ongoing process through which femininity and masculinity are constructed in everyday practices. She cautions, however, that common misrepresentations of what critical media literacy should entail are the crux of the matter. The misrepresentations have to do with teachers' tendencies to associate critical media literacy with helping students learn how to liberate themselves from texts that are designed to dupe them. She sees a pedagogical trap looming large for students, particularly when they are asked to critique media texts that are disapproved of or "looked upon with disfavor by those who are in positions of authority," such as the teacher, priest, or father figure. For this reason, she challenges teachers to examine more critically gendered texts because they are part of the larger context in which popular culture is "read" through and into the media's representation of the male and female subject.

Chapters 8, 9, and 10 focus on the key concepts of media literacy. In Chapter 8, Carolyn Layzer and Judy Sharkey provide analysis of media artifacts from advertising and illustrate how to go about teaching critical media literacy in an English classroom. This chapter adds to the richness of this volume, particularly in its detailed descriptions of a Japanese English classroom. Furthermore, this chapter focuses on process rather than content in its attempt to help students see how media shape cultural values and opinions and enables them to deconstruct messages inherent in media products and making sense of relevant cultural information.

In Chapter 9, Semali emphasizes the need for taking a critical stance in media education. He demonstrates how teachers can use critical viewing as a language of criticism to sift through multiple layers of text and be able to go beyond surface impressions, traditional myths, and clichés, applying the meaning to one's own social context. He then concludes that critical viewing, critical reading, and critical authoring are pivotal components by which to integrate media literacy across the curriculum of intermedial classrooms.

In Chapter 10, Roberta Hammet discusses the role of hypermedia authoring in critical media literacy. In this context, hypermedia is taken up from a constructivist perspective, in which the acquisition of knowledge is viewed as incremental, socially and culturally mediated, and individually situated. In the context of intermediality, Hammet's project goes to show that in the intermedial classroom students are empowered by the multimedia environment with multiple texts from personal media and printed texts, including literature and the Internet, to have a far wider range of cultural references at their disposal than any single teacher will ever have. The future that teachers have dreaded for a long time seems now to be upon us when technology could replace the classroom teacher. The expertise that once was confined to the classroom is now widely dispersed. Furthermore, teachers alone are no longer the only key holders of the approved body of knowledge, ready to pass it down to students. It is this shift of the teacher-centered classroom toward virtual classrooms and the possibilities for curriculum, instruction, and learning that make teaching in these times so challenging.

Douglas Kellner's Afterword is a synthesis of many key intermedial concepts. He explains that educators must develop critical pedagogies and new understandings of literacy in response to changing technologies and conditions in schools and society. He further asserts that teachers, through critical reflection and action, are potential leaders for countering media manipulation and promoting justice in social institutions. Most important, Kellner stresses that new classroom roles and forms of interaction are crucial to emancipatory pedagogies that empower students, teachers, and citizens. He points out that all the studies presented in this book show diverse ways students and teachers may learn together and thus create highly participatory, empowered roles. For Kellner, educational participants who collaboratively learn, examine, and reflect on new perspectives, literacies, pedagogies, and possibilities engage in critical behaviors needed in a truly democratic nation. Last, Kellner encourages educators to consider, employ, and adapt ideas and practices presented here so that they may transform their own classrooms into more relevant and egalitarian places.

It is our hope that these case studies and the attendant analysis will provide insights to practicing teachers and encourage them to develop dynamic learning environments. But the authors of these chapters are cognizant that teachers, who may have been trained in other theories and methodologies, may not be ready for their quite different role and expectations in intermediality. We invite the readers of this book to take up the illustrations from our classrooms and evaluate them critically so as to make sense of what works for their individual needs and particular social contexts.

References

Altheide, D. L., & Snow, R. P. (1986). The grammar of radio. In G. Gumpert & R. Cathcart (Eds.), *Inter/media: Interpersonal communication in a media world* (3rd ed., pp. 273–281). New York and Oxford, UK: Oxford University Press.

Althusser, L. (1986). Ideology and ideological state apparatuses. In H. Adams & L. Searle (Eds.), *Critical theory since 1965* (pp. 239–251). Tallahassee: Florida State University Press.

American Association of School Librarians. (1988). *Information power: Guidelines for school library media programs*. Chicago: American Library Association.

Ball-Rokeach, S. J., & DeFleur, M. (1986). The interdependence of the media and other social systems. In G. Gumpert & R. Cathcart (Eds.), *Inter/media: Interpersonal communication in a media world* (3rd ed., pp. 81–96). New York and Oxford, UK: Oxford University Press.

Barthes, R. (1957). *Mythologies* (A. Lavers, Trans.). New York: The Noonday Press. Farrar, Straus & Giroux.

Barthes, R. (1971). *Image, music, text* (S. Heath, Trans.). New York: Hill and Wang.

Barthes, R. (1974). *S/Z* (R. Miller, Trans.). New York: Hill and Wang/The Noonday Press.

Benveniste, E. (1986). Subjectivity in Language. In H. Adams & L. Searle (Eds.), *Critical theory since 1965* (pp. 728–732). Tallahassee: Florida State University Press.

Bakhtin, M. M. (1988). Intertexuality. In T. Todorov (Ed.), *Mikhail Bakhtin: The dialogical principle* (pp. 60–74). Minneapolis: University of Minnesota Press.

Bianculli, D. (1992). *Teleliteracy.* New York: Continuum.

Bissex, G. (1980). *Gnys at work.* Boston: Harvard University Press.

Bopry, J. (1994). Visual literacy in education—A semiotic perspective. *Journal of Visual Literacy, 14*(1), 35–49.

Brand, A. G. (1987). The why of cognition: Emotion and the writing process. *College Composition and Communication, 38*(4), 436–443.

Britton, J. (1985). Viewpoints: The distinction between participant and spectator role. *Research in the Teaching of English, 18*(3), 320–331.

Britzman, D. P. (1991). *Practice makes practice: A critical study of learning to teach.* Albany: State University of New York Press.

Buckingham, D. (1993). Introduction: Young people and the media. In D. Buckingham (Ed.), *Reading Audiences: Young people and the media* (pp. 1–23). Manchester, UK: Manchester University Press.

Burton, G. (1990). *More than meets the eye: An introduction to media studies.* London: Edward Arnold.

Calhoun, Craig. (1995). *Critical social theory.* Cambridge, MA: Blackwell.

Calkins, L. (1983). *Lessons from a child.* Portsmouth, NH: Heinemann.

Carpenter, E. (1960). The new languages. In M. McLuhan & E. Carpenter (Eds.), *Explorations in communication* (pp. 162–179). Boston: Beacon.

Cheyney, A. B. (1992). *Teaching reading skills through the newspaper* (3rd ed.). Newark, NJ: International Reading Association.

Considine, D. M. (1987). Visual literacy and the curriculum: More to it than meets the eye. *Language Arts, 64*(6), 34–40.

Considine, D. M., & Haley, G. E. (1992). *Visual messages: Integrating imagery into instruction.* Englewood, CO: Teacher Ideas Press.

Considine, D. M., Haley, G. E., & Lacy, L. E. (1994). *Imagine that: Developing critical thinking and critical viewing through children's literature.* Englewood, CO: Teacher Ideas Press.

Cooper, M. (1986). The ecology of writing. *College Composition and Communication, 36*(3), 364–375.

Davis, F. (1992, December 7–9). *Media literacy: From activism to exploration.* Background paper for the National Leadership Conference on Media Literacy. Queenstown, MD: The Aspen Institute.

Derrida, J. (1986). Structure, sign, and play in the discourse of the human sciences; Of grammatology; Difference. In H. Adams & L. Searle (Eds.), *Critical theory since 1965* (pp. 83–137). Tallahassee: Florida State University Press.

Dewey, J. (1933). *How we think.* Chicago, Henry Regnery.

Dobbs, B. (1988). Video friend or foe: How to teach the reading of seeing. In R. Braden et al. (Eds.), *Readings of the 21st Annual Conference of the International visual Literacy Association* (pp. 12–16). Blacksburg: Virginia.

Duncan, B. (1993). Surviving education's desert storms. Adventures in media literacy. *Telemedium, 39*(1–2), 13–18.

Duncan, B. (1997). Learn more about popular culture. *Telemedium, 43*(2), 20.

Edwards, B. L., Jr. (1991). How computers change things: Literacy and the digitalized word. *Writing Instructor, 19*(2), 68–76.

Elbow, P. (1985). The shifting relationship between speech and writing. *College Composition and Communication, 36*(3), 283–301.

Emig, J. (1983). *The web of meaning.* Upper Montclair, NJ: Boynton/Cook.

Evans, E. (1987). Readers recreating texts. In B. Corcoran & E. Evans (Eds.), *Readers, texts, teachers* (pp. 22–40). Portsmouth, NH: Boynton/Cook.

Farber, P., Provenzo, E. F., Jr., & Holm, G. (Eds.). (1994). *Schooling in the light of popular culture.* Albany: State University of New York Press.

Fehlman, R. H. (1996). Viewing film and television as Whole Language instruction. *English Journal, 85*(2), 43–50.

Fiske, J. (1987). *Television culture.* New York: Methuen.

Fiske, J. (1989). *Understanding popular culture.* Boston: Unwin Hyman.

Fiske, J., & Hartley, J. (1989). *Reading television.* New York: Routledge.

Flood, J., Heath, S. B., & Lapp, D. (Eds.). (1997). *Handbook of research on teaching the communicative and visual arts.* New York: Macmillan.

Flood, J., & Lapp, D. (1995). Broadening the lens: Toward an expanded conceptualization of literacy. In K. A. Hinchman, D. J. Leu, & C. K. Kinzer (Eds.), *Perspectives on literacy research and practice: Forty-fourth yearbook of the National Reading Conference* (pp. 1–16). Chicago: National Reading Conference.

Flower, L. (1989). Cognition, context, and theory building. *College Composition and Communication, 40*(3), 282–311.

Foster, H. M. (1979). *The new literacy: The language of film and television.* Urbana, IL: National Council of Teachers of English.

Frye, N. (1957). *Anatomy of criticism.* Princeton: Princeton University Press.

Giroux, H. (1988). *Teachers as intellectuals: Toward a critical pedagogy of learning.* South Hadley, MA: Bergin & Garvey.

Giroux, H. (1991). Postmodernism as border pedagogy: Redefining boundaries of race and ethnicity and rethinking the boundaries of educational discourse: Modernism, postmodernism, and feminism. In H. Giroux (Ed.), *Postmodernism, feminism, and cultural practice: Rethinking educational boundaries* (pp. 211–256). Albany: State University of New York Press.

Giroux, H., & McLaren, P. (Eds.). (1989). *Critical pedagogy, the state, and cultural struggle.* Albany: State University of New York Press.

Giroux, H., & Simon R. (1989). *Popular culture, schooling, and everyday life.* New York: Bergin & Garvey.

Goffman, I. (1981). *Forms of talk.* Philadelphia: University of Pennsylvania Press.

Goodman, J. (1992). Towards a discourse of imagery: Critical curriculum theorizing. *Educational Forum, 56*(3), 269–289.

Goody, E. N. (1978). Towards a theory of questions. In E. N. Goody (Eds.), *Questions and politeness: Strategies in social interaction* (pp. 16–43). Cambridge, UK: Cambridge University Press.

Greene, M. (1988). *The dialectic of freedom.* New York: Teachers College Press.

Gumpert, G., & Cathcart, R. (1985). Media grammars, generations, and media gaps. *Critical Studies in Mass Communication, 2*(1), 23–53.

Guralnik, D. B., & Friend, J. H. (Eds.). (1964). *Webster's new world dictionary of the English language* (College edition). Cleveland and New York: The World Publishing Company.

Heath, S. B. (1983). *Ways with words: Language, life and work in communities and classrooms.* Cambridge, UK: Cambridge University Press.

Herber, H. L., & Herber, J. N. (1993). *Teaching in content areas with reading, writing, and reasoning.* Boston: Allyn and Bacon.

Himley, M. (1991). *Shared territory: Understanding children's writing as works.* New York and Oxford, UK: Oxford University Press.

Hyerle, D. (1996). *Visual tools for constructing knowledge.* Alexandria, VA: Association for Supervision and Curriculum Development.

Kellner, D. (1995). Preface. In P. McLaren, R. Hammer, D. Sholle, & S. S. Reilly (Eds.), *Rethinking media literacy: A critical pedagogy of representation* (Vol. 4, pp. xiii–xvii). New York: Peter Lang.

Kervin, D. (1985). Reading images: Levels of meaning in television commercials. In N. Thayer & S. Clayton-Randolph (Eds.), *Readings from the 16th annual conference of the International Visual Literacy Association* (pp. 36–43). Bloomington, IN: Western Sun.

Lakoff, G., & Johnson, M. (1980). *Metaphors we live by.* Chicago: Chicago University Press.

Lester, P. M. (1995). *Visual communication: Images with messages.* Belmont, CA: Wadsworth.

Leveranz, D., & Tyner, K. (1966). What is media literacy? Two leading proponents offer an overview. *Media Spectrum, 23*(1),10.

Levinson, M. E. (1994). Needed: A new literacy. *The Humanist, 54*(3), 3–5, 34.

Lickona, T. (1991). *Educating for character: How our schools can teach respect and responsibility.* New York: Bantam.

Lusted, D. (Ed.). (1991). *The media studies book: A guide for teachers.* London and New York: Routledge.

Lutz, W. (1989). *Doublespeak.* New York: Harper Perennial.

McCaleb. (1994). *Building communities of learners: A collaboration among teachers, students, families, and community.* New York: St. Martin's Press.

McLaren, P., Hammer, R., Sholle, D., & Reilly, S. (1995). (Eds.), *Rethinking media literacy: A critical pedagogy of representation.* New York: Peter Lang.

McLuhan, M. (1962). *The Gutenberg galaxy: The making of typographic man.* Toronto: University of Toronto Press.

McLuhan, M. (1964). *Understanding media: The extensions of man.* New York and Toronto: McGraw-Hill.

McLuhan, M. (1978). The brain and the media: The Western hemisphere. *Journal of communication, 28*(4), 54–60.

McLuhan, M., & Fiore, Q. (1967). *The medium is the massage.* New York: Random House.

McMahon, B., & Quin, R. (1990). *Monitoring standards in education.* Ministry of Education, Western Australia.

McMahon, B., & Quin, R. (1993). Knowledge, power and pleasure: Direction in media education. *Telemedium, 39*(1–2), 18–22.

Messaris, P. (1994). *Visual literacy: Image, mind & reality.* Boulder: Westview Press.

Moffett, J. (1968). *Teaching the universe of discourse.* Boston: Houghton Mifflin.

Moline, S. (1995). *I see what you mean: Children at work with visual information.* York, ME: Stenhouse.

Mosenthal, P. B. (1993). Understanding agenda setting in reading research. In A. P. Sweet & J. I. Anderson (Eds.), *Reading research into the year 2,000* (pp. 115–128). Englewood Cliffs, NJ: Lawrence Erlbaum.

Neuman, S. B. (1991). *Literacy in the television age: The myth of the tv effect.* Norwood, NJ: Ablex.

Ohlgren, T. H., & Berk, L. M. (1977). *The new languages: A rhetorical approach to mass media and popular culture.* Englewood Cliffs, NJ: Prentice-Hall.

Ong, W. (1986). Knowledge in time. In R. Gumpert & G. Cathcart (Eds.), *Inter/media* (pp. 630–647). New York and Oxford, UK: Oxford University Press.

Papert, S. (1980). *Mindstorms: Children, computers, and powerful ideas.* New York: Basic Books.

Perl, S. (1980). Understanding composing. *College Composition and Communication, 31,* 363–369.

Pettersson, R. (1992). Describing picture content. In J. Clark Baca, D. G. Beauchamp, & R. A. Braden (Eds.), *Visual communication: Bridging across cultures* (pp. 153–160). Blacksburg, VA: International Visual Literacy Association.

Pike, K., Compain, R., & Mumper, J. (1997). *New connections: An integrated approach to literacy* (2nd ed.). New York: Longman.

Pope, C. A. (1993). Our time has come: English for the twenty-first century. *English Journal, 82*(3), 38–41.

Postman, N. (1993). *Technopoly. The surrender of culture to technology.* New York: Knopf.

Pritchard, D. R. (Ed.). (1994). *The American heritage dictionary* (3rd ed.). New York: Dell.

Reinking, D. (1995). Reading and writing with computers: Literacy research in a post-typographic world. In K. A. Hinchman, D. J. Leu, & C. K. Kinzer (Eds.), *Perspectives on literacy research and practice* (Vol. 44, pp. 17–33). Chicago: National Reading Conference.

Reutzel, D. R., & Cooter, R. B. (1992). *Teaching children to read: From basals to books.* New York: Merrill.

Rosenblatt, L. (1978). *The reader, the text, the poem: The transactional theory of the literary work.* Carbondale: Southern Illinois University Press.

Rushkoff, D. (1996). *How kids' culture can teach us to thrive in an age of chaos.* New York: HarperCollins.

Saint-Martin, F. (1990). *Semiotics of visual language.* Bloomington and Indianapolis: Indiana University Press.

Schmidt, P. R. (1993). Literacy development of two bilingual ethnic minority children in a kindergarten program. In D. J. Leu & C. K. Kinzer (Eds.), *Examining central issues in literacy research: Theory and practice* (pp. 189–196). Chicago: The National Reading Conference.

Schmidt, P. R. (1997). *Exploring values through literature with inquiry learning.* Paper presented at the International Reading Conference Institute: Exploring Values Across the Curriculum with Mass Media and Literature, Atlanta.

Schnitzer, D. K. (1990). Integrating reading, writing, speaking, art, music, and the content areas: Animation in the classroom. In P. Kelly & W. P. Self (Eds.), *Media and technology in the English language arts* (Vol. 40, pp. 25–29). Blacksburg, VA: Virginia Association of Teachers of English.

Schön, D. A. (1983). *The reflective practitioner: How professionals think in action.* New York: Basic Books.

Schön, D. A. (1987). *Educating the reflective practitioner.* San Francisco: Jossey-Bass.

Semali, L. (1994). Rethinking media literacy in schools. *Pennsylvania Educational Leadership, 13*(2), 11–18.

Sholle, D., & Denski, S. (1993). Reading and writing the media: Critical media literacy and postmodernism. In C. Lankshear & P. L. McLaren (Eds.), *Critical literacy: Politics, praxis and the postmodern* (pp. 297–321). Albany: State University of New York Press.

Sinatra, R. (1986). *Visual literacy connections to thinking, reading, and writing.* Springfield, IL: Charles C. Thomas.

Sinatra, R. (1990). Combining visual literacy, text understanding, and writing for culturally diverse students. *Journal of Reading, 33*(8), 612–617.

Smith, F. (1984). Reading like a writer. In J. Jensen (Ed.), *Composing and comprehending* (pp. 47–56). Urbana, IL: National Council of Teachers of English.

Spring, J. (1992). *Images of American life: A history of ideological management in schools, movies, radio, and television.* Albany: State University of New York Press.

Vacca, R. T., & Vacca, J. A. L. (1996). *Content area reading* (5th ed.). New York: HarperCollins.

Vygotsky, L. S. (1978). *Mind in society.* Cambridge, MA: Harvard University Press.

Watts Pailliotet, A. (1997). Questing toward cohesion: Connecting advertisements and classroom reading through visual literacy. In R. E. Griffin, J. M. Hunter, C. B. Schiffman, & W. J. Gibbs (Eds.), *Vision quest: Journeys toward visual literacy* (pp. 33–41). State College, PA: International Visual Literacy Association.

Watts Pailliotet, A. (1998). Deep viewing: A critical look at texts. In S. Steinberg & J. Kincheloe (Eds.), *Unauthorized methods: Strategies for critical teaching* (pp. 123–136). New York: Routledge.

Weber, S., & Mitchell, C. (1995). *"That's funny, you don't look like a teacher": Interrogating images and identity in popular culture.* London: The Falmer Press.

Witkin, M. (1994). A defense of using pop media in the middle school classroom. *English Journal, 83*(1), 30–33.

Worth, S., & Gross, L. (eds.) (1981). *Studying visual communication.* Philadelphia: University of Pennsylvania Press.

Zeichner, K., & Liston, D. (1996). *Reflecting teaching.* Mahwah, NJ: Lawrence Erlbaum Associates.

2 Deep Viewing: Intermediality in Preservice Teacher Education

Ann Watts Pailliotet

Deep viewing is a method for critical construction and analysis of textual understanding of children's writing. Deep viewing extends Himley's (1991) notions to all visual texts. I (and others) have employed it to analyze electronic media such as film, videos, television, newscasts, and commercials; print media such as textbooks, children's literature, and newspapers; and visual or mixed media such as artwork, software, web sites, comics, and magazine advertisements as well as for observations of instruction and social interactions in classrooms and schools.

Deep viewing embodies many intermedial principles and processes. The method draws from varied theories for its procedures. Participants "read" or deconstruct textual meanings and "write" or construct new ones (Barthes, 1974) through discourse analysis and personal responses, within a heuristic framework (Lusted, 1991). Understandings are guided by semiotic codes for print and visual information (Barthes, 1974; Saint-Martin, 1990) and three-leveled comprehension models (Herber & Herber, 1993; Kervin, 1985). The use of varied texts fosters active meaning construction of multiple signs, symbols, and signification (de Saussure, 1986; Silverman, 1983) and promotes literacy learning in multiple modalities (Flood & Lapp, 1995; Pike, Compain, & Mumper, 1997; Sinatra, 1986; Watts Pailliotet, 1997).

Deep viewing is a structured process through which participants first identify textual elements and discourse forms such as language (Stubbs, 1983), sound (Barthes, 1971), images (Messaris, 1994), and structures (Lusted, 1991), then interpret and respond to them through varied transactions (Rosenblatt, 1978). Through deep viewing, individuals build connections among texts (Bakhtin, 1988) and media forms (Neuman, 1991), literacy environments (Flood, Heath, & Lapp, 1997; Witkin, 1994), and their own and others' points of view (Johnson, Johnson, Holubec, & Roy, 1984) as well as present and possible social realities (Dyson,

1997). Central to the method is critical analysis of the textual, personal, and social representations participants construct (Kellner, 1988). As a critical pedagogy, deep viewing is incomplete unless it leads to reflection, learning, and praxis through positive personal and collective social action (Goodman, 1992; Sholle & Denski, 1993).

Elsewhere I have discussed at length deep viewing's theoretical premises (Watts Pailliotet, 1998). Here, I first explain procedures and adaptations for its use with varied texts. I then draw from research data to show how preservice teachers used the method to analyze print textbooks, social contexts of classrooms, and videotapes of their own teaching. By providing descriptions of instructional processes and results, I hope that teachers and educators may develop their own purposes for deep viewing and promote critical media literacy in their own classrooms.

Deep Viewing Methodology: Guidelines

Deep viewing is a three-leveled process. Participants first observe, identify, and describe elements in the text. Next, they respond and interpret their data in varied ways. Finally, they evaluate and apply their findings. The method is highly adaptable. Participants may deep view individually (one person examines all codes); partially (one person examines selected codes); collaboratively (each member of a group examines one code); or in a cooperative learning, Jigsaw II format (groups examine each code). Participants write notes and/or draw diagrams as they view and talk. In an individual or partial format, they discuss findings at the end of Level 3.

It is essential that participants follow the full sequence to develop grounded, critical understandings. In a collaborative format, after each level of discussion groups share their observations with the whole group, thus creating broad, varied understandings. Designate a facilitator, recorder and reporter in each group, especially when learning this technique. The facilitator keeps members focused on specific tasks of each level and makes sure all participants speak; the recorder takes notes about group findings; the reporter conveys ideas to others.

Codes for Analysis

Use the following codes, recording methods, and guiding questions to structure data and collect ample evidence:

1. *Action/Sequence*—This group notes events, patterns, sequences, order, and relationships of time through oral discussion; written notes; and/or visual devices such as flow charts, timed notes, story framing,

sketch to sketch, storyboards, and time lines. For films, television broadcasts, or software programs, the group records order, content, and duration of events. For textbooks, print narratives, or magazines, the group notes sequencing of information, in table of contents; chapter titles; and throughout the text, plot, and topics. For newspapers, the group would note order and pages of stories. In social observations, the group looks at what occurs, when, and for how long, asking, what happens? In what order? When and how long do events take place?

2. *Semes/Forms*—Semes are units of visual meaning. This group records visual forms—both objects and people—then examines their characteristics: colors, textures, repeated, emphasized, and contrasted forms (i.e., objects that are paired with other objects, such as lightness with darkness), as well as the appearance, types of dress, and features of actors. Semantic webs, storyboards, captioned pictures, or intersected lists are good ways to record information for this category. When examining films, advertisements or illustrations, this group focuses on symbols, use of color, or repeated images. When analyzing software, the group looks at icons, graphics, and visual content. When reading literature, the group focuses on character development and imagery. In newspapers, it would look at content of photographs. In a classroom observation, it might examine instructional materials, objects in the room and on the walls, how the teacher and students are dressed, and so on. The group asks, what objects are seen? What are their traits?

3. *Actors/Discourse*—This group examines what characters, actors, or texts say, through semantic feature analysis, tallies, or a selective verbatim. Group members note words and phrases that sum up main ideas or themes, repeated language, terms particular to a group or discipline, and language that is unfamiliar or seems out of place. In films, TV commercials, broadcasts, and social observations, they also note qualities of what is heard: the tone, rate, pitch of voices, and so on. In commercials, music videos, or film, they might examine song lyrics. For textbooks, literature, and software, they focus on how language conveys concepts and information, through chapter headings, repeated words, captions, quotes, and key ideas. For newspaper analysis, they might focus on titles, leads, and quotes. In social observations, they might record content of talk, tally who talks to whom, or focus on qualities of talk. They ask, what is said, written, or conveyed? By whom? How is it communicated? How is it heard or understood?

4. *Proximity/Movement*—Using storyboards, diagrams, or flow charts, this group examines uses of space and all movement, including gestures and movements of characters/actors and other forms. Group members note *vectorality* (where objects or actors move), relationships (how the forms move in relation to each other), and dimensions and relative sizes

(does one form dominate in front?). In advertisements, textbooks, computer programs, film, television, or illustrated literature, they examine how space usage creates meanings. They might examine size, borders, and white space of visual and print information. In newspaper analysis, this examination of space is key; where articles are situated in the paper (which page, what part, and what section) as well as their relative sizes sends many messages about their content and importance. During classroom observations, group members record when, where, and how teachers and students move. They ask, what sorts of movements occur? How is space used?

5. *Culture/Context*—This group notes symbolic and discourse references to cultural knowledge such as science, art, educational practice, or popular culture. Devices like Herringbone charts, who/what/where/when/why and how lists, or character trait graphics should be used here. This code is essential to critical analysis, because participants examine many tacit and explicit discourses and thus issues of control, equity, and representation. For instance, in textbooks, films, or newscasts, they would look for symbols or imagery that evoke stereotypes and undefined language that assumes audience understanding, as well as visuals, terminology, or rhetorical devices (such as the use of "we") that privilege certain points of view while neglecting or downplaying others. When reading literature, they examine setting and point of view. When analyzing newspapers, they focus on who, why, how, and where questions: Whose point of view is represented and left out? Why is this story presented as being important and how is it presented? Where does it occur and how is that place and its people represented? They might analyze textbook content for gender or racial biases, newscasts or commercials for content accuracy and target audiences, or classrooms to determine what content and values are conveyed through the formal and hidden curricula. They ask, what social knowledge is referred to and assumed? What is implied? What is missing? Where are the creators and actors in this text situated historically and culturally?

6. *Effects/Process*—In commercial texts, such as film, software, and television broadcasts, this group examines artistic and production devices: the use and repetition of techniques, quality of visuals, sound effects, musical accompaniments, camera angles, technological enhancements, and so on. In less sophisticated productions, viewers examine camera or observer angles, noting what is seen and missing, then posit how perspectives influence understanding. In print texts such as newspapers or textbooks, they examine production devices used to structure the text and further the creators' purposes, such as bold print, font, and illustration style. In fieldwork or naturalistic observations, they seek to understand how the observer's perspective and participation affects un-

derstanding and outcomes. Storyboards, cause-effect charts, or decisionmaking models are best here. This group should also focus on the quality of the text, that is, how do factors such as sound, angle of perception, devices, and focus affect meaning? Group members ask, what production devices and elements are in the text? What meanings do these devices construct? How do my own and the creators' points of view influence meaning?

First Level: Literal— Describing and Summarizing

Form groups according to codes. Select facilitators, recorders, and reporters. In a group setting, students focus on one category, using a variety of responses, including talk, writing, and pictures. For very small groups, ask participants to observe more than one code. For individual observations, create a paper with six vertical columns and record observations under each heading.

Level 1 is *literal*. Its purpose is to gain as much data as possible for subsequent analysis. I have found, however, that individuals of many ages and abilities often have difficulty simply recording what they observe; instead, they attempt to move directly to interpretation or evaluation. Most teachers have encountered students who make comments like, "I feel this way about it," or, "This is good/ bad," but who cannot connect their responses to specific textual examples. For literacy skills, content learning, and critical analysis to develop, students must learn to ground personal responses in specific textual evidence. Preservice teachers must also show how their beliefs arise from real-life outcomes. Therefore, it is likely that teachers will need to instruct students how to collect and record data through modeling and practice, using varied graphic organizers, note-taking strategies, and observational techniques noted above in the code categories.

Before deep viewing, remind participants of the following: Describe only what you see and hear. Gather as much data as possible. Do not interpret or evaluate. While viewing the text, take notes and/or draw pictures of aspects you notice. Record questions that puzzle you. Observe within your group's assigned focus or code.

After viewing, give the following directions: During this level there is no cross talk in groups. First, take turns speaking in your groups. Each person shares notes about what he or she has seen and heard in the text. This level is literal. Describe only what you perceive in the text—interpretation will come later. The recorder should write down observations, particularly those that are repeated. Next, summarize. Remain brief, but remain as true as possible to what each participant feels or perceives is the main point of his or her observation. Recorder underlines or notes main ideas. Third, each group reports findings to the whole group through oral, pictorial, and/or written means. Other groups take notes, draw pictures, and/or formulate questions for subsequent discussion.

Second Level: Interpretation: Responding, Exploring, and Constructing Meanings

The purpose of Level 2 is to explore multiple responses to findings made explicit in Level 1. There are no single "right answers," but many possible interpretations. Some deep viewing response strategies are similar to those employed with traditional print texts. They may be modeled by teachers or group facilitators before beginning this level. Examples include summarizing; questioning; exploring meanings of key words, images, or ideas; comparing and contrasting; forming hypotheses; connecting textual elements; positing meanings of repeated data; recalling responses to other texts and experiences; identifying purposes and intended audiences; noting what is missing; locating text in social, historical, cultural, or intellectual contexts; noting author devices and possible motivations for their use; and articulating intellectual and emotional responses. Any strategy may be used for any of the codes.

At this level, teachers may also develop specific questions or prompts to focus response, depending on their instructional purposes (e.g., noting persuasive strategies, stereotypes, point of view, or a theme stressed in readings or guiding inquiry into connections between the current text and others). I have developed guiding questions to help students comprehend textual elements in all media (Watts Pailliotet, 1998), to promote content area reading skills (Watts Pailliotet, 1997) and to enable preservice teachers' critical analysis of effective teaching (Watts Pailliotet, 1995).

Stress that students need to cite data from Level 1 observations to support and explain their interpretations. Often, responses drawn from the codes will begin to overlap at this level, as participants begin to discover relations between textual elements and their observations about them. This overlap is desirable, but in Level 2, focus on a single category until all code-specific remarks are completed. There is no cross talk in groups until each participant has had a minimum of three uninterrupted turns to speak.

Teachers should facilitate the following progression: First, each viewer makes an observation based on explicit aspects of the text. Note what is present *and* what is missing. Begin with observations that are readily apparent and then move to more inferential levels. Talk until all members agree their observations are complete and are ready to move into the third level. Groups again stop and share their observations with the whole group.

Third Level: Synthesis, Extension, Evaluation, and Application

At Level 3, participants synthesize, extend, evaluate, and apply information and interpretations made explicit in the first two levels. Each person should have several uninterrupted turns before open group discussion begins. Teachers may also frame inquiry here by identifying key Level 2 comments or topics or providing students with a specific task (e.g., "Identify and evaluate point of view, author purposes," etc.). Participants should also question each other, starting with their code focus and then progressing to discussions of other categories.

Teachers should offer the following directions: In groups, express broader inferences about meanings. You may now indicate personal likes and dislikes, citing aspects of the text you recorded earlier. Be explicit about textual content and personal responses. Say "I" when expressing an opinion or observation; say "the text" when expressing what you noted at the literal level. Evaluate this text by comparing it with others or certain criteria, draw on personal experiences, identify disagreements and shared views in your groups. Pose questions and develop ways you would change the text or might act in the future, based on your assessments.

At this level, the codes will overlap, as participants make connections among their own observations and those of others. They should relate the text to their own experiences, expectations, feelings, purposes, and knowledge. Often, at this stage, participants construct larger themes. All participants should have ample opportunities to listen and respond. There may be breaks in conversations. Facilitators should allow these reflective pauses for participants to assimilate and formulate ideas. Discussion continues until group members agree that the topic has been exhausted, and then the groups report back to the whole group, describing findings, themes, questions, or issues they see as particularly interesting or important. Teachers may then facilitate a whole group discussion, summarize key points, or ask students to summarize.

At this point, teachers should connect the deep viewing experience to future learning and action. For instance, they might ask students to write a formal summary or compare/contrast paper, convey their findings through a different medium or genre; devise strategies for reading content textbooks or critically viewing a text, rewrite part of a text from a different point of view, build a vocabulary word bank, construct an artistic or dramatic response, complete a creative writing assignment or other project that employs devices they identified, begin a research project to learn more about topics and points of view missing from the original text, or create personal goals and a plan for future learning or skills development.

In the next section, I demonstrate how I applied deep viewing's intermedial premises and procedures to my instruction of preservice teachers.

Methods for the Study

Research Context: College, Program, and Course

I teach at a small liberal arts college in the Pacific Northwest. Our preservice teacher program embodies many intermedial goals. We strongly believe educators must actively and critically think about *why* they are doing things—simply knowing *how* to implement instruction is not enough. We want our students to become informed agents of social change, so we have entire courses devoted to examining how current educational issues are presented in diverse media, as well as ethics of teaching and educational equity. Our students learn to observe and connect contexts early on; they learn varied research methods, engage in ongoing school observations, and complete teaching practica throughout their coursework, so that they can understand, critique, and address actual social conditions in schools. Our students are also highly literate with varied media; we require much writing, impose a heavy reading load, and utilize computers and mass media throughout our classes. Since our state has developed performance-based standards for reading, writing, communication, and content, students learn how to observe, record, and assess learning outcomes and their own teaching capacities in multiple ways. Based on notions of social learning, much of our instruction is cooperative in nature. Last, we require much critical analysis of varied print, experiential, and electronic texts, because we believe good teachers are good communicators. By the time our students get to methods courses, most are predisposed to look at the world critically, "reading" possible meanings in many ways and "writing" diverse texts (print, visuals in print, and electronic).

I teach a semester-long course entitled "Resources in Secondary Education," required for all secondary teacher candidates. It combines traditional content area reading instruction with mass media, technology, and popular media. Our two required texts are Vacca and Vacca's (1996) *Content Area Reading* and Considine and Haley's (1992) *Visual Messages: Integrating Images into Instruction*. Students also read numerous articles about uses of specific media for literacy instruction. They attend 1-1/2-hour classes three times a week and engage in an ongoing, 10-week high school practicum that involves weekly observation and teaching assignments.

Participants

Six students in my spring 1997 class were seniors; four were juniors. All were fairly high achieving and motivated, with minimum grade point averages of 3.0 in their education and content major coursework. There were nine Caucasian students and one African American enrolled, four males and six females, with majors including biology, English, French, psychology, history, politics, and environmental studies. I am a middle-aged, Caucasian, female assistant professor with an English education background.

Data Collection and Analysis

Over one semester, I collected multiple data that informed my teaching and allowed me to assess students' learning from varied perspectives. This dynamic interaction among research and practice, with observations informing reflection and instruction, was a core intermedial concept I wished to instill in these future educators.

First, my course syllabus, daily lesson plans, instructional materials, and assignment handouts served as a basis to understand what we did in class. I compared these materials with three sets of students' class notes (from one male and two females who volunteered to share them) to see if what I thought I was teaching was what students were understanding. All notes reflected structures and content similar to the lesson plans. As the course progressed, I noticed an increasing use of questions and annotations in student notes, suggesting they were engaging class ideas in critical and active ways.

Second, after lessons, I wrote biweekly reflections (three to five single-spaced pages) in which I recalled and summarized student comments, behaviors, and outcomes during classes. These notes allowed me to better understand patterns and changes in their behaviors and thus perhaps in their understandings or perspectives. For instance, by Week 4, I noted a shift away from my own teacher-directed talk and behaviors to more student-initiated talk, questions, and actions. Additionally, students began to challenge or disagree with me and question each other instead of turning to me "for the answer," indicating that they were beginning to act, think, and speak from empowered, dynamic, and discriminating stances. In response to these data, I scheduled more student-directed discussions and projects as the semester progressed.

Third, I collected all students' weekly practica reflection papers. Here, I focus on two—an observation of social context and interactions in a secondary classroom and a textbook analysis. Each week, I read, reread, and commented on the reflections, then noted common elements, themes, and ideas and unusual comments (negative cases) and also looked for what was missing—a process similar to constant comparative analysis (Glaser & Strauss, 1967). I offered my themes and notes as student feedback each week and used them as a basis for teaching subsequent classes, reviewing or extending concepts as needed.

Next, I gathered data from students' end-of-the-semester, in-class microteaching. I took participant observation field notes while each taught. I then deep viewed their 10 videotapes, taking notes according to code categories. All students also created an "effective teaching rubric" and assessed peers by noting examples observed during lessons. All students took their peers' rubrics, deep viewed their own tape, and wrote a reflection paper. After observing in class and viewing the tapes, I read student rubrics and reflection papers. I combined these sources using a grid and written comments (Miles & Huberman, 1984) to construct a multifaceted picture of my students' teaching practices and understandings.

Fifth, I compared similarities and changes in content, length, language, and concreteness (connecting real-life observation and action to theory or personal belief) of students' "I believe papers," written in Weeks 2 and 14. In these, they wrote about their definitions of literacy and purposes for instruction and schooling, what students and teachers should do in classrooms, preferred methods, materials, assessment, and desired educational outcomes. I compared these at the end of the semester, identifying themes and changes, to gain an idea if and/or how students' instructional beliefs and practices had changed.

Last, I used course evaluations and students' self-assessments to identify what concepts, learning, practices, and personal or professional changes they felt were most important. These last three data sources offered me insights into the effectiveness of my own teaching practices, helped me reflect on what changes I needed to make in future classes, and provided clues as to what kinds of teachers my students might become (Britzman, 1991).

Intermediality in Preservice
Education: Three Deep Viewings

Textbook Deep Viewing

In Week 3, students engaged in a group deep viewing analysis of the content area textbooks used in their practica classrooms. This assignment served many purposes: It helped them understand required content, scope, and sequence in their chosen disciplines; made them aware of varied meta-cognitive and comprehension strategies for reading; assisted them to identify structures and elements common across varied media; enabled them to critically read a text for point of view, content, bias, and missing information; and, perhaps most important, allowed these future teachers to articulate plans, adaptations, alternative materials, and practices for using textbooks in their own classrooms.

Despite considerable past training in observation and analysis, these preservice teachers initially had a great deal of difficulty simply describing textual content—all attempted to move directly to evaluation. Eight were highly critical of their texts and said they were "boring," "lower order," "watered down," "biased," "basic," "irrelevant," "sexist," or "stupid." This finding shows the importance of teaching and modeling observational and analytic processes.

I immediately stopped the session and retaught observation and data collection strategies for Level 1, tying these processes to the content analysis needed by secondary teachers to plan, and reading strategies— such as previewing and note taking—needed by students to learn. I made a grid on the board and asked students to connect their critiques first to specific textual elements, then to a personal response, and finally to evaluation. By asking questions like, "What elements make this boring?" (examples of lower-level questions at the chapter's end, muted color, and consistent style of layout) or " biased" or "sexist?" (predominance of white male figures in a history text and male authors in an English anthology, smaller size of pictures that included women, captions, lack of pictures or facts about ethnic minorities, isolation of short chapter about "famous women" toward back of book). I next asked, "What is your response to these elements?" and we wrote each response to specific textual content.

Once they could anchor and connect interpretations to specific textual content, students then returned to Levels 2 and 3 discussion. After the session, they wrote textbook analyses that revealed common themes: articulation of what was missing in terms of content, representation, and point of view; identification of specific examples from texts to illustrate point of view and cultural bias; textual citations directly linked to personal response; and time lines, summaries, or lists of curricular scope and sequence, with suggested revisions or additions.

Additionally, eight explained specific actions they would take when teaching with their text. These included using it as a guide for planning curriculum, as an anthology from which they would select readings or activities, as "one of several resources," as a "basic source of information if I'm not sure about initial facts," as a "starting point for discussion," and (my favorite) as "a means to teach my students how to read between the lines critically and start asking questions . . . I'm going to teach them the strategies we learned in class."

Analysis of Social Contexts and Interactions in a Secondary Classroom

In Week 5, students individually deep viewed the social contexts and interactions in their high school classrooms. This assignment also had many purposes, including practice of informal assessment techniques, a chance to compare the idealized physical layouts and guidelines for student/teacher interaction described in course texts with the realities of a classroom setting, critical inquiry into formal and hidden curricula, and an opportunity to appreciate the complexities of teaching.

Students submitted data (3–12 pages) suggesting they were highly observant and competent in gathering information. Their notes were organized according to the six deep viewing codes and reflected diverse techniques learned in previous classes as well as mine: selective verbatim, checklists, flow charts, diagrams, lists, summaries, pictures, tallies, ratios of talk, and timed notations of classroom sequences.

During class, after they had collected data, I instructed them to organize their notes in some way. I gave them guiding questions: What's there? What's missing? What's repeated? How do you feel about what you observe? What personal or educational beliefs of teachers and students do these observations convey? Have you experienced similar situations? What are the limits of your observations? What works in this context? What doesn't? For whom? Why? What would you change or keep? Students formed groups, discussed data, and then color-coded, made grids, summarized, added observer comments, or used numerical codes to organize observations.

Their subsequent written reflections shared common traits. All began with sequential outlines or lists of events, perhaps as a way to structure and convey their experiences. Learning transfer from our earlier textbook analysis likely took place. All described specific objects, materials, and classroom layout (particularly arrangement of student desks and access to and use of materials, as well as classroom adornment). All identified specific student behaviors (kid watching) and teacher actions in detail, using comments, gestures, movements, and events, rather than merely reporting vague accounts like "s/he was studying," "off task," or "teaching." These observational and recording skills are in keeping with the performance-based assessment required by our schools.

Additionally, all also demonstrated critical analysis in several ways: by noting elements missing from their classrooms—student work on walls, teacher interaction with certain groups or individuals, use of varied media, student/student interaction, active learning, or higher-order questioning. All articulated strengths and weaknesses of specific methods, materials, interactions, or objects. None made blanket statements that a certain teaching strategy or interaction was solely "bad" or "good." Instead, all discussed trade-offs and articulated practical alternatives and additions to the physical layouts, teaching methods, materials, and teacher behaviors they perceived, suggesting they were thinking about teaching in critical, complex ways. They then applied their observations to actual practices. For instance, several described how they would change the configuration of desks, post student work on the walls, or "move around the room more." After observing a teacher-directed lecture, one wrote he would "add more scaffolding, active involvement and make the lesson have more multiple modalities. I'd start with a web so students could generate ideas and see responses, then they could go back in pairs after reading and discuss their predictions. At this point, I'd jump in and fill in the gaps with guided questions and an overhead and they could take notes."

Students' foci also varied widely. Six recalled personal experiences in their own schooling and compared or contrasted them with data in their observations. Eight discussed themes generated through data. Three explored points of view among different students and variations in how they might have perceived the lesson; two wrote about possible teacher motivations; one discussed the hidden curriculum in terms of gender and race; four noted the limits of their observations (length, "a onetime thing," or where they were sitting); one detailed the larger context ("it was assembly day"); four wrote not only how they would change what they observed but why. One compared and contrasted examples of effective and ineffective teaching; another cited positive and negative social interactions tied to her "I believe" teaching guidelines; two gave multiple examples of data to critique—quite harshly—teachers they felt were "ineffective" or "racist."

I was highly pleased with the depth and completeness of data; the students' abilities to connect observations to analysis; and their varied, critical, and complex responses. Certain topics were notably absent from their papers, however. Although they focused on their own or students' affective responses to social conditions, they largely neglected student academic learning outcomes, descriptions of student products, in-depth accounts of content, examples or discussion of assessment techniques, and analysis of how contexts influenced discipline and management. In subsequent weeks, we covered these topics through readings, class activities, and practica.

Videotaped Microteaching

In the last two weeks, all students engaged in 30- to 40-minute in-class microteachings for their peers. This project allowed them to demonstrate learning and observation skills, reflect on their own teaching and that of others, formulate assessment criteria, communicate their pedagogical beliefs, and evaluate varied teaching styles and lessons.

We began this assignment by identifying aspects of good teaching and critical reflection and then negotiated assessment criteria. In this way, we identified clear objectives and outcomes. I required a scaffolded instructional framework, active student involvement, efficient time use, quality content area learning, evidence of effective management strategies, and relevant assessment for lessons, but asked the students to identify further traits of effective teaching. Each created a rubric based on 7 to 10 criteria he or she felt were most important and then described how superior, fair, and poor outcomes might look, in terms of behaviors, lesson plan and structure, comments, materials used, and so on. (Common categories included active learning; multiple modalities; use of varied, interesting, or relevant media; scaffolding; clear directions/modeling; higher-order thinking in student response; and professional presentation through dress, movement, and voice.) These were copied and shared with classmates.

We engaged in the same procedure for video analysis and reflection papers. Some of my requirements included evidence of data observation and analysis through coding, summary, and so on; clear examples from data to illustrate interpretations in papers; synthesis of findings and course learning into themes; and connections among theory or ideas and actual practice. Students added further criteria, such as identifying their teaching strengths and weaknesses, a minimum length, and clarity of description. Again, we discussed what superior, average, and poor papers would look like; both I and students generated oral and written examples.

The microteachings reflected intermedial concepts through their use of varied texts, literacy modalities, and methods. One student connected meanings of symbols in *The Dark Crystal* to those in several American poems. Another asked us to examine the green light imagery in the closing page of *The Great Gatsby* by employing advertisements, film clips, a graphic organizer, paired reading, discussion, and writing. A science major began with current articles about cloning, collected from the Internet, popular magazines, and newspapers, to engage us in a debate about scientific ethics before launching into a genetics lesson. During a French lesson, we smelled varied perfumes, developed vocabulary lists of our descriptors, then wrote copy and drew advertisements for them. A history major connected television coverage of the O. J. Simpson trial to textbook readings about Civil War reconstruction. We used comprehension guides, discussion, and written narratives to develop historical and present understandings of race and civil rights. We learned much about politics and environmental studies when we studied local maps, read newspaper articles posing competing views about land use, wrote arguments, and then engaged in a role-playing exercise to determine an action plan for local development. In another lesson, about body image and nutrition, we viewed a sequence from *Clueless* and examined print advertisements to identify dominant social messages about food and appearance. We then assessed the validity of these images through discussion and written response. Next, we heard a brief lecture on nutrition, read a text that demonstrated examples of healthy diets, used newspapers to shop for a day's meals, and defended our choices, drawing from prior content.

After each lesson, students had 10 minutes to write observations in their rubric categories and to grade each other. Nine connected specific data from peers' lessons to each of their criteria, citing comments, behaviors, events, gestures, and so on to support assessments. Eight wrote additional remarks. The tenth student checked off categories on his rubric and offered a summary statement of strengths and weaknesses at the page bottom. All identified varying student points of view, assuming the stances of one or more of their classmates and responding from their perspectives. All then made constructive, concrete suggestions to improve lessons, no longer delivering harsh, unsupported criticisms as they had during textbook analysis. Thinking complexly and translating observation into praxis are at the heart of intermediality and critical literacy for me. One student typifies these aims when he wrote:

> This lesson definitely promoted higher order thinking and interest. You used images and metaphor well by showing how they were repeated in a movie and the book. . . . It showed good scaffolding and relevance when you began with the [film] clip and asked us to watch for colors, then discuss their meanings and how we felt. . . . However, people like [names classmate] who don't have an English background had a hard time with this. You can tell because he kept asking questions. . . . [Another classmate] was drawing and off task most of the time. . . . You spent a lot of time on the green light metaphor at the end of *Gatsby,* but we read it to ourselves and then you went right into discussion. . . . This lesson would be good for college students or [an] AP high school class, but it might not work for an average high school student. Definitely needs more support like line by line analysis or vocabulary for middle school.

Like the example above, all rubrics recorded clear, observable phenomena and connected them to specific evaluation criteria. After analyzing my in-class and deep viewing notes, I was also pleased that all students' microteachings embodied core course concepts: use of multiple literacy modalities, texts, and methods; active, critical thinking; scaffolding through planning and delivery; content knowledge; clear communication of criteria and desired outcomes; relevance and active student learning; ongoing monitoring; and varied, appropriate assessment.

Four students later deep viewed their videotapes in a group; six did so individually. After reading their peers' comments, they wrote three- to five-page reflection papers. Again, there were certain common themes. First, all cited specific data from their own lesson plans, peer rubrics, and deep viewing notes to discuss at least one aspect of each code category. For instance, one talked about lesson pacing and gaps in her anticipatory set under Action/Sequence; her rationales for using varied materials in Semes/Forms; comments that illustrated her "unclear" directions and resultant vague student responses under Actors/Discourse (as well as the "annoying" fast rate and high pitch of her voice); how she used Proximity/Movement to get two students back on task; and how the context (Culture/Context) may have influenced her lesson—"It was a spring day and many of us were burned out from working on theses." She summed up the limits of the video recording under Effects/Process: " I couldn't see what [names student] was doing because she was out of camera range and I can't remember." Second, after citing data observations, all could articulate strengths, weaknesses, and multiple alternatives for future lessons. Additionally, five noted that the deep viewing process was positive, because it helped them "structure," "focus," "organize," "pick apart," and "think about" their data.

Seven went farther and discussed teaching guidelines or principles they had learned through the experience, linking them to specific practices or future goals. One reported, "I learned how important planning is. . . . [Describes at length peer comments and instance in lesson where she "lost" her "place" and "forgot a step."] In the future I know I have to write my directions and questions out more, play the lesson in my head before I teach it, and anticipate what students will say."

But not all students responded with such concrete plans for future action. Only three were as specific as the individual above. The remainder made no mention of goals or identified only vague aspirations for "better management," "structure," "experience," and "practice." Most had no discussion about how they might accomplish needed learning or demonstrate future professional growth. During our last class, we collectively made a huge semantic web of course learning, which covered the board. I then asked students to make individual grids, identifying what they still needed to learn, how they would learn it, and how they would demonstrate this learning. Although we shared the grids and discussed goals, many remained fairly intangible in terms of action. In the future, I will develop much more instruction in this area.

Conclusion

The three applications of deep viewing detailed here might easily be adapted for other preservice settings and school classrooms. Analysis of textbooks might help students learn critical reading strategies such as previewing and comprehension techniques, as a KWL (*k*now, *w*ant to know, *l*earned) exercise to begin an inquiry project or thematic unit or for teachers to identify content and plan lessons. Deep viewing of social contexts enables students and teachers to assess the effectiveness of cooperative learning, daily instruction, and classroom behaviors. The microteaching process is easily adaptable to varied oral or video student presentations, as well as providing a means for teachers to reflect on their own instruction.

The students' final "I believe" papers indicated they had learned and implemented many intermedial concepts of the deep viewing method. In their initial versions, eight defined literacy as merely "reading and writing" or "content." Two originally discussed literacy in more global terms: as "communication" or "experiencing the world." Now, all defined literacy in broadened ways—as "empowerment" or "power"; "action"; "multiple modalities" or "media"; "critical 'reading' of the world—not just a book"; "interactions among students, teachers, texts, and contexts"; "communication and conversation in many forms"; "something that is everywhere, not just in classrooms"; "change growth movement"; and "creating, understanding, critiquing, and acting." Additionally, all papers were longer and more detailed than initial ones. All students now used relevant terminology and multiple, specific examples of methods, materials (all now cited many mass media), assessment, and student outcomes to support their definitions and beliefs.

The deep viewing process of linking literal observation to interpretation and evaluation may have aided in the creation of these well-grounded papers.

The changes in "I believe" papers, the varied deep viewing reflections, my own data and student notes, rubrics, student self-assessments, and course evaluations seemed to demonstrate that these preservice teachers had honed their abilities to observe, analyze, respond, think complexly and critically, evaluate, and teach using many texts. Five students specifically made positive comments about deep viewing on their course evaluations or self-assessment, noting it was one of the most important things they had learned.

I'm certain that the deep viewing process alone did not lead to the results reported here. Whatever changes and outcomes these preservice teachers exhibited were the result of sustained, interdisciplinary foci inherent in our program and reinforced over time, as well as the participants' own willingness to work hard; take risks; and engage with the course, me, and each other. But the deep viewing method does indeed embody many of the practices, theories, texts, and outcomes needed by both theorists who wish to explore notions of intermediality and classroom teachers who wish to implement critical literacy pedagogy.

References

Barthes, R. (1971). *Image, music, text* (S. Heath, Trans.). New York: Hill and Wang.

Barthes, R. (1974). *S/Z* (R. Miller, Trans.). New York: Hill and Wang/The Noonday Press.

Bakhtin, M. M. (1988). Intertexuality. In T. Todorov (Ed.), *Mikhail Bakhtin: The dialogical principle* (pp. 60–74). Minneapolis: University of Minnesota Press.

Britzman, D. P. (1991). *Practice makes practice: A critical study of learning to teach.* Albany: State University of New York Press.

Considine, D. M., & Haley, G. E. (1992). *Visual messages: Integrating imagery into instruction.* Englewood CO: Teacher Ideas Press.

de Saussure, F. (1986). Course in general linguistics. In H. Adams & L. Searle (Eds.), *Critical theory since 1965* (pp. 646–663). Tallahassee: Florida State University Press.

Dyson, A. H. (1997). *Writing superheroes: Contemporary childhood, popular culture and classroom literacy.* New York: Teachers College Press.

Flood, J., Heath, S. B., & Lapp, D. (1997). Preface. In J. Flood, S. B. Heath, & D. Lapp (Eds.), *Research on teaching literacy through the communicative and visual arts* (pp. xv–xvii). New York: Macmillan.

Flood, J., & Lapp, D. (1995). Broadening the lens: Toward an expanded conceptualization of literacy. In K. A. Hinchman, D. J. Leu, & C. K. Kinzer (Eds.), *Perspectives on literacy research and practice: Forty-fourth yearbook of the National Reading Conference* (pp. 1–16). Chicago: National Reading Conference.

Glaser, B. G., & Strauss, A. (1967). The discovery of grounded theory: Strategies for qualitative research. Chicago: Aldine.

Goodman, J. (1992). Towards a discourse of imagery: Critical curriculum theorizing. *Educational Forum, 56*(3), 269–289.

Herber, H. L., & Herber, J. N. (1993). *Teaching in content areas with reading, writing, and reasoning.* Boston: Allyn and Bacon.

Himley, M. (1991). *Shared territory: Understanding children's writing as works.* New York and Oxford, UK: Oxford University Press.

Johnson, D. W., Johnson, R. T., Holubec, E. J., & Roy, P. (1984). *Circles of learning: Cooperation in the classroom.* Minneapolis: Association for Supervision and Curriculum Development.

Kellner, D. (1988). Reading images critically: Toward a post-modern pedagogy. *Journal of Education, 170*(3), 31–52.

Kervin, D. (1985). Reading images: Levels of meaning in television commercials. In N. Thayer & S. Clayton-Randolph (Eds.), *Readings from the 16th annual conference of the International Visual Literacy Association* (pp. 36–43). Bloomington, IN: Western Sun.

Lusted, D. (Ed.). (1991). *The media studies book: A guide for teachers.* London and New York: Routledge.

Messaris, P. (1994). *Visual literacy: Image, mind & reality.* Boulder: Westview Press.

Miles, M. B., & Huberman, A. M. (1984). Qualitative data analysis: A sourcebook of new methods. Newbury Park, CA: Sage.

Neuman, S. B. (1991). *Literacy in the television age: The myth of the tv effect.* Norwood, NJ: Ablex.

Pike, K., Compain, R., & Mumper, J. (1997). *New connections: An integrated approach to literacy* (2nd ed.). New York: Longman.

Rosenblatt, L. (1978). *The reader, the text, the poem: The transactional theory of the literary work.* Carbondale: Southern Illinois University Press.

Saint-Martin, F. (1990). *Semiotics of visual language.* Bloomington and Indianapolis: Indiana University Press.

Sholle, D., & Denski, S. (1993). Reading and writing the media: Critical media literacy and postmodernism. In C. Lankshear & P. L. McLaren (Eds.), *Critical literacy: Politics, praxis and the postmodern* (pp. 297–321). Albany: State University of New York Press.

Silverman, K. (1983). *The subject of semiotics.* New York: Oxford University Press.

Sinatra, R. (1986). *Visual literacy connections to thinking, reading, and writing.* Springfield, IL: Charles C. Thomas.

Stubbs, M. (1983). *Discourse analysis: The sociolinguistic analysis of natural language.* Chicago: University of Chicago Press.

Vacca, R. T., & Vacca, J. A. L. (1996). *Content area reading* (5th ed.). New York: HarperCollins.

Watts Pailliotet, A. (1995). "I never saw that before." A deeper view of video analysis in teacher education. *The Teacher Educator, 31*(2), 138–156.

Watts Pailliotet, A. (1997). Questing toward cohesion: Connecting advertisements and classroom reading through visual literacy. In R. E. Griffin, J. M. Hunter, C. B. Schiffman, & W. J. Gibbs (Eds.), *Visionquest: Journeys toward visual literacy* (pp. 33–41). State College, PA: International Visual Literacy Association.

Watts Pailliotet, A. (1998). Deep viewing: A critical look at texts. In S. Steinberg & J. Kincheloe (Eds.), *Unauthorized methods: Strategies for critical teaching* (pp. 123–136). New York: Routledge.

Witkin, M. (1994). A defense of using pop media in the middle school classroom. *English Journal, 83*(1), 30–33.

Appendix One:
Student Comments About Deep Viewing

Deep viewing is "a means to teach my students how to read between the lines critically and start asking questions."

"I will teach this method so my students can 'read' and 'write' in many ways."

"The textbook analysis made me stop and think about who's story gets told and who's gets left out. . . . It also made me very aware that I can't take the text for granted, I have to be critical . . . I need to show this to my students."

"Deep viewing helped me structure a huge amount of information so I could see repeated data. After that, it was easy to start thinking about the themes and patterns."

"I couldn't believe how much I saw in there [the school classroom observation]. The [deep viewing] categories were the only way I could make sense of all of it."

"The deep viewing took my microteach to a deeper level. . . . I got past the surface things like the way I sounded or looked. . . . It helped me be more objective and more positive. . . . I could see how what I did impacted the class, then break it down and think about it in more real practical ways."

"I felt empowered when I deep viewed my tape and that's what I want for my students."

"One of the best things about this class was deep viewing. It made me 'read beyond the lines' and think about what was missing from textbooks and teaching. It helped me express what I believe, my materials and methods, what I want to my students to do, and what kind of teacher I want to be."

"At first it was really hard watching myself [on the teaching video]. . . . I'm glad I went through the whole [deep viewing] procedure though because getting feedback and watching the tape made me realize I have some good teaching strengths. . . . Hearing and seeing it in different ways made things more real than just listening to someone write or talk about it."

"I liked how Pailliotet really taught what she preached. The deep viewing was rad—multiple modalities, scaffolding, activating schema—all the BIG HITS!"

"Deep viewing was one of the best methods we learned because it really typifies what the course was about and my own beliefs about literacy. . . . It is active, crosses disciplines, involves students, makes people think, and can be applied in lots of ways."

Appendix Two:
Student Definitions. Literacy is. . . .

"Empowering students to read and write the many worlds around them. . . . [It is] creating, understanding, critiquing and acting."

"Critical 'reading' of the world—not just a book but using multiple modalities."

"Literacy is the multiple modalities of reading, writing, speaking, listening, viewing, moving, acting, thinking, feeling. Literacy is being aware of life. . . . It is thinking, feeling, and action. . . . It's having the tools and using the tools to understand, learn and create."

"Literacy is interactions among students, teachers, texts and contexts."

"Literacy is communication and conversation in many forms."

"Literacy is social and personal power. . . . Analyzing both mass media and academic materials will let my students access and use that power in positive ways."

"Literacy is potential. It is not a static set of facts. It is Change growth [and] movement. . . . The world outside my classroom is constantly changing. I can't ignore it and I don't want to. I want to empower my students to discover their own unique potential as human beings and also make them aware of the many future possibilities in society. To do this, I have to show them connections between their lives in school and out of it. . . . Media literacy is a bridge between students and teachers, classrooms and society, the present and the future."

"I began this class thinking my job was to teach content, period. To be honest with you, I wasn't interested in 'touchy feely' or 'pc' education. But in my practicum I learned right away I can't just stand up there and deliver information in a lecture or book all the time. The kids won't accept it or learn it. . . . My beliefs have changed. I agree 'every teacher is a teacher of literacy' [quote from syllabus] and literacy is more than teaching content. I've learned my own teaching involves knowing content but also understanding students and where they come from. . . . Literacy is something that is everywhere, not just in classrooms. . . . Using different mediums adds a human side like relevancy and interest. My students will learn more content and think more critically about it (which are still my main goals) if they have different ways of seeing and hearing information."

"Media literacy helps students understand their own and other people's cultures."

"I want my students to know that history isn't just some dry 'objective' set of facts and literacy isn't just reading a book and regurgitating answers on multiple choice exams. History is essential in their daily lives. So is literacy. My main goal is for students to be able to identify and critique multiple points of view presented by various groups throughout history. They have to be able to use many kinds of texts to do this, because textbooks generally only present one point of view. I will use strategies like modeling, graphic organizers, alternative readings, creative writing, group projects, role playing and discussion. Media literacy will definitely be a large part of my instruction, because it shows students how the same idea or event can be represented in radically different ways."

"Media literacy works. I've seen it firsthand."

Intermediality in the Classroom: Learners Constructing Meaning Through Deep Viewing

Sherry L. Macaul
Jackie K. Giles
Rita K. Rodenberg

Since the mid-1980s, we have witnessed significant and transformative changes in literacy. The definition of literacy has become dynamic and ever changing. Innovations range from the ways in which information is accessed and viewed to the processes and mediums by which messages are constructed and represented. In this chapter, we present a case study of how a multiage class of seventh/eighth graders perceive and interpret a variety of media during viewing. Applying the *deep viewing* approach developed by Ann Watts Pailliotet, we consider individual and group-generated interpretations of students' deep viewing of commercial/ad/web site. The commercial/ad/web site have been created by the same company. They promote the same products in three different media namely, TV (videotaped commercial), a newspaper ad, and a product web site. We then compare what our students know about and can do with the concepts and processes that English/language arts and other standards suggest for literacy and technology. Finally, we propose new directions for curricular projects.

Purpose of Case Study

The purpose of our study is to explore elementary/middle-level learners' perceptions, interpretations, and critiques of various types of media and sign systems as they apply the deep viewing approach to construct meaning while viewing a video, reading a text, and browsing a web site. We begin by discussing the current literature that supports the concept

that we are proposing, *intermediality*. We consider several new definitions of literacy as well as perspectives on "viewing" and "visually representing," the two most recently acknowledged areas of English/language
arts. We then present our case study findings as well as support for the
concept of intermediality. Next, we examine related national and state
standards created by national professional associations that pertain to
English/language arts, speaking/listening, and media literacy as well as
the visual arts. Finally, we propose ideas for teaching and learning.

Questions posed by this deep viewing study are concerned with how
elementary and middle-level learners

1. Perceive, analyze, and evaluate mass media and interpret messages when commercials/ads are presented via TV/video, newspapers, and web sites
2. Respond to "intramediality," the impact that a variety of interactive media (visual and auditory representations such as voice,
   music, graphic or digital images, animation, morphing, etc.)
   within a particular message have on interpretations and meaning construction of the message
3. Respond to "intermediality," the impact that a variety of interactive media (visual and auditory representations such as voice,
   music, graphic or digital images, animation, morphing, etc.)
   from our prior knowledge and experience with mass media have
   on interpretations
4. Interpret ads differently individually versus through social collaboration in viewing discussion circles

Students

The students in this case study are seventh/eighth graders attending a
Pre-K–8 elementary/middle school. These students possess similar experiences with viewing but varied backgrounds in exploring and applying new technologies for creating visual representations of meaning.
Some of the students are familiar with on-line services and web sites
and one student has created his own web page. The majority of the students have had minimal experience accessing and evaluating on-line resources. The school is located in a Midwest community of 50,000 people.
The students represent various socioeconomic backgrounds. Students
enrolled in these classes are primarily of Caucasian and Hmong descent.
The school relocated to its newly constructed building in fall 1997. There
is a library/media center with approximately 16 Windows computers
with one active modem line in the library/media center.

New Definitions of Reading/Literacy

Currently, we perceive reading as a transactive, constructive process. But definitions of reading/literacy are constantly evolving. Barton (1994, p. 5) speaks of "new, more complex views of what is involved in reading and writing" and asks us to consider them in the context of human activity, social life position in history, language and learning. He recommends a shift "to studying literacy as a set of social practices associated with particular symbol systems and their related technologies." He asserts that a social view of literacy involves "literacies and domains, roles and networks, literacy as communication, values and awareness" as integral components. An integrated view of literacy, according to Barton, begins with people's use of literacy in their everyday lives versus their formal learning of it. Bruce (1997) perceives literacy as "sociotechnical practice" (p. 303). He offers a conception of literacy as the evolution of social and technological changes. He suggests that "literacy is expressed by its technologies rather than determined by them" (p. 294). Willinsky (1990) recognizes the "new literacy as increasing students' control over text its meaning which alters the relationship between teacher and student" (p. 7). He envisions literacy as connecting school, community, and one's life.

Flood, Heath, and Lapp (1997, p. xv) introduce the notion of a broadened or "expanded view of literacy" that includes the visual and communicative arts as well as recognizing the social influence on language and literacy. They address the idea of "commingled forms/representations" such as sound, animation, images, and meanings constructed through students' everyday lives outside of school and through the mass media. They refer to this as "multiple layered information" requiring a variety of interpretation skills and recognition of the importance of visual literacy. Flood, Heath, and Lapp advocate the need to recognize and promote the importance and integration of both the visual and communicative arts in the schools, whether student created or technology enhanced. They suggest the need for further research analyzing how different kinds of visual arts promote learning.

Messaris (1997) indicates that we need to move beyond considering literacy as the "ability to read and write" to entertaining the notion of "multiple literacies" (p. 3). Reinking, Labbo, and McKenna (1997) suggest that emerging forms of electronic literacy may require us to abandon our traditional conceptualizations of literacy. Calfee (1997) in refining his definition of critical literacy calls it "the capacity to use language and other media for representing ideas to think, to solve problems, and to communicate" (p. 145). In addition, he offers Olson's (1995, p. 292) definition of writing as "any graphic form used to convey meaning" and literacy as "getting meaning as well as understanding how a text works."

Hobbs (1997, p. 7) believes that mass media have been largely omitted from the curriculum. She compels us to consider teaching "about media" versus just with media, analyzing and evaluating the messages created by such literacies that influence our "emotional responses." She urges us to consider a new definition of literacy from the media literacy movement as suggested by Firestone (1993): "the ability to access, evaluate and communicate messages in a variety of forms" (quoted in Hobbs, 1997, p. 7). Such learning experiences can provide effective samples on which students may base their own creations. Hobbs (1997) and Gilster (1997) encourage us to guide students toward relevant and authentic inquiry-based issues and problems of study that can bring about social change. Newman's (1997, p. 19) "theory of synergy" suggests that each medium has its own unique structure and processing strategies. She has found that through practice, learning through the medium is enhanced and transferred to new learning environments. Sweet (1997) suggests that the dual coding theory expands literacy to include the visual and communicative arts with "multiple codes and images that deepen students' understanding" (p. 273). She further asserts that "the convergence of multiple disciplines accommodates an evolving and expanded view of literacy" (p. 280). Eisner (1991), citing Broudy (1987) contends that "the image—visual, tactile, auditory—plays a crucial role in the construction of meaning through text" (quoted in Eisner, 1991, p. 125). He asserts that "those who cannot imagine, cannot read." Eisner further suggests that each form of representation can be used in a different way and calls for different skills and forms of thinking. His conception of literacy is a way of conveying meaning through and recovering meaning from the form of representation in which it appears. Eisner (1997) states, "Each form of representation can be used in different ways, and each way calls on the use of different skills and forms of thinking" (p. 352). Gee (1996) defines a discourse as a "socially accepted association among ways of using language, other symbolic expressions and 'artifacts' of thinking, feeling, believing, valuing, and acting that can be used to identify oneself as a member of a society meaningful group or 'social network' or to signal a socially meaningful 'role'" (p. 131). We need to consider how media messages may promote and include versus exclude individuals and groups from various discourses. Finally, Gilster (Pool, 1997) defines "digital literacy" as "the ability to understand information—and more important—to evaluate and integrate information in multiple formats that the computer can deliver" (p. 90). He adds, "Being digitally literate in multidimensional and interactive" (p. 6).

Intermediality

Beach et al. (as quoted in Harris & Hodges, 1995, p. 122) define the term *intertextuality* as constructing meaning by making text connections based on one's prior knowledge of "literary and social conventions of texts." "Intermedia" is defined by Weiner (1996) as "a combination of art forms such as audiotape and print material or film and live performance, also called mixed media or multimedia" (p. 308). In this chapter, we refer to intermediality as suggesting that meaning is constructed based on one's prior knowledge of a variety of media messages, social experiences, and conventions. It is our belief that intermediality represents making connections across a convergence of various media. Meaning is based on a person's or group's media life experiences, which may include sound, voice, music, graphics/images, animation, hypermedia/multimedia, and live performances. The term *intramediality* suggests to us the way in which individuals or groups make connections among various media within a given media message and how these media interact with one another to create unique individual or collective group meanings.

Deep Viewing

The deep viewing approach developed by Watts Pailliotet (1995) was used as the basis for this case study. The deep viewing analysis code titles, descriptions, and questions were modified to meet the ages and grade levels of the learners as shown:

1. *Action/Sequence* (time relationships)—What happens? When and for how long?
2. *Semes/Forms* (visual meaning units)—What objects are seen? What are their characteristics?
3. *Actors/Words*—What is said and by whom? How is it said and heard?
4. *Closeness/Distance and Movement* (directionality and relationships of movement)—What types of movements occur?
5. *Culture/Context*—To whom might this video be targeted? What symbols do you notice?
6. *Effects/Processes* (artistic devices, visual and audio)—What is seen? What is missing? What is the quality?

   Comments and Questions (not part of deep viewing but aimed toward eliciting critical responses to media) What impact does this video have on you? What effects influenced you most? What do you want to know about this video?

The seventh-/eighth-grade students in this case study applied the deep viewing approach and responded to three types of mass media, including a TV commercial/video, a newspaper ad, and a web site over a three-week period. The commercial, ad, and web site were created by the same company and promoted the same products. The ad is recent and has been featured via the national and local mass media between November 1996 and spring 1998.

1. *Deep Viewing:* TV commercial/video—*Time*—The New Dodge (BBDO Advertising, 1996)

The commercial begins with a red ball traveling through a rectangular transparent object that the children referred to as "glass" or " the window of time." The background is black. The ball turns into a car as it moves through the "glass." Each time the red car or truck passes through the glass, it morphs into a different car or truck and the name of each newly created vehicle is shown in white print on the screen beside or under the vehicle. The ball begins in the upper left-hand corner of the screen and moves toward the bottom right-hand corner. Subsequent vehicles rotate among the upper and lower left quadrants of the screen, which are the areas of the screen where viewer's eyes tend to focus often during viewing. The music and sounds build as the ad continues. The commercial ends with a chorus and the last few seconds show what the children refer to as "pieces of swirly things," forming the New Dodge symbol. During the 60-second commercial, a voice describes how the cars and trucks have undergone change through time.

2. *Deep Viewing:* Newspaper ad—The New Dodge—"Steel Medals"

The horizontal, full-page ad features the same series of red vehicles lined up side by side. Above the vehicles in huge letters is written "Steel Medals" and below are the 8 to 10 titles and graphics of the awards won by the Dodge cars and trucks, indicating the categories for which they are recognized.

3. *Deep Viewing:* Web site—The New Dodge (www.4adodge.com)

The web site shown to the students had a graphic of a New Dodge vehicle with a red motion streak behind the car to create the illusion of movement. In addition to the company name and symbol, there are at least 10 to 12 hot links to take the viewer to areas for additional information about each vehicle as desired.

Case Study: Intermediality in Elementary/Middle-Level Education

1. Deep Viewing—Personal Responses to New Dodge TV commercial/video Time—The New Dodge (BBDO Advertising, 1996)

Students in the multiage seventh/eighth grade were given a sheet of paper with the words "deep viewing" on it and asked to record their name and grade level. They were asked to respond to the video individually in writing and/or with drawings in terms of its meaning for them. The responses were collected.

Findings: Deep Viewing—Personal Responses. We classified the students' free responses under the six deep viewing analysis areas listed above. We found three patterns to emerge from their responses, namely the content of their responses, the order/sequence, and the overlap or connection of a particular response with one or more other categories. (For example, movement, action, semes, and effects often contained statements that could have been classified in more than one of the six categories that may be related to intermediality.) In general, the seventh-/eighth-grade students freely responded earlier in their responses (usually their first 1–4 responses) to the effects/process, action/sequence, and semes/forms categories. Next in order of sequence came actors/words and closeness/distance and movement. Finally, culture/context was only rarely responded to and did not appear to fit this commercial. As we analyzed the students' individual free responses, we noted that music, visuals, and action/movement were the codes that students attended to overall. Although there were no actors present, the students were attuned to the words spoken by the narrator.

When we categorized students' open-ended responses, they clustered under the deep viewing categories as follows:

Action/Sequence
found the way they changed shape to be intriguing
changes every time and you get to see many different automobiles
shows many different things, not boring

Semes/Forms
the color red and the clear/transparent windows or glass
how the vehicles looked like a pool of water as they moved through
  the glass
bright colors, black and red, made it stand out
it looked expensive
red cars and sparks

Actors/Words
talks about time
it's about time and music changes with it
good slogan
did not have information on prices

Closeness/Distance and Movement
seeing the different glass, at the end, made me think there would be
  more and better cars in the future
showed how they turned a red ball into trucks and cars
going through time and releasing cars

very catchy
sparks, now the RAM came together
how each car went through the glass and it changed the car

Effects/Process
music was good
ripples in the glass
background music fit the commercial
cool, unreal, futuristic
type of music and camera angles
how they made a splash, the music gets you excited
it's good and has cool music
neat music, cool camera shots
voice in control loudish and deep "unreal"
good sound effects, lasts longer, goes fast and looks smooth
said how they lasted longer
computer animation was excellent
high tech, something from the future
three dimensional view was cool very convincing

The students' responses indicate that they are aware that the slogan focuses on time and change. Many grasp the notion of how the music and images change together and connect with the slogan. They are especially perceptive of the camera shots, animation, and high-tech effects. One student comments on the commercial as being convincing. Another suggests that it shows a transformation. Comments by several students indicate that they see how the media work together to create/reinforce meaning.

2. Deep Viewing—Individual Responses to New Dodge TV commercial/video Time—The New Dodge (BBDO Advertising, 1996)

Next, the students received a copy of Watts Pailliotet's (1995) deep viewing guide containing the six codes with a brief description and one to two questions related to each level as shown above. The students were given an opportunity to view the video again and were asked to respond individually in writing to the deep viewing categories. Finally, the students met in viewing discussion circles, shared their responses, and completed a group deep viewing guide and submitted that as well.

Findings: Deep Viewing—Individual Responses. Data analysis of the students' individual responses indicates that the students are able to classify their ideas and thoughts about the ad into the six analysis code areas. The responses that individual students share in writing on their deep viewing personal responses also appear in categorization on the new code sheet. The guide words assist students read and respond. The students readily identify the author's purpose. They mention media effects such as the camera, colors, and movement. One student mentions the idea of transformation and others address change. A diverse range of responses to the three questions emerge as follows:

What impact does this video have on you? Why?
I want a car. I have always wanted a car.
Dodge is a good make.

What effects influence you the most?
camera movement
the effects are the transformation
cars splashing through glass
music
cars morphing, computer animation
how it changes, the cycle, and the music
sound influenced me the most and relaxed me

What do you want to know about this video?
Who is the narrator?
the price
How did they make it?
How much do the cars cost?
the swirlies
How long did it take to make?
Has the ad helped sales?

3. Deep Viewing—Group Response to New Dodge TV commercial/video Time—The New Dodge (BBDO Advertising, 1996)

The students met in groups of three to four to share individual deep viewing responses and submitted a combined record of their discussion. The guides were turned in and a whole class discussion took place.

Findings: Deep Viewing Guide—Group Response—Social Constructivist Perspective. Each one of the five group deep viewing guides was compared to the individual guides of each member of that particular group. A review of the individual responses indicates that the group recorders constructed representative responses that tended to be all-inclusive. In one case, the group response represents a collective listing. Other groups collapse data with broader terms being used to summarize. Overall, there appears to be a consensus in the ideas compiled and recorded by these elementary/middle-level students.

The students seem to be won over by the ad. Only a few students actually question the product. It is evident that these learners will need to engage in learning experiences to help them become critical viewers, conscious consumers, and honest producers of media. Critical analysis and evaluation are content objectives and processes suggested in the Wisconsin English/Language Arts Standards (McCallum & Benson, 1998) and the Speaking, Listening, and Media Literacy Standards for K Through 12 Education (Speech Communication Association, 1996), as well as the Wisconsin Visual Literacy Standards (Driscoll, 1998).

4. Newspaper Ad Versus Television Commercial—New Dodge

In the next session, the students were provided with individual copies of a full-page newspaper ad for the same products advertised in the commercial. The students were given an analysis/evaluation activity entitled, "What Is It Saying?" from *Messages and Meaning: A Guide to Understanding Media* (Garrett, Frey, Wildasin, & Hobbs, 1996). The students responded to the following questions after viewing the commercial and reading the newspaper:

Newspaper   *TV*

Name the product
What is used to get your attention?
What is used to make you interested in the product?
What is used to make you want to own the product?
What is used to make you want to buy the product very soon?
Would you buy this product? Why or why not?

Findings: Newspaper Ad and TV Commercial (same products).
Newspaper Ad—The students indicate that the newspaper ad indicates the accomplishments of the company's cars and trucks. One student exclaims, "If you don't buy soon it will be the old Dodge." They comment on the bold letters and word play, "Steel Medals." The students address the importance of the awards since they represent quality.

TV Commercial—The students note that in the commercial the names of the cars appeared and that the setting of the video was high tech, futuristic, transformational, and convincing.

5. Comparison and Contrast of Newspaper Ad, TV Commercial, and Web Site http://www.4adodge.com (same products)

At the final session, the students viewed the company's web site to see how the product was portrayed in this new media. The students then engaged in an activity from *Messages and Meaning* (Garrett et al., 1996) focused on comparing and contrasting the newspaper ad, TV commercial, and web site.

Findings: Web Site—Student Group Responses.

website goes into more detail
more cars and lots of information
buttons, little things you could push to take you up to a section
cars, awards and articles
same thing as video and newspaper
it's written
no movements, no speech
car speeding around (motion streak)
for people who want a car
you choose what you want to see for as long or short as you want
scroller, illusion of speed, Dodge icon, music is missing
website should have more
I choose what I want to see as long as I want to stay
car's fake motion until we change the screen

Next we examine how students interpret ads presented across the three media.

TV/Video Commercial.

Action/Sequence
different time frame
cars floating, moving, and changing
sixty seconds
car moving through window/glass

Semes/Forms
different cars, trucks and a sign
red ball, glass, cars, sparks

Closeness/Distance
cars displacing cars going through the glass
morphing
goes through glass
slow movements that look 3-D

Culture/Context
anyone
car buyers
everyone
people who need cars
people watching TV
adults watching TV

Effects/Process
cars—good camera movement
red cars, glass, more real
cars, red ball, glass
people
good music
cars and trucks

Newspaper.

Action/Sequence
red cars in a row with words
cars in a line until you turn the page
cars in a line with writing at bottom of the page

Semes/Forms
medals and red cars, glass
awards
cars, trucks and bold letters

Closeness/Distance
cars all lined up and show medals won
cars lined up sideways at an angle

Culture/Context
anyone
safety, people, and Dodge symbol

adults and older kids
people reading
medals, trophy, and vehicles

Effects/Process
nice format, smooth, shiny cars
awards, nice touch
red cars
shadows
cars and trucks
cars and words
metal spelled medal

Web Site.

Action/Sequence
buttons
looks like cars moving
moving icons
select what want to see for as long as want to see it
display cars
cars speeding

Semes/Forms
same
lots of information
red cars and icons
icons
scroller

Closeness/Distance
cars speeding
icons
illusion of speed
looks like it is moving

Culture/Context
anyone
Dodge symbol/icon
car buyers
gives more detail
people who have Internet

everyone on the web
people online, on the Internet
looking for cars with medals

Effects/Process
it had things to push to get the section wanted, convenient
red cars
sound is missing
cars and trucks
cars and words
should have more

Looking across the student responses to viewing across the three media, it becomes apparent that the students see how time and action can be denoted through movement and through streaks of color creating an illusion of movement. They perceive that bold letters attract the attention in text and that movement attracts attention in video. They understand that icons/buttons lead to additional information. Under the web site, they use descriptive words such as display and scroller. Under culture and context, the students were able to differentiate among the roles of viewer, reader, and browser as the active audience of the messages. Finally, in terms of effects, several students noted that the sounds seemed to be missing from the web site. They knew that such media could incorporate sounds but may be unaware of the memory constraints. These cross-media comparisons/reflections help students begin to perceive how media are in some ways unique. They are also beginning to understand how various media are beginning to converge and share qualities and types of information that can enhance the message.

As is evident from the student comments above, the students were able to note many benefits and advantages of ads/commercials appearing on a web site. Students who possess more experience with electronic media are able to use the terms such as "morphing" and "scroll bar" to more accurately describe their responses. The students have begun to realize how various media provide different types of access as well as important forms of information that we all must begin to understand and apply.

6. Comparison of a Traditional Newspaper with Its On-Line Version

During the third week, we asked the students to compare and contrast their local newspaper in traditional paper format with its on-line format. The students were provided with a copy of that day's local newspaper. Then, via a large screen projector, the students were shown their same local paper on-line. After an introduction and demonstration as to how the on-line version functions, the students used a Venn diagram to compare and contrast the newspaper with its on-line version.

Leader Telegram
can carry around and save specific articles
cheaper, wording larger, read faster and can move
you do not have to go to the computer
indexed pages. easier to use
not easier to use
takes longer because you need to flip pages

Leader Telegram On-Line
better
easier to follow, can pick spots really fast
faster and options
do not have to turn pages, easy access, more information
easier to find an article, do not have to go buy it
more color and more attractive
icons easily scroll, links, color, and animations
quicker, doesn't get crumpled up
easier to read, gets to article right away, links everything together
quicker way to use
choose articles you want to see, hard to read if small, can do it
    faster

Comparison of Leader Telegram *and* Leader Telegram On-Line
inform
news and pictures
good news, names, and the same stories and reporters
you still read
information and pictures
tells where everything is

Responses from the students indicate that they perceive many of the advantages of each medium. In addition, it is evident that they perceive the commonalities across media and also the convergence of media that is occurring.

Case Study Questions

In response to our initial questions we found that
1. Students were able to perceive and analyze but only somewhat evaluate information presented in the three different media namely, TV/video, newspapers, and web sites.

2. Many students applied the concept of intramediality, identifying and applying the interactivity of the various media in the commercials and ads (visual and auditory representations such as voice, music, graphic or digital images, animation, morphing, etc.) to construct meaning ("built-in meaning" by designers).

3. Many students applied the concept of intermediality, associating and applying the interactivity of the various media from one's background knowledge and experience as well as in the commercial or ad (visual and auditory representations such as voice, music, graphic or digital images, animation, morphing, etc.) to construct meaning ("built-on meaning " by the viewer).

Intermediality

The term intermediality to us suggests that we apply a variety of media when interpreting mass media messages. Our prior knowledge and experience with various media and combinations of media and their conventions influence our interpretations. Sound, words/voices, images, graphics/photos, animations, and morphing all contribute to the meanings that we collaboratively construct, refine, and negotiate with others. We must critically evaluate such messages to be certain that we are not inappropriately influenced by the surface structure of the media. New definitions of literacy must include the use of visual, auditory, and performance media. Our schools must help students not only perceive, analyze, and critically evaluate mass media messages but also construct and communicate visual representations through significant issues and problems in their world.

Standards and Intermediality

Inquiry, research, and problem-based learning are important components of the most recent standards in such areas as math, science, social studies and English/language arts. Applying inquiry, research, or problem-based learning approaches guides students to focus on relevant issues and learning experiences that allow them to apply the communicative and visual in authentic real-life contexts.

The standards related to the present study include:

- English/language arts, namely reading, writing, speaking, listening, viewing, and visual representation (International Reading Association & National Council for Teachers of English, 1996)
- Speech communication standards for speaking, listening, and media (Speech Communication Association, 1996)
- Visual arts (Driscoll, 1997).

The Model Academic Standards for the English Language Arts Draft No. 3 (McCallum & Benson, 1998) for the state of Wisconsin offers the following guidelines related to intermediality:

1. Media and technology for elementary/middle level include:

   A. use computers to acquire, organize, analyze and communicate information
   B. make informed judgments about media and its products
   C. create products appropriate to audience and purpose
   D. demonstrate a working knowledge of media production and
   E. distribution
   F. analyze and edit media work as appropriate to audience/purpose

2. Inquiry/research

   A. conduct research and inquiry on self-selected or assigned topics, issues, or problems and use an appropriate form to communicate their findings

The national Speech Communication Association Standards, focused on speaking, listening, and media, offer the following guidelines. They indicate that these must be both studied and practiced if children and adults are to become wise media consumers.

1. Speaking—effective communication processes include:

   - designing coherent messages
   - clearly delivered
   - adaptable to listeners

Standards related to this study include:

   - the relationships among the components of the communication process
   - the various levels of the meanings of messages
   - role of personal responsibility in making ethical communication decisions

2. Listening—active process of

   - receiving
   - interpreting

- responding

Standards related to this study include:

- the ability to use language that clarifies, persuades, and/or inspires while respecting the listener's backgrounds, including their culture, gender, and individual differences.

3. Media literacy—critical, reflective consumers understand how words, images, graphics, and sounds work together in subtle and profound ways

- mass media influence how meanings are created and shared in society
- selecting how to send a message and evaluating its effect— must be aware of the distinctive features of each medium
- communication changes when moving from one medium to another
- to process information critically
- create messages appropriate for both the medium of transmission and the audiences of those messages

Standards related to this study include demonstration of

- the effects of the various types of electronic audio and visual media including television, radio, the telephone, the Internet, computers, electronic conferencing, and film on media consumers
- the ability to identify and use skills necessary for competent participation in communication across various types of electronic, audio, and visual media

The visual literacy standards final draft for the state of Wisconsin (Driscoll, 1997) suggest the following guidelines related to intermediality:

1. Doing

A. visual design and production
B. practical applications

2. Communicating

A. visual communication and expression
B. visual media and technology

3. Thinking

   A. art criticism
   B. visual thinking

4. Understanding

   A. personal/social development

5. Creating

   A. making connections
   B. visual imagination and creativity

As is evident from reviewing these excerpts from the standards, there are many connections and commonalities across the various communication processes. How do children and adolescents use these processes to interpret and construct media messages? How do they respond to the "convergence" of these new media?

Moving from Deep Viewing to Visual Representation and Media Design

The next phase of our project with the seventh-/eighth-grade students will involve analyzing and evaluating three informational types of media productions used to promote this fall's 50-year celebration of our local Beaver Creek Reserve Nature Center. A video of the two-minute TV news spot shown in October has been accessed along with copies of the special weekend insert from the *Leader Telegram*. Students will read the newspaper and then view the Beaver Creek web site to see how the celebration is depicted in each of the three media. Students will work in teams to analyze and evaluate the processes and effective communication and visual techniques involved in each media production.

Finally, following several of the standards listed above, teams of students will select an inquiry-based project focused on issues and problems in their local community of interest to them. They will research their issue and present their perspectives by creating a video/TV clip, a newspaper story (traditional or on-line), or a web site. After the students have created their media representations and reflected on their practices, a media professional from the *Leader Telegram* will provide them media production techniques and tips to enhance their representations. The three teacher-researchers in this study will be establishing learning environments and activities to provide learning experiences to guide students in creating well-designed media. We will select activities from *Messages and Meaning: A Guide to Understanding Media* (Garrett et al., 1996) and *Mastering the Message: Performance Assessment Activities for Understanding Media* (Garrett, McCallum, Yoder, & Hobbs, 1996). Then, the students will use multimedia programs, video, digital cameras, and web page software to produce their media. Finally, students will share them with their peers and self-reflect on their work.

Evaluating Media Productions

The recent literature provides numerous suggestions and guidelines for evaluating and designing media from critical content and issues to the organization and design features of the message (Glister, 1997; Caruso, 1997; Harris, 1997). In addition, the question of ethics arises when we consider such design techniques as morphing, which is digital alteration of an image or text. As critical consumers, students need to evaluate the use of such design techniques both in the media they view as well as in the media that they design. Our goal is to assist students in becoming skillful, critical, and ethical consumers and designers of media.

References

Barton, D. (1994). *An introduction to the ecology of written language.* Cambridge, MA: Blackwell.

BBDO Advertising. (1996). *The new Dodge* [Television commercial].

Broudy, H. (1987). *The role of imagery in learning* (Occasional Paper No. 1). Los Angeles: Getty Center for Education in the Arts.

Bruce, B. C. (1997). Literacy technologies: What stance should we take? *Journal of Literacy Research, 29,* 289–309.

Calfee, R. (1997). Assessing development and learning over time. In J. Flood, S. B. Heath, & D. Lapp (Eds.), *Handbook of research on teaching through the communicative and visual arts* (pp. 144–166). A project of the International Reading Association. New York: Simon & Schuster Macmillan.

Caruso, C. (1997). Before you cite a site. *Educational Leadership, 55,* 24–25.

Driscoll, V. (1997). *Wisconsin's model academic standards for the visual arts.* Madison: Wisconsin Department of Public Instruction.

Eisner, E. W. (1991). Rethinking literacy. *Educational Horizons, 69,* 120–128.

Eisner, E. W. (1997). Cognition and representation: A way to pursue the American dream? *Phi Delta Kappan, 78,* 349–353.

Firestone, C. (1993). *Media literacy: A report of the National Leadership Conference on Media Literacy.* Washington, DC: The Aspen Institute Communications and Society Program.

Flood, J., Heath, S. B., Lapp, D. (Eds.). (1997). *Handbook of research on teaching through the communicative and visual arts.* A project of the International Reading Association. New York: Simon & Schuster Macmillan.

Garrett, S. D., Frey, J., Wildasin, M., & Hobbs, R. (1996). *Messages and meaning: A guide to understanding media.* Newark, DE: Newspaper Association of America Foundation, International Reading Association, and National Council for the Social Studies.

Garrett, S. D., McCallum, S., Yoder, M. E., & Hobbs, R. (1996). *Mastering the message: Performance assessment activities for understanding media.* Newark, DE: Newspaper Association of America Foundation, International Reading Association, and National Council for the Social Studies.

Gee, J. P. (1996). *Social linguistics and literacies: Ideology in discourses* (2nd ed.). Bristol, PA: Taylor Francis.

Gilster, P. (1997). *Digital literacy.* New York: John Wiley.

Harris, J. (1997). Content and intent shape function: Designs for web-based educational telecomputing activities. *Leading and Learning with Technology, 24,* 17–20.

Harris, T. H., & Hodges, R. (Eds.). (1995). *The literacy dictionary: The vocabulary of reading and writing.* Newark, DE: International Reading Association.

Hobbs, R. (1997). Literacy for the information age. In J. Flood, S. B. Heath, & D. Lapp (Eds.), *Handbook of research on teaching through the communicative and visual arts* (pp. 7–14). A project of the International Reading Association. New York: Simon & Schuster Macmillan.

International Reading Association & National Council for Teachers of English. (1996). *Standards for the English Language Arts.* Newark, DE, & Urbana, IL: Author.

McCallum, S., & Benson, J. (1998). *Wisconsin's Model Academic Standards: English Language Arts* (Draft No. 3). Madison: Wisconsin Department of Public Instruction.

Messaris, P. (1997). Introduction. In J. Flood, S. B. Heath, & D. Lapp (Eds.), *Handbook of research on teaching through the communicative and visual arts* (pp. 3–6). A project of the International Reading Association. New York: Simon & Schuster Macmillan.

Newman, S. (1997). Television as a learning environment: A theory of synergy. In J. Flood, S. B. Heath, & D. Lapp (Eds.), *Handbook of research on teaching through the communicative and visual arts* (pp. 15–22). A project of the International Reading Association. New York: Simon & Schuster Macmillan.

Olson, D. (1995). Conceptualizing the written word: An intellectual biography. *Written Communication, 12,* 277–298.

Pool, C. R. (1997). A new digital literacy: A conversation with Paul Gilster. *Educational Leadership, 55,* 6–11.

Reinking, D., Labbo, L., & McKenna, M. (1997). Navigating the changing landscape of literacy: Current theory and research in computer-based reading and writing. In J. Flood, S. B. Heath, & D. Lapp (Eds.), *Handbook of research on teaching through the communicative and visual arts* (pp. 77–94). A project of the International Reading Association. New York: Simon & Schuster Macmillan.

Speech Communication Association. (1996) *Speaking, listening, and media literacy standards for K through 12 education.* Annandale, VA.

Sweet, A. P. (1997). A national policy perspective on research intersections between literacy and the visual/communicative arts. In J. Flood, S. B. Heath, & D. Lapp (Eds.), *Handbook of research on teaching through the communicative and visual arts* (pp. 264–285). A project of the International Reading Association. New York: Simon & Schuster Macmillan.

Watts Pailliotet, W. (1995). I never saw that before. A deeper view of video analysis in teacher education. *The Teacher Educator, 31,* 138–156.

Weiner, R. (1996). *Webster's new world dictionary of media and communication.* New York: Macmillan.

Willinsky, J. (1990). *The new literacy: Redefining reading and writing in the schools.* New York: Routledge.

4 *Preservice Teachers' Collages of Multicultural Education*

Ramón A. Serrano
Jamie Myers

The growing trend of cultural diversity in the United States requires us to recognize and embrace issues regarding multicultural education. Teachers must know how to work with children from different cultural backgrounds to support learning and break the reproduction cycle of inequality and injustice in our society (Sherritt, 1989). But the specific experiences that would constitute adequate teacher education multicultural preparation in programs are shrouded in differences of belief regarding the goals of multicultural education. In addition, even if educators could agree about the nature of multicultural education, the students preparing to become teachers in U.S. classrooms hold beliefs that shape any educational experience aimed at developing their sense of multicultural education. Both popular perspectives on multicultural education and predominant perceptions of students must be more fully examined to better integrate multicultural education into the school experience.

One of us, Serrano, was a graduate assistant from Puerto Rico who worked with students in the elementary teacher education program at the Pennsylvania State University and was always interested in integrating multicultural education into his preservice course. Yet, as he continued to develop students who were culturally aware of differences, he observed that every mention of or reference to multicultural education was met with body language that reflected a resistance to the whole concept. He felt a sense of self-exclusion on the students' behalf as if saying, "Here we go again. I have nothing to gain and everything to lose." With this concern, we began to wonder just what perceptions preservice teachers have about issues of diversity. How do these perceptions shape their definitions of multicultural education? How might their definitions reflect various theoretical positions about multicultural education recently advanced by educators?

The research reported here describes the perceptions of multicultural education held by a group of 13 white middle-class preservice students who volunteered as participants in the study. The similarities and differences between these students' perceptions and the five popular theoretical definitions of multicultural education are of particular interest. Differences between the students' perceptions and the five definitions should help us understand sources of resistance to the multicultural ideas advocated. A close similarity to any one definition might suggest some support for beginning with an examination of that position in planning educational programs; we believe, however, it will also point to the underlying perceptions, and educational approaches that support the reproduction of societal opportunities on the basis of cultural differences. We argue that educational programs should not be planned on the basis of any match between students' original perceptions and any of the theoretical definitions of multicultural education but on the definition of multicultural education that supports the most democratic future for citizens (Nieto, 1992; Suzuki, 1984). This study provides critical information about how teacher educators might explore the underlying perceptions of students to design curricular experiences that might help transform the students' perceptions about multicultural education. In that respect, we also argue that the method by which we studied the students' perceptions of multiculturalism is also an excellent pedagogical experience in multicultural education.

Multicultural education is defined in various different forms: as an educational reform (Banks, 1993); from a critical perspective (Nieto, 1992); as an educational strategy (Tiedt & Tiedt, 1990); as developing one common culture (Ravitch, 1989); and from a social context (Suzuki, 1984). Each definition represents a significantly different perspective on the goals and means of multicultural education, although they share some aspects.

Banks' (1993) definition of multicultural education argues for educational reforms that produce changes in the educational structure; it also addresses equality between gender, race, ethnicity, and cultural groups so that they may succeed in schools.

Nieto's (1992) definition of multicultural education also stresses issues of school reform and challenges racism and other forms of discrimination in schools and society. It advocates critical pedagogy as its underlying philosophy, enacted through interactions among teachers, students, and parents. The main focus is that of knowledge, reflection, and action when addressing social issues for change. According to Nieto, this form of multicultural education expands the democratic principle of justice. Although similar to Banks' (1993) definition, Nieto's (1992) stresses the importance of critical pedagogy as the primary tool in examining inequalities.

Tiedt and Tiedt (1990) have a different view of multicultural education. They see it as a form of developing awareness of national diversity. They believe students must identify a personal culture to build self-esteem, learn about different cultures, and appreciate contributions to the growth of the United States. Understanding the "other" is the basis of this "humane education," as they call it, and in their view this is important to develop a democratic society that fosters world harmony. Tiedt and Tiedt differ from Nieto (1992) in their promotion of awareness of differences and similarities to understand and accept the "other," whereas Nieto pushes examination—and change—of the more fundamental underlying beliefs that lead us to fail to understand or accept others.

Ravitch (1989) refers to multicultural education as a term that means schools must recognize diversity among cultures and teach children to tolerate the "other." By "other," she refers to those who have a different skin color, religion, language, or heritage from the dominant population. Issues of race, ethnicity, and religion are central to her definition of multicultural education, and learning toleration is very important in order to form one common culture. Although the other definitions also stress the need to understand and accept differences, Ravitch (1989) pushes the "other" into an assimilation in which differences are washed away. In her definition, we find that beyond just learning how to understand and accept differences, we need to learn how to tolerate others to help them blend in and become participants of a common culture.

Suzuki's (1984) definition of multicultural education addresses a need to match the academic, social, and linguistic needs of students. He stresses the importance of helping students understand their own backgrounds as well as the backgrounds of others. His goals for multicultural education are to help students learn to respect and appreciate cultural diversity and understand the factors that produce contemporary conditions of ethnic polarization, inequality, and alienation. With the use of a critical perspective, students will move society toward greater equality and freedom. Rather than advocating a model that aims at assimilating people into the dominant culture, Suzuki stresses the need to examine inequalities from a social context. His definition is similar to that of Nieto (1992) in that a critical perspective should help understand and change the conditions that foster inequalities and affect the lives of people.

Theoretical and Analytical Frame

We define perception as the basis by which we interpret everything that surrounds us. Perception provides the contextual ground for signifying (interpreting a text and constructing a text for others to interpret) the signs in each new experience. This contextual ground is a momentary array of ideas and experiences with relationships to each other that are constructed through prior cultural and individual experiences and are connected to the present signs with respect to, or in the capacity of, those relationships. Perception gives signs their textuality. And of interest in this study are the texts students create about multiculturalism, as they reveal the underlying perceptions used to support the signs they identify, or signify, as multicultural education.

This definition of perception as the contextual ground for the production of meaning in signs is based on the semiotic definition of C. S. Peirce (1955), who defines a sign as "something which stands to somebody for something in some respect or capacity" (p. 99). As Figure 4.1 illustrates, the *sign* (the single word, action, or image) represents the *object* (the intended meaning) with reference to a third sign called the *interpretant* (contextual relationships). In this study of students' visual collages about multicultural education, signs are the images or words in the collage, objects are the interpretations of students about the meaning of collage signs, and interpretants are the contextualizing perceptions that shape their meanings about multicultural education.

The interpretation of text, especially visual text (as is the case in this study), is contextualized by signs that are socially and culturally produced as part of our perceptual ground. According to Bal and Bryson (1991), human culture "is made up of signs, each of which stands for something other than itself, and people inhabiting culture busy themselves making sense of those signs" (p. 174). These signs of human culture form the perceptual ground (interpretants) by which intentional meanings are signified for new signs, such as words and images, in each new experience. Based on this semiotic frame, we designed an activity in which preservice teachers developed and responded to visual poster-size collages that represented multicultural education. We then analyzed the students' artifacts to articulate their underlying perceptions about multiculturalism that influenced the meanings they signified in the collage experience.

In Serrano's 8 A.M. reading methods class, 13 white middle-class students volunteered as participants in the study. The group consisted of 2 male and 11 female preservice teachers. They began by constructing collages outside of class to "represent their perceptions of multicultural education." They were asked to use whatever they felt necessary to develop their collages. The students used such materials as magazines, pictures, ribbons, clay, and paint to illustrate their perceptions of multiculturalism. Along with their collages, the students also prepared a rationale of why and how they constructed their collages the way they did. Two weeks later, they exhibited their collages during class. The collages

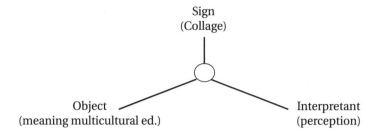

Sign
(Collage)

Object
(meaning multicultural ed.)

Interpretant
(perception)

FIGURE 4.1

were then assigned numbers and posted throughout the room. Once this was completed, the class was asked to move around the room and examine each collage. The students were also instructed to select the three collages they each felt best represented the concept of multicultural education. After the collage selection was completed, the responses were tallied to determine the three most popular representations of multicultural education. We chose to focus on these three collages and their authors as the greatest points of class consensus about the meaning of multicultural education.

We first analyzed the responses to three collages written by the authors of the three most popular collages, and for each author we constructed a network of ideas that were connected across her three written explanations (see Figure 4.2). We hypothesized this perceptual ground as the basis by which the authors defined signs as instances of multiculturalism in their own collage as well as the three class collages they selected as most representative of multicultural education.

We sought to confirm the network of ideas in the perceptual ground constructed for each of the three popular collage authors through interviews in which each author was asked to (1) give a definition for multicultural education, (2) explain the thinking used to construct the collage of images and words representing multicultural education, (3) share reasons for selecting the three collages that best represented multicultural education, and (4) critique the network of ideas hypothesized from their written responses. These data collection and analysis procedures converged in a definition of multiculturalism as held by the popular authors in class and, by extension, the class as a whole. We then juxtaposed the students' perceptions with the various definitions of multicultural education promoted by educational theorists. We focused on ideas and connections in the students' underlying network of ideas that were incongruent with particular definitions and thus might cause resistance. In this way, we could later make these perceptions problematic in class instructional activities with multicultural education as a goal.

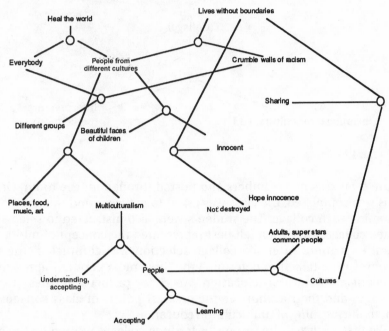

FIGURE 4.2   Ann's perceptual ground

Perceptions of Multicultural Education

The three most popular collages in class were authored by Ann (46 percent responses), Kim (62 percent responses), and Mary (62 percent responses). The responses from the class to all three collages shared a belief that children must learn to accept differences: "If we help children understand and value these differences, imagine how the world could be for our children" (Ann's interview, April 26, 1993). Within this common emphasis on accepting differences, the three authors emphasized different aspects of life as the perceptual ground for signifying differences among people. Ann emphasized how everyday clothing, food, and activity defined different cultures. Kim emphasized how gender, age, and other physical attributes shape different identities (both in and across different cultures). And Mary emphasized how family traditions and race defined different ethnicities (which then resulted in different cultures). Yet, even though the three authors perceived multiculturalism differently, with respect to a person's activity, identity, and ethnicity, their collages and responses highlighted the perceptual practice of segregation and self-exclusion in thinking about others. They defined difference and grouped others without any recognition of their own cultural activity, identity, and ethnicity; they remained invisible as a standard by which otherness and difference were defined.

Ann's Case

Ann's interview began with her definition of multicultural education as "teaching acceptance, learning about other cultures and accepting other cultures" (Interview, April 26, 1993). She believed these concepts were important because they would lead to mutual respect among people. As a consequence of her underlying beliefs (interpretant signs) about understanding, accepting, learning, and sharing other cultures, Ann suggested there is a need to make students aware of cultural differences so that they will accept these other cultures and not see themselves as the center. Although she conveyed some understanding of self-exclusion, she did not include the need to study one's own culture but just the need to examine others. When asked to talk about her collage and its construction (see Figure 4.3) Ann indicated, "It represented the differences among people, foods, animals, children, and countries." She also indicated that while constructing the collage she made sure that it "included anything that stood out as being different" (Interview, April 26, 1993). This last sentence reinforces Ann's self-exclusion by making reference to differences in others. She did not include herself as possibly being different, but rather saw the others as being different from her accepted cultural norm. According to Ann, her construction of the collage was driven by looking at different people of all ages, different cultures, and different children. This was also affirmed in her written responses to class collages, where she wrote,

> The variety of pictures and quotes encompasses a wide range of what multiculturalism is to me. It's people, places, food, music, art. It's understanding, accepting, sharing, and learning. Culture is formed through all of these things. (Written response, February 15, 1993)

When asked if she thought these signs influenced her selection of other collages, she replied, "The ones that really sprung out . . . the ones that included different aspects of my own perceptions and that would be, different cultures, different children, and people" (Interview, April 26, 1993). Ann also indicated that these signs were important because "the things I had included in my own [collage], despite branch out or enhance what I thought was important" (Interview, April 26, 1993).

In her written responses to class collages and in her interview, Ann indicated that what she liked about these other collages was that they

> included a wide variety of interesting depiction of multiculturalism, i.e.: maps of the world, different groups of people from different cultures, chil-

FIGURE 4.3   Ann's collage

dren, etc. Because children are our future and it will be through them that the wall of prejudice and racism will crumble. (Written response, February 15, 1993)

It's something that I feel very strongly about, educating children about different issues, multiculturalistic issues. (Interview, April 26, 1993)

Ann sees as vital the need to educate children about different, everyday activities of other cultures to eliminate prejudice and racism in the world. Her comment is very important because it is an example of how Ann, while examining other collages, used the signs that formed her perception of multiculturalism as a guide to make meaningful connections to other collages. Images of different children, clothing, and activity were noticed by Ann and therefore signified as the basis of multicultural education. These interpretations were made with respect to her underlying perceptions that differences involve everyday activity and appearance and that children are the future chance for world harmony.

Ann's definition of multicultural education is influenced by signs that represent people, children, food, animals, and countries. For her, they signify acceptance, learning, understanding, and sharing of other cultures as the basis of multicultural education. What is evident in the semiotic analysis of Ann's collage (see Figure 4.4) is that her perception of multiculturalism is heavily influenced by the underlying beliefs that differences are represented by the everyday activity of people and that only children can change the future by learning to understand and ac-

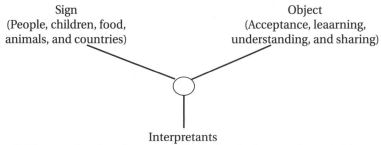

Sign
(People, children, food,
animals, and countries)

Object
(Acceptance, leaarning,
understanding, and sharing)

Interpretants
(Differences involve what people do and make in everyday activity,
children are the future hope to end prejudice and racism)

FIGURE 4.4 Semiotic representation of Ann's perception of multicultural education.

cept these differences. Of the three participants, Ann was the only one to chose her own collage as one of her favorites. This was influenced by the branching effect she asserted earlier, in which she felt that the other two collages expanded and made clearer her perceptions of the meaning of multicultural education.

While analyzing Ann's perceptions of multicultural education, Serrano noted that she did not make reference to issues like child labor, poverty, politics, environmental resources, and assimilation. She instead focused on surface-level appearance differences and how these subsumed the racial and cultural issues that needed to be understood and accepted by everyone, especially children. But the images and words in her collage could be interpreted in vastly different ways when connected to these social and political issues that seem to be outside of Ann's perception about her own cultural self, as well as the lives of others.

The pictures Ann used could very easily represent child labor and poverty throughout the world instead of the need for children to understand construction and homes in different cultures. In her collage, Ann placed pictures of the British royal family and different U. S. presidents with their families on opposite sides. Above these pictures there were labels that read, respectively, "All the President's Kins" and "Caught in the Act." Politics in this collage are represented by this contrast between the U.S. and British political environments. Her images could represent the political ideal of the dominant Eurocentric culture or differences between democracy as seen by Americans and the British. Her collage might also imply that racial differences are the foundation of diversity's meaning, because of her emphasis on pictures of people from different racial backgrounds. The rhinoceros might be a call for awareness about endangered species instead of the simple appreciation of strange animals living in different geographic regions of the world. The chefs sitting around a table could very well represent not just exotic foods from all over the world but also the economic structure that supports the chefs and their delicacies while simultaneously starving those who cannot afford to purchase basic staples. One striking picture is that of a tribal mask topped by a Santa Claus cap. The position of this figure at the top of the collage, as well as the expressions surrounding it of "American style" and "Santa Safari," clearly signify Ann's acceptance of assimilation of all other cultures. In sum, it could be easily argued that with different underlying interpretants, the images and words of this collage could be signified as defining a multicultural education that assimilates the differences of others' everyday activity into one consumer-oriented market economy epitomized by the students' very own, unexamined, American culture.

Kim's Case

Kim's definition of multicultural education focused on respecting individuals who are different (see Figure 4.5). She, like Ann, emphasized "understanding" others. But Kim's understanding was more in reference to individual uniqueness and identity, whereas Ann contextualized understanding in reference to everyday cultural activity. Kim indicated,

> Multicultural education is everything, it's more than just teaching about racism or teaching about different cultures. It's making children understand them and respecting them. Personally I think it's about respecting individuals, everything about that person. It's learning to learn from them and respecting them. People need to learn to respect others, no matter what they do, I think that's a big thing. (Interview, April 28, 1993)

Kim clearly excluded herself from the focus of learning in multicultural education when she continually referred to "them" and to "others" as the target of learning. By also bringing ideas of learning, understanding, and respecting others into her definition of multiculturalism, Kim held a position similar to Ann's, that people do not naturally understand, accept, or respect others, but must learn to do so. As Kim described how she represented multiculturalism in the construction of her collage, she revealed her underlying perception of difference as involving individual identity:

> I wrote multiculturalism on top and the way I did it was that I cut out all the letters differently, like I didn't want any of them to be the same. Which means that everyone is different in the world and everybody is made differently, physically and emotionally. So that's what I put on top and that was important to me. I put living without boundaries in the middle because I think that's a big part of what we have do. People tend to put walls up in

FIGURE 4.5   Kim's collage

front of each other and don't let them down, they don't really get to know the other people around them. I think I have everything on here, I have politics, children where we need to start, the world, and women. I notice I did have a lot of women on this side, mostly because I had all women magazines, but I did put them over here. (Interview, April 28, 1993)

Kim indicated that people tend to put up walls and don't really get to know each other, yet she admitted she herself grouped women to one side of her collage. Whether she was aware of this or not as she created her collage, the act of isolating women in the text constitutes a barrier or wall based on an underlying perception of gender as an important characteristic of individual identity. When Kim referred to "everybody" being "made differently," we suspect that she did not mean every person was entirely unique and could not be included in some cultural group. Kim did not group people on the basis of shared cultural activities; instead, she defined the need to respect others on the basis of a similarity in gender.

When choosing and responding to other collages, Kim found that the signs that had influenced her selection were people, children, and culture. When asked why she had chosen these particular collages she indicated,

I think people in general called my attention. I think that for me that seems to be natural. Children also called my attention because, I'm going to be a teacher and sometimes when you look at things you look at it in the aspect of being a teacher or as being an educator. (Interview, April 28, 1993)

Kim stressed her perspective as a teacher in signifying meaning in the collages about multicultural education:

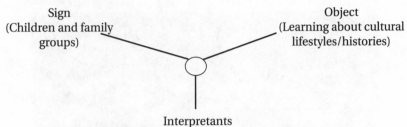

Sign
(Children and family
groups)

Object
(Learning about cultural
lifestyles/histories)

Interpretants
(Differences involve peoples' race and ethnicity,
children are the future hope to end prejudice and racism.
Instruction isolates each group for learning. Familiarity brings
acceptance and respect.)

FIGURE 4.6 Semiotic representation of Mary's perception of multicultural education.

> I really liked the Quote by John Lennon. I think it says a lot about how we should educate everyone. We need to reach out to our children, they will be the future, they will make the difference. It meant understanding and respecting everyone no matter what. It also meant being able to learn from everyone and every culture, from every idea and every person in the world. (Written response, February 15, 1993)

Kim interpreted the collage images and words with respect to her own future work with children and with respect to her emphasis on the unique individuality of every person in the world. Kim's perceptions of multicultural education involved teaching children to understand and respect others who are different, where difference is signified with respect to individual identity and gender more than culturally shared activities like food and clothing (although certainly clothing is a gendered sign). A representation of the sign relationships in her definition of multicultural education is presented in Figure 4.6.

Kim's collage addressed issues relating to race, children, ageism, homeless people, controversy, sex, politics, world and national events, and issues regarding sexual preference. It included many aspects of life that are similar across boundaries of ethnicity and race. Kim used a more passive form of representing issues of oppression and inequality, however. She did not include images or words that would represent the abuse common toward children, women, or certain races. Ageism and homeless people were also presented in a nonchallenging form, and her references to controversy were limited to representations of political leaders and words with opposite meanings. Sexual preference was made problematic by using the military as a heterosexual sign and showing homosexuality by a picture of two sailors standing together.

Throughout the interview process and in her responses to other collages, Kim focused on respecting differences in people and culture, as well as the need to educate children. Ann clearly did not try to make problematic any of the signs representing people's clothing and everyday activity by connecting them to issues of oppression or inequality; instead, she focused merely on needing to learn how others live. It might be argued that even though Kim was most concerned with just learning about others, her collage did attempt to make gender differences a problematic issue for people in all cultures.

Mary's Case

During the interview with Mary, she defined multicultural education in ways very similar to Ann and Kim, but she based this definition on perceptual beliefs somewhat different from cultural activity or unique identity. Her definition was also based on a group's race and ethnicity. This was very apparent in her collage, in which different ethnic groups were labeled and separated spatially (see Figure 4.7). She also viewed multicultural education as a supplementary activity to be incorporated into a lesson, then taught within the standard school subjects. Mary defined multicultural education as "taking others from different cultures and explaining to them that they are different. Everybody is different, each culture is different and trying to incorporate that somehow into a lesson whether it be math or social studies" (Interview, April 28, 1993). Mary's definition suggests an add-on approach in which the traditional lessons are not changed, but special interest lessons are developed about each ethnic or racial group and used as supplemental material at the appropriate time in the mainstream dominant curriculum. Neither Ann nor Kim showed any indications in their definitions as to whether they would attempt to integrate understanding and respecting differences in every lesson or develop add-on lessons to learn about others.

Mary said that one important element in the construction of her collage was the use of children:

> Kids need to learn about it [differences] and you have to start them real young, you have to learn about different cultures. . . . I put them into small groups because each group is different. I separated them into different groups like the Amish, Chinese, and African American. (Interview, April 28, 1993)

Mary clearly defined differences with respect to ethnicity and race, indicated by the spatial separation of cultural groups on her collage. Kim also separated women in her collage, defining difference with respect to gender, and Ann separated images with respect to everyday activities that might be done differently across cultures. Yet, all three thought about multiculturalism with respect to the age of people who are prejudiced, believing that young children are the main hope in creating a more peaceful world. All believed that children need to be taught to re-

FIGURE 4.7   Mary's collage

spect others by learning about them while still young and in school. Their belief is based on the questionable assumption that individuals only need to become familiar with something, then will automatically accept and respect it.

> This display of multiculturalism depicts all children from a variety of cultures such as African-Americans, Chinese, and Amish. I decided to create it with all children because I believe children have the power to break down the barriers in our prejudiced country. The earlier on we educate children that everybody is equal regardless of their skin color or culture, then can there be an end to hatred and violence that surrounds them in this world. (Mary, written response, February 15, 1993)

Mary defined differences among people as "belonging" determined by skin color (race) or ethnicity, then extended the source of this ethnicity to the family as a unit of cultural belonging.

> I was looking at things that stood out and caught my attention. Things that make up the world like children, culture and families. Children and families are definitely number one, because we have to educate the children if we are going to break the barriers that separate people and keep us judging other people and making prejudices. (Interview, April 28, 1993)

Even though Mary called for an education of children that will break down barriers, she never made problematic the spatial separation of cultural groups in her own collage. Even as she responded to other collages in class, families that shared race and ethnicity were signified as the hope for ending racism.

Provocative pictures from around the world. The images of people joined together in caring arms, the family as a focal point toward an end to racism. The use of the world as a central point. (Written response, February 15, 1993)

Mary's perception of multicultural education revealed that children need to learn about the lifestyles of families in each different cultural group (see Figure 4.8). Group difference was defined with respect to race and ethnicity. Learning was defined as children being more open to accepting different lifestyles, breaking down barriers of prejudice between groups of adults, and isolating different groups in instructional activities to learn their particular histories and contributions to mainstream cultural life.

Mary presented a positive representation of children from different cultural backgrounds, without signs of suffering from hunger, pain, abuse, or war. Her view was a neutral one that only presented the side that everyone likes to see. Her collage representations showed children enjoying life, having fun, and always accompanied by a family member. There were some single-parent families in her collage, but in all of the pictures, it was the mother with her child and not the father. Mary extended her own beliefs about families to all other cultures and narrowed the meaning of multicultural education to learning about traditional family lifestyles. Such learning, she believed, would strengthen the children and their current and future families, bringing about an acceptance of others and world peace.

Mary's collage unproblematically segregated children from different countries and ethnic backgrounds. For example, children and families representing African Americans were grouped together, as were Eskimo, Native Americans, Chinese, and Amish children and families. This grouping system represented a colonialism, supporting Mary's comments about adding into the standard curriculum educational activities about the "other." Mary's collage did not contain a grouping of Anglo-Saxon, white, Protestant children and families. This exclusion of one's self from multiculturalism was most marked in Mary's collage, but none of the most popular collages or responses highlighted the need to include one's own culture as anything other than the standard from which all difference originates.

Classmate Responses to Collages

The collages of Ann, Kim, and Mary were the most popular representations of multicultural education in the class. Their classmates' writings interpreted how the collages best represented multicultural education. These responses reveal several of the same perceptions as the more in-

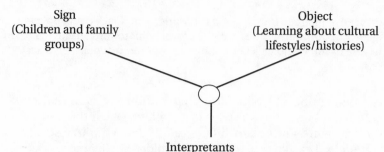

Sign
(Children and family
groups)

Object
(Learning about cultural
lifestyles/histories)

Interpretants
(Differences involve peoples' race and ethnicity,
children are the future hope to end prejudice and racism.
Instruction isolates each group for learning. Familiarity brings
acceptance and respect.)

FIGURE 4.8 Semiotic representation of Mary's perception of multicultural education.

depth analysis of Ann's, Kim's, and Mary's texts. Responses focused on pictures of children; differences in people, food, customs; the forms people live in; changing attitudes; and the notion of children as a resource in changing the world. The following examples illustrate a broader sense of the entire group's perception of multicultural education.

Here, Louise's perception focuses on a global view of culture:

> I really did like it more than a lot of them. I think the variety of pictures and quotes encompasses a wide range of what multiculturalism is to me. It's people, places, food, music, art, it's understanding, accepting, sharing, and learning. It included pictures of children and adults, superstars, and common people as well as animals! Culture is formed through all of these things. (Written response about Kim's collage, February 15, 1993)

Amy's view is based on living in harmony:

> I like the many cultures of the world. When I think of multiculturalism I think of many cultures together, living together to survive. These murals represent many cultures and their daily life activities and even some struggles to survive. I think they are good representations. (Written response about Mary's collage, February 15, 1993)

Barbara indicates that the focus in culture should be to examine differences that lead to better understanding:

> Children and their cultures expresses what I hope to express as a teacher. We are all the same but yet unique. If we help children understand and value these differences, imagine how the world could be for our children. (Written response about Mary's collage, February 15, 1993)

And finally, Amy shows children as resources for the future:

> I like Kids and Their Cultures because I also agree that kids are our future. The mural represents many different cultures of children and has a very important theme. If we want peace and acceptance in this world we need to start with the young, the children who don't have any preconceived biases. It's easy to change their attitudes than older people. (Written response about Mary's collage, February 15, 1993)

In sum, their classmates' responses to the collages echoed the semiotic analysis and perceptions of Ann, Kim, and Mary. The students as a whole based their definitions of multicultural education on beliefs that (1) children especially can be taught to accept others; (2) others should be the focus of study; (3) study should examine one group at a time (perhaps as it connects to something in the traditional curriculum); and (4) difference originates in appearance (including race), everyday activity, ethnicity, and family traditions.

Discussion: Defining Multicultural Education

By comparing the ideas from the semiotic analysis of Kim's, Ann's, and Mary's representations of multicultural education (Figures 4.4, 4.6, and 4.8), we constructed three issues that inform theoretical definitions of multiculturalism and pedagogical designs for multicultural curricula. Together, they present a view of multicultural education as the shaping of young, innocent minds by dispensing information about "others" based on unproblematic surface-level differences while ignoring the origin of standards in one's own cultural history.

First, all three participants defined multicultural education as teaching awareness of difference. They believed students must learn about different people and cultures in the world so they can understand, accept, and respect them. Within this theme, the source of differences was defined somewhat differently by the three collage authors. Ann focused on everyday activities that are done in different ways by members of other cultures; her collage had the greatest variety of signs—objects, activities, animals, people. Kim focused on identity differences, without regard to cultural group membership but with some attention to gender membership; her collage signs focused more on people but included more words with the potential of making problematic the concepts by which we divide, segregate, and privilege. Mary focused on differences in family belonging and traditions along clearly separated racial, ethnic, or national groups; her collage signs were even more uniform in their content focus on children and families.

Second, the concept of the "other" was used frequently by the authors and other class respondents. They excluded themselves from the concept of multicultural education, reproducing the belief that it is just a supplementary program aimed at helping dominant culture students see the differences of other people and countries, without critically examining their own personal backgrounds. This supports and develops a perception that multicultural education is only about other people and is limited to an awareness of surface-level racial, ethnic, and cultural characteristics that obviously differ from an unquestioned norm. Other aspects of cultural existence, such as age, gender, sexual preference, education, class, discourse, goals, ethics, and values, are not examined in their origin or reproduction in one's own identity and cultural belonging.

Finally, the third theme that emerged was that of educating children about differences so that they could get along with each other and live in harmony. The collage authors saw a great need to work with children so they would become agents of change for the future. Based on their perceptions, these changes were limited to ending racism and learning how to get along with others. The participants felt that to accomplish this it would be necessary to focus on children's education, because they were not old enough to be prejudiced and they would be forming the future families of the world.

These three themes in the students' perceptions of multicultural education can be compared to the five dominant definitions of multicultural education advocated by scholars. By making such comparisons, we can better understand how students' perceptions will impact the instructional activity defined, and accepted, as multicultural education. This will support the planning and critique of educational activity aimed at convincing teachers to adopt multicultural education goals for their classrooms.

All three authors saw a strong need to focus instruction on the awareness, understanding, acceptance, and respect of differences in others. For example, Ann indicated that it was important to learn about and accept differences among cultures. Kim not only believed it was important to teach acceptance, understanding, and sharing, but she emphasized the need for teaching respect. Mary asserted understanding others would reduce barriers of prejudice. This definition falls under the *human relations approach* (Sleeter, 1991), which aims toward sensitivity training and has little to say about empowerment—people learn about others but do not examine any circumstances by which others and themselves are oppressed. In this definition, multicultural education uses information resources to develop understanding about differences and how to accept these differences. Its main purpose is to change attitudes through loving and harmonious relationships made possible by exposing students to the human qualities of others' lives. In aligning themselves with the *human relations approach*, the collage authors emphasized the end point of Tiedt and Tiedt's (1990) definition, in which "students can extend their learning to include knowledge of diverse cultures and the contributions that members of different cultural groups have made to the growth of the United States. Such understanding forms the basis for a humane education, extending over twelve or more years, that has the possibility of educating students to participate in creating a truly democratic society that contributes to world harmony" (p. 6). The students did not, however, emphasize the first step of Tiedt and Tiedt's definition, which "begins with helping each student to identify a personal culture and to build his or her self-esteem. From this base, students can extend their learning to include knowledge of diverse cultures" (p. 6). Kim was the closest to including herself in the definition of multicultural education by her inclusion of pictures and words related to life in her own culture and her emphasis on gender as an important characteristic by which difference is constructed.

Mary's case included perceptions that linked to a second definition. She defined multicultural education as explaining to "others" (those who have a different racial or ethnic background) that they are different, emphasizing that everyone is also different, yet should still work together. She also saw a need to incorporate multicultural education into different subject areas. Mary's definition is closely tied to Ravitch's (1989) definition, which views multicultural education as

> a term that means that schools must recognize that this nation is a society of many different cultures, and that one of our strengths as a nation is our extraordinary diversity. As the world grows ever smaller and ever more interdependent, it becomes clear that America's experience in creating a multi-racial, multi-ethnic, multi-religious society is of international importance. Most wars in the history of the world have derived from the inability of people to tolerate others who are different: who have a different skin color, a different religion, a different language, or a different heritage. (p. 3)

Many participants supported the separation of groups in Mary's collage and her focus on teaching children about these others to bring about a more peaceful world. The students, in echoing Ravitch's (1989) definition, subscribe to a *teaching the culturally different* approach. This approach would empower students with the skills needed to survive in schools, society, and the work place to assimilate the "others" into one common culture (Sleeter, 1991). Ann and Kim indicated during interviews that when they were looking at the collages, they were looking for signs regarding different cultures, children, and people. Mary looked for representations of different families, feeling strongly about the role families play in preparing children to accept diversity. Mary believed that any changes in peoples' attitudes about accepting those who are different must start at home with children and continue throughout their schooling. Both believed schools must provide children with the information about those who are different.

Definitions of multicultural education that involve social and critical perspectives, such as Nieto's (1992) and Suzuki's (1984), remained outside the perceptions of the collage authors and class respondents. The students' perceptions in understanding and accepting the "other" were limited to issues of racial, ethnic, and cultural differences. They excluded themselves from the concept of multiculturalism and instead saw themselves as administrators of cultural awareness to students. They visualized multicultural education as a resource for helping people understand and accept the "other." They did not make problematic the conditions of life (their own and others') that they used to characterize cultures in stereotypical ways.

Their perception may be due to the lack of understanding regarding multicultural education and the reproduction of the two commonly used approaches in teacher preparation courses: the *human relations* and the *teaching the culturally different* approaches (Sleeter & Grant, 1987; Sleeter, 1991). Both approaches focus on developing awareness about the differences among people; they fail, however, to address conditions that empower some groups, to challenge forms of institutional oppression, or to examine the underlying sociopolitical and historical basis for defining any one particular act or word as culturally different. For example, most courses developed for preservice teachers talk about people as members of "other" cultural groups and detail how each group contributed to the development of the United States. Preservice teachers learn techniques for teaching about Blacks, Hispanics, Asians, or other national or ethnic groups and the contribution they have made to U.S. progress ("progress" defined with respect to the dominant "other" who sees all the "others" as different). Seldom mentioned are the oppressive conditions in which these groups lived and continue to live in a nation that is far from complete. Along with Sleeter (1991), we strongly argue against these two theoretical definitions of multicultural education and their pedagogical consequences.

To more fully examine perceptions of multicultural education in teacher education, it is necessary to develop experiences that will help students examine their own cultural identity, its formation, and its impact on the definition of the identities of others. We believe that the experience of constructing a collage to represent multiculturalism opened up just this type of possibility in our students' thinking. In another course, "Ethnic Cultures: Fiction and Fact," we used students' responses to literature written by ethnic authors to examine their own assumptions in finding specific events or people important enough to write about (Nelson & Myers, 1993). Once the culture of one's own self is made problematic as a source of difference, students can benefit from the study of the five theoretical positions on multicultural education (Sleeter & Grant, 1987; Sleeter, 1991). Through the examination of these approaches, preservice teachers will be able to connect the various curricular philosophies and the social agendas that underlie and support the implementation of these approaches in specific curricular activities (Serrano, 1993). These pedagogical experiences can position us to challenge and address diverse forms of cultural and institutional oppression defining our possibilities as teachers in a multicultural world.

Preservice teachers must be given the opportunity to examine and deconstruct definitions of multicultural education to understand that it is not limited just to learning about the "other" but rather includes learning about the self in the other and the other in the self. In doing this, the problem of self-exclusion can be challenged through an understanding that we too are culturally diverse even though we may be part of a dominant "invisible" culture. Multicultural education addresses more than just issues of race and ethnicity; it addresses a wide range of issues regarding oppression, inequalities, and unequal access to a better life. At each moment we signify differences in others, we must simultaneously make problematic the interpretive ground from which difference is perceived. Multicultural education must be driven by the questions, what leads us to believe a particular difference exists and why should we support its continued existence? It must become an open struggle in defining the self in relationship to others, and all of us in relationship to the social, political, and historical contexts that shape the possibilities of our cultural identities. Inasmuch as these possibilities are constructed visually through our media lives, visual collages become tools for critically examining the cultural values and beliefs that underlie our perceptions and representations of the "others" in our self.

References

Bal, M., & Bryson, N. (1991). Semiotics and art history. *Art Bulletin, 73*(2), 174–208.

Banks, J. A. (1993). Multicultural education: Characteristics and goals. In J. A. Banks & C. A. Banks-McGee (Eds.), *Multicultural education: Issues and perspectives* (pp. 3–28). Needham Heights, MA: Allyn and Bacon.

Nelson, M., & Myers, J. (1993). Teaching ethnic cultures. *Teaching Education, 5*(2), 23–32.

Nieto, S. (1992). *Affirming diversity: The sociopolitical context of multicultural education.* White Plains, NY: Longman.

Peirce, C. S. (1955). Logic as semiotic: The theory of signs. In J. Buchler (Ed.), *Philosophical writings of Peirce* (pp. 98–119). New York: Dover.

Ravitch, D. S. (1989). *Multiculturalism in the curriculum* (Report No. UD-027-871). Andover, MA: Network, Inc. (Eric Document Reproduction Service No. ED 329 622).

Serrano, R. A. (1993). *Multicultural education and literacy: Connections for equality.* Unpublished manuscript, Pennsylvania State University, University Park.

Sherritt, C. E. (1989). Multicultural teacher preparation: A study of teacher migration patterns and certification requirements. *The Teacher Educator, 25,* 16–21.

Sleeter, C. E. (1991). *Empowerment through multicultural education.* Albany, NY: State University of New York Press.

Sleeter, C. E., & Grant, C. A. (1987). An analysis of multicultural education in the United States. *Harvard Educational Review, 57*(4), 421–444.

Suzuki, B. H. (1984). Curriculum transformation for multicultural education. *Education and Urban Society, 16*(3), 194–323.

Tiedt, P. L., & Tiedt, I. M. (1990). *Multicultural teaching: A handbook of activities, information, and resources.* Needham Heights, MA: Allyn and Bacon.

5

A Late-'60s Leftie's Lessons in Media Literacy: A Collaborative Learning Group Project for a Mass Communication Course

Arnold S. Wolfe

The personal is the pedagogical: "Love, love, love . . . "
(Lennon & McCartney, 1967)

He was a child of the 1960s, schooled at a private university in the East. To-day, he teaches mass communication at a state university in Middle America. In the early '60s, inspired by Brian Wilson's visions and the Beach Boys' sonorities, he dreamed of endless summer California Girls-on-the-Beach while landlocked in January Northeast snowdrifts six feet high. In the mid-'60s, stylized urgencies of the Temptations singing "Ain't Too Proud to Beg" (Whitfield, N., & Holland, E., 1966) electrified his apple autumn nights. "I *know* you're gonna leave me. . . . " Later, the Doors' "The End" (1967) gave him an even more urgent call: "You may be studying *Oedipus* in your English class, man, but don't you, too, really *want* to 'kill father' and . . . *yaaaaeeeehhhh*?" For nearly 30 years, he's claimed the Beatles changed his life. He even wrote his dissertation about one (see Wolfe, 1988). And as memory faded and his back continued to ache, as his son fled from sweet soul melodies to the multiple Ices of rap (T, Cube, Vanilla), he still some-times felt fool enough to wonder: Was it still at all possible that "all you need is love?" (Lennon & McCartney, 1967). "Mercy, mercy, me."

Wolfe was thinking about including a collaborative learning group experience in a mass communication theory class he was to teach when a song from his college days blared from the skyrise dorm near his work-place. More than 30 years before, he'd walked to class hearing that tune. Thirty years later, he walks to class, now its teacher, hearing the same tune. "What's it like," he thought, "being an undergraduate *today* and hearing this 'blast from the past' on your way to class?" The question first came up more than five years ago. He searched the library back then for studies tracing what he came to call the cultural history of any '60s song that was still being played in the then-early '90s. He found none.

Wolfe refers to himself in the third person not merely in tribute to the late '60s New Journalism style of the likes of Mailer (1968). Wolfe uses the third person to stress that any teacher in his position can choose to structure a new preparation around either "the canon of acceptable litera[ture] far removed from students' experiences" (Semali & Watts Pailliotet, 1995, p. 2) or texts closer to those experiences. At the time he was first preparing the course, Oliver Stone's '60s-set *JFK* was being experienced by millions of U.S. college students (Doherty, 1997). Another film then in release, *My Girl*, not only referred to but deployed the Temptations' eponymous mid-'60s hit. Even Wolfe's then-15-year-old son bought himself a Doors' greatest hits CD and was wearing that sucker to woe.

Perhaps the timing was right. For his course's cooperative learning project, his students would write a cultural history of a '60s song, a history that would include the responses of students their age to such "tracks." A '60s expression kicked in: "Don't fight the feelin'." Wolfe didn't, and here's what happened:

Pedagogical Origins: "Nothing You Can Make That Can't Be Made"

At Illinois State University, a course titled "Mass Communication: Theory and Effects" is required of all mass communication majors. It has tended to function in the communication curriculum as the site of majors' indoctrination in the "media effects" literature. Typically, that literature has conceptualized media "effects" as behavioral or attitudinal in character, and quantitative approaches have been the privileged, if not the exclusive, research methods students have been asked to come to know (see, e.g., DeFleur & Ball-Rokeach, 1989; for a critical intellectual history of mass communications studies, see Pietila, 1994). Absent a broadly shared agreement on a definition of media literacy, proponents of the dominant school of media effects could argue that the media literate were those with a (never-determined) quantity of knowledge of this literature. Opposing them were the media illiterate who had none, some, or any less knowledge of this literature than any particular proponent thought he or she possessed.

By the early '90s, however, Marxist and other media scholars of many inflections (British cultural studies, French pre-Derrideans, feminists) had been criticizing dominant paradigm approaches to mass communication for more than 15 years (see Carey, 1985; Fiske, 1982; Hall, 1977;

Steeves, 1987; for a good example of the late-'70s/early-'80s assault on the dominant, quantitative, grasp of mass communication from a Marxist perspective highly influenced by semiotic theory, see Fry & Fry, 1985). Beyond the shifty boundaries of mass communication scholarship, education researchers such as Semali and Watts Pailliotet (1995) had not experienced the vaunted benefits of the dominant approaches to media effects. "American education," they wrote, has failed to meet "the challenge" of helping "young people navigate the sea of messages flooding into their lives daily through TV, movies, radio, video games, magazines, newspapers, even billboards, bumper stickers, and T-shirt logos" (pp. 3–4). In other words, the effects of dominant paradigm media effects research on two generations of American young—the generation that grew up with TV in the '50s and the generation that followed—were either not positive or not visible to these educators. Ten years earlier, communication scholar James Carey (1985) identified the plausible cause: The dominant "effects tradition" in mass communication research "has been a failure on its own terms. [It] has not generated any agreement on the laws of behavior or the functions of [mass] communications of sufficient power and pertinence to signal to us that success has been achieved" (p. 28). Three years thereafter, one critical mass communication scholar could argue credibly in one of the discipline's premier outlets that the mass media audience, the privileged dependent variable in the effects tradition, "exists nowhere" (Allor, 1988, p. 228).

In light of these intellectual historical developments, Wolfe initially regarded his assignment to teach the "effects" course with all the mirthful anticipation most would reserve for a proctology exam. What was more, after his nearly 20 years' experience teaching undergraduates, Wolfe was convinced he didn't "do" negation well for them: To teach the dominant paradigm only to debunk it would not be a class he'd want to take, much less teach. The experience would be more likely too negative, too student *dis*abling rather than enabling. A Beatles memory lit a path, though: "Take a sad song," sang Paul, "and make it better" (Lennon & McCartney, 1968). Right. But how?

A colleague recommended Pauly's (1991) "Beginner's Guide to Doing Qualitative Research in Mass Communication." In Pauly, Wolfe found an ally who was also critical of the quantitative, demographic thinking that *still* dominates students', the mass media industry's, and academics' grasps of media audiences (for the latter, see, e.g., Edwards & Singletary, 1989). Whether the effects under study were, or are, individual, group, or cultural, demographic approaches never explained media message reception—or production—satisfactorily. For Pauly (1991), real social groups are not now, nor have they ever been, identical to demographic categories: "For qualitative researcher[s], living social groups cannot be [defined] as statistical . . . aggregat[ions]—here, an old age/low income/frequent media user; there, a middle age/medium income/high information-seeking user." Rather, for the qualitative scholar, living social groups, such as Beatles fans, *X-files* addicts, or high school students must be grasped on their *own* terms (pp. 6–7). As for the production side, though John Lennon when he formed the Beatles could have been counted as a member of the 18- to 24-year-old, college-educated, middle-income demographic, this categorization did not, indeed, *could* not predict either the media messages he would make or their effects on Anglo-American culture. The same held true for Spielberg before he cut his teeth on *Jaws*.

In Wolfe's lifetime, no living social group galvanized a mass medium *as* a group and reshaped it to its image more than the Baby Boomers reconstructed the recording industry (see Chambers, 1985; Frith, 1981; Gillett, 1970; Grossberg, 1983–1984, 1984, 1985, 1986a, 1986b). As Chambers (1985, p. 107) put it, rock and roll began because a real social group with a sense of itself *as* a group collectively opposed "the 'rational' and 'normal' rules of everyday life" their parents—and their parents' media—thrust upon them. In the words of *Rolling Stone*'s Mikal Gilmore, "The parents of this generation had worked and fought for ideals of . . . security and affluence, and they expected their children not only to appreciate and benefit from this bequest but also to affirm and to extend th[e] prosperous new world [the older generation] created." But the older generation also thrust onto the newer "a legacy of fear and some unpaid debts—anxieties about nuclear obliteration and leftist ideologies and sins of racial violence—and in the push to stability priceless ideals of equality and justice had been compromised" (1990, p. 63). The young, "the best informed, the most intelligent, and the most idealistic [generation] the country has ever known . . . assumed responsibility for passing judgment on American policies, and we found them criminal" (McConnell, 1985, p. 40). And we said so in our music. (For excellent reviews of the antiestablishment, or countercultural, views expressed in '60s popular music, see Bloodworth, 1975; Chambers, 1985; Hibbard & Kaleialoha, 1983.)

That this music was recorded and released by divisions of such establishment firms as CBS, which sponsored the biting social criticism of Bob Dylan, and defense contractor RCA, which distributed Jefferson Airplane's radical call for *Volunteers*, testifies to a "moment . . . when the music business was bewildered by its market. Musicians gained a measure of control of the production of rock simply because they seemed better able than the established [recording company executives] to predict what would sell" (Frith, 1978, p. 189). To borrow terms from an early communication scholar, this moment signifies as great a victory of the *vernacular* as against *monopoly* (see Innis, 1950) as the history of U.S. mass communication over the past half century yields. If one of the purposes of this anthology is to challenge pedagogy that would impose on Americans a uniform, univocal, classics-privileging, print-limited, white, patriarchal definition of literacy, then the popular music of this moment, and others, offers educators a golden vein of texts, genres, and other resources to "deliver us from" such Bill Bennett–blessed "days of old" (Berry, 1957). If we wish to foster a "critical media literacy" that invites students to become "actors in the struggle to expand the possibilities of human life and freedom" (Giroux, quoted in Semali & Watts Pailliotet, 1995, p. 4), then popular music grasped as expression of the vernacular, as opposed to corporate mono*logy,* can help.

So, to counter the dominant quantitative orientation of DeFleur and Ball-Rokeach's (1989) account of mass communication theory, which Wolfe's department required, Wolfe also assigned Pauly (1991), and, informed both by Pauly and by Rau and Heyl's (1990) pedagogical article advocating collaborative learning, designed a collaborative learning experience, titled "A Cultural History of a Popular Song from the 1960s." Excerpts from the syllabus Wolfe used in his "Theory and Effects" class may best explain his objectives for the course and design of its collaborative learning experience.

In connection with the latter, pay particular attention to the following matter in the fourth column in the "Class Schedule" section of the syllabus (Figure 5.1). The column is labeled "Project Activity": Week 1., "questionnaire"; 3.,"Source List assignment"; 4., "3000-word reading"; 5., "close textual analysis of song (due 10/6)," and "reports of work based . . . on assignments i), ii), iii) (due 10/13)"; 7., "Discuss, modify field research protocols I've handed back." 8., "Editor to compose edited CTA. [close textual analysis]/literature review, due 11/10. . . ."

Excerpts from Syllabus for "Mass Communication: Theory and Effects" (Wolfe, 1997)

Course Objectives

1. To identify several ways in which the term *mass media effects* can be conceptualized.
2. To deepen your grasp of some mass media effects that researchers have been able to verify.
3. To improve your research and writing skills by participating in a unique research project.
4. . . . .

The COM 360 Research Project: A Cultural History of a Popular Song from the 1960s

Groups will be formed to investigate the cultural effects of certain songs first released in the 1960s. As you know, any number of songs from that decade can be heard on any number of media channels every day. In popular cultural history, this is a remarkable fact: Thirty-year-old music is far more popular today than 30-year-old music was 30 years ago. The major task for groups choosing this project is to account for the lasting popularity of the chosen song.

To write your cultural histories, groups will investigate no fewer than five (5) sources:

(a) the popular press from the first release of your group's song onward, (b) scholarly literature covering the same period, (c) radio station program directors and music directors [working at radio stations in the region] that still air your group's song, (d) former '60s students, and (e) current college students. . . .

Required Readings: Pauly (1991), (P), and DeFleur & Ball-Rokeach (1989), (DBR)...

Explication of Collaborative Learning
Group Project Components

Week 1: "Questionnaire"

Before the end of the first class, during which the course and the collaborative learning experience were introduced, Wolfe assigned a 500-word essay that had several purposes:

- To get students to think in writing about their experience with '60s popular songs, which students were to consider a mass communication form
- To encourage students to problematize and focus on the question of the meaning(s) of mass communication as the cardinal issue of the course (cf. Semali & Watts Pailliotet, 1995)
- To acquaint Wolfe with the compositional skills of his students, so that he could have fresh writing samples with which he could make informed choices for the pivotal post of project editor
- To enable Wolfe to form groups based on similarities in musical tastes

A copy of the assignment can be found in Appendix One.

The class consisted of 25 students; Wolfe did not expect any two of them to select the same song. No two did. But following Rau and Heyl's

FIGURE 5.1 Class Schedule (assumes two 75-minute meetings/week)

Week Starting Date	Class Topic(s)	Readings	Project Activity
1. 8/18	Introduction;	DBR, chapter (ch.) 5 to p. 131	Answer questionnaire—due 8/20. (See pp. 9-10, below for an explication of this assignment).
2. 8/25	Introduction;	DBR, ch. 5, remainder	Groups formed, meet 8/25 to: a) Elect Leader and Recording Secretary (Scribe) for next Group Meeting (GM), 9/8; b) leader gets song recording and playback unit (tape or CD player) for GM, 9/8.
3. 9/8	DBR, ch. 5 Qualitative Research	P, to p. 14	GM, 9/8 to: a) Play song, discuss; b) Each group member given Source List assignment. (Due 9/15). They are: In correct MLA or APA bibliographic form, list: i) *five* relevant *books* about song or song performer(s), genre, influences, etc.; ii) no fewer than three relevant, *scholarly* articles about song, performer, genre, influences, etc.; iii) ten popular periodical articles about song, performer, etc.; iv) develop a list of five former '60s students (at least one of whom must be a university professor or administrator), who are willing to be interviewed about their recollections and interpretations of your Group's song; v) develop a list of five to eight small and/or mid-size market Midwestern radio station Program Directors (PDs) and Music Directors (MDs), who work for stations that continue to play your Group's song. List must be complete with full addresses and phone numbers. *(Gather information only; try a printed source that contains the information needed. For purposes of this assignment, do not ask any of these persons or their co-workers if they would be willing* *(continues)*

104

FIGURE 5.1 Class Schedule *(continued)*

Week Starting Date	Class Topic(s)	Readings	Project Activity
			to be interviewed! When we have developed a questionnaire (protocol) later this term, we will contact the names on these lists then.); vi) develop a similar list of five to eight PDs and MDs at similar major market Midwestern radio stations. *(Same caution as above applies.);* vii) print-out of Group's song's lyrics, names of main personnel on recording (artist's group name, e.g., the Beatles, not acceptable; get names of individual performers, esp. back-up musicians, if any), chief engineer, producer. *Each Group (G) must have some one do assignments vii, i, ii, iii, & v.*
4. 9/15	DBR, ch. 5	P, remainder	GM, 9/15 to: a) discuss Source Lists, make additions or corrections on them before they are turned in. b) G decides on one 3000-word reading to read: The reading can be a book chapter, a scholarly article, or several shorter popular articles—to be discussed at GM, 10/6. c) G Leader and/or Editor *assign* work for GM, 9/22: One G member will make copies of reading(s). Each other G member will write five questions to ask current students, five to ask former '60s students, and five to ask radio PDs and and MDs for purposes of our field work later this term. G Member (Mbr) #3's minutes must be turned in to me on 9/22, noting each G Mbr's assignment.
5. 9/22	Intro to P; intro to quantitative research methods	Your G's reading; Wolfe (1995)	GM, 9/22 to discuss my comments on Source Lists, including my recommendations. Also: a) review, modify field research questions and turn them in to me.

(continues)

FIGURE 5.1 Class Schedule *(continued)*

Week Starting Date	Class Topic(s)	Readings	Project Activity
			b) Copies of G Reading(s) handed out; and c) assign G member to write 4–6 pp. *scholarly* close textual analysis of song (due 10/6), and three other G Mbrs to write 4–6 pp. reports of work based on lists. Reports will be written on assignments i), ii), iii) (due 10/13).
6. 9/29	Fundamental differences between quali-quantitative research	Review P, to p.14	GM, 9/29 to discuss your G's Reading. Each G member *must* bring a copy to me; make copies for your fellow G Mbrs. The G will help the G Scribe write a typed, 1-page *Group* Response to the G Reading.
7. 10/6	Living social groups (lsgs), not demographic categories	Review P, remainder	GM, 10/6 to discuss, modify G Response to G Reading. Also: a) hear textual analyst present a 5-minute oral summary of paper. Discuss if and how analysis should affect composition of other reports, due 10/13. b) Discuss, modify field research protocols I've handed back. Revised protocols due 10/13.
8. 10/13	What counts as evidence & knowledge in quantitative and qualitative (qual) research	DBR, ch 9; pp. 240–58	GM, 10/13 to a) discuss my comments on textual analysis; b) hear G Members who've written book, scholarly, and popular literature reviews each present a 5-minute oral summary of their papers; c) G Member #3 (or EDITOR) to compose edited c.t.a./ literature review, *due 11/10*; d) Review, modify 1st revision, field research protocols.
9. 10/20	Purpose of qual research in mass communication	DBR, ch 9; remainder	

(continues)

FIGURE 5.1 Class Schedule *(continued)*

Week Starting Date	Class Topic(s)	Readings	Project Activity
10. 10/27	Wrap-up P; DBR, ch 9; intro	Wolfe & Haefner (1996)	GM, 10/27 to help G member #3 assigned to compose edited c.t.a/ literature review; final draft must reflect my comments on reports i), ii), and iii). C.t.a./literature review due 11/10.
11. 11/3	DBR, ch 9; The general meaning paradigm	DBR, ch 1, pp. 17–27	GM, 11/3 to review, modify revised field research protocols, assign interviews of PDs, MDs, students, and former '60s students (to be interviewed between 11/4-11/20, only after final drafts of protocols accepted).
12. 11/10	DBR, ch 9; Principles of written communication; differences between writing & speech	DBR, ch 1	GM, 11/10 field research protocols returned; review, modify remainder accordingly; schedule interviews.
13. 11/17	DBR, ch 9; Knowledge, action; intro to semiotics	Any needed to help Editor revise	Field interviewing.
14. 11/24	DBR, ch 9; semiotics		GM, 11/24 to report on fieldwork (Field semiotics reports due 12/1).
15. 12/1	DBR, ch 1		GM, 12/1; field worker(s) give 5-minute oral presentation of results.

Failure to turn in a G assignment on the due date will result in 5 points off your Group Research Participation grade for the first incident, 10 points for the second, 15 for the third, etc. "Free riding" on others' work is strongly discouraged. Each G member is required to submit copies of *each* assignment to *all* other members of his/her G. The Communication Department cannot defray your copying costs. No hand-written work will be accepted on any assignment....Stay tuned.

(1990) recommendation that collaborative learning groups (CLGs) number from four to eight students (p. 145), Wolfe decided to organize four or five CLGs and attempted to classify the students' song selections. In the nine terms he has taught the course, Wolfe has developed four classifications he's used more than once: (1) "Soul," in which he includes such student selections as "Stand by Me" by Ben E. King and "My Girl" by the Temptations; (2) "Love Songs," in which he includes such songs as "California Girls" by the Beach Boys and "Brown-eyed Girl" by Van Morrison; (3) "Counterculture," in which he includes songs by the likes of Jefferson Airplane and the Doors; and (4) "British Invasion," in which he includes selections by the Beatles and the Rolling Stones.

He announced the formation of these groups the following class period, noting that musicologists and fans alike could quarrel with his classifications and that individual students could too: Certainly "My Girl" could have just as easily been fit into the "Love Song" as the "Soul" category. No student, however, voiced any objection, perhaps in part because all were assured they would have a say in deciding which single songs each group would research. "I don't care which one song of the five or six in each group you choose," Wolfe told the class. "Majority rules." Ultimately, during one of the first terms he taught the course, a class divided itself into four groups: The "Soul" group chose "My Girl," the "Love Song" group "California Girls," the "Counterculture" group "The End" by the Doors, and the "British Invasion" group the Beatles' "All You Need Is Love."

Before the groups' first meeting, Wolfe handed out and discussed a written job description that detailed the duties of Group Leader and Scribe (cf. Rau & Heyl, 1990, p. 146). The description details instructions for an ice-breaking activity as well as a breakdown of responsibilities for conducting group meetings and composing their minutes. A copy of this handout can be found in Appendix Two. In addition, Wolfe prepared a schedule of meetings that, among other things, explains how the positions of Group Leader and Scribe would rotate each succeeding meeting. Rotation permits last week's Scribe to be this week's Leader, and another group member is appointed this week's Scribe. Optimally, each student in each group gets a turn being both Group Leader and Scribe.

This latter handout also specifies the "admission tickets" required of group members for each meeting (see Rau & Heyl, 1990, pp. 147–8): Group Leaders and Scribes are required to produce typed or word-processed minutes of the meetings they led in order to participate in the following group meeting. Other group members are required to produce such items as photocopies of bibliographic lists of scholarly articles on, say, the Beatles or "All You Need Is Love." The syllabus and schedule of meetings specifies the range of acceptable admission tickets required for each group meeting.

Wolfe selects editors based on the quality of writing students displayed in the initial essay and his experience with those students enrolled in the course that he had taught in other courses. Editors are responsible for producing a coherent scholarly essay that integrates a close textual analysis of the song (using any recognizably scholarly approach) with the literature reviews other group members compose on (1) books about the song, song performer(s), or popular music genre into which the chosen song can be plausibly fit; (2) scholarly articles about the song, performer(s), or genre; and (3) popular periodical articles on the above. I shall begin to elaborate the term, "close textual analysis" (CTA) by first discussing the second Project Activity Item.

Week 3: "Source List Assignment"

Consistent with sound writing pedagogy (see Barry, 1989; Hesse, 1994), the task of composing the papers that make up each group's project is divided. The first phase of each group member's contribution would be called "building a bibliography," if the role of at least one student in each group were not to compile a list of interview respondents rather than literature citations. As the syllabus excerpt notes, each member of each group takes on one of the following Source List assignments:

In correct Modern Language Association (MLA) or American Psychological Association (APA) bibliographic form, list:

i) five relevant books about song or song performer(s), genre, influences, etc.;
ii) five relevant, scholarly articles about song, performers, genre, influences, etc.
   (Only two scholarly outlets, one less than fifteen years old, consistently publish scholarly popular music research. They are *Popular Music and Society*, published by Bowling Green State University's Popular Press, and *Popular Music*, published by Cambridge University Press.);
iii) ten popular periodical articles about song, performer, etc.;
iv) five former '60s students (at least one of whom must be a university professor or administrator), who are willing to be interviewed about their recollections and interpretations of your Group's song;
v) five to eight small and/or mid-size market Midwestern radio station Program Directors (PDs) and Music Directors (MDs), who work for stations that continue to play your Group's song. List must be complete with full addresses and phone numbers.
   (Educators in other nations or in regions of the U.S. other than the Midwest should modify this assignment—and the next—accordingly.)

As the syllabus excerpt indicates, I supply written instructions designed to maximize the possibility that these sources will be available to be interviewed later in the term by insisting that students choosing this assignment only gather information at this stage, rather than contact prospective interviewees directly. *Broadcasting* magazine publishes an annual that lists the executive personnel who work at particular stations. Such information should be followed up by a telephone call to the station receptionist to verify names, positions, and spelling. (The names of the position of, say, a "program director," may have changed since publication of the annual. Even more likely, given the high rate of turnover at radio stations, the name of the role occupant may have changed since publication.)

In my experience as both a journalistic and scholarly interviewer as well as an educator, media professionals are far more likely to grant you or your students interviews if you or your students are prepared with a sound protocol when the actual request for an interview is made, generally by means of a telephone call. Media professionals often prove more willing to be interviewed if they know a few of the questions they may be asked; for this eventuality, a researched, even if not completed, protocol is necessary. Questions are more likely to interest a professional if they are the product of library research rather than spontaneously generated. The more "customized" the sample question to a given prospective interviewee, the greater the likelihood of winning an agreement to be interviewed.

Effective fieldwork depends on (1) knowledge of the literature, (2) knowledge of sound field methodology, and (3) a well-written questionnaire or protocol (McCracken, 1988; Pauly, 1991). Therefore, the fieldwork phase of the project does not start until after the separate papers that will be blended into the CTA/literature review have been turned in and the fieldworkers have had the opportunity to read the reviews of books (Assignment i), scholarly articles (ii), and popular articles (iii) their fellow group members have composed. When members of a collaborative learning group (CLG) seeking to account for the lasting popularity of a Beatles' song sought interviews during the fall 1997 semester, for instance, they were able to respond to a source's inquiry about what sorts of questions would be asked with, "Beyond a standard question, such as, 'When I mention the song, "Strawberry Fields Forever," what comes to your mind?' I'm also planning to ask you if you've seen *The Beatles Anthology* (Aspinall, 1995), and, if so, whether you recall the use of 'Strawberry Fields Forever' in that." Such a response demonstrates (1) the student's genuine interest in the personal views of the prospective respondent; (2) the student's preparation for the prospective interview (he or she has learned that the song was visualized in the *Anthology*); and, perhaps most important, (3) enough sensitivity to the professional's position to assure the respondent that the interviewer's prime purpose is not to seek employment.

Scholarly Defenses. Before describing the final two Source List assignments, I should like to defend for the project under discussion my choices of scholarly method and respondents. As I wrote in the first publication that evolved from one student rendition of the project (Wolfe, 1995):

> An increasing number of mass communication and cultural studies schol-
> ars are contending that the meanings of popular culture artifacts cannot be
> read off their textuality alone (see Barkin & Gurevitch, 1987; Fiske, 1987;
> Gitlin, 1983; Grossberg, 1986a, 1986b; Jensen, 1987). Those meanings that
> specify the constituents of the lasting popularity of such artifacts, particu-
> larly for living social groups that still find them worthy, are even less likely
> to emerge through textual analysis alone. The specification of such con-
> stituents requires analysis of the reception of texts by consumers other than
> critics; mass communication scholar Klaus Bruhn Jensen (1987) has argued
> that "the combined analysis of textual structures *and audience responses*
> can become the basis of a more comprehensive approach to reception" (p.
> 27; emphasis added). Cultural studies scholar John Pauly (1991) concurs
> and in his "Beginner's Guide to Doing Qualitative Research in Mass Com-
> munication" calls for popular communication researchers to explain how
> living social groups, as opposed to demographic categories, use popular
> texts in a continuing effort at "making . . . meaning" (p. 11, see also pp. 7, 10,
> 14; and Kreiling, 1978).
>
> Such inquiries have value insofar as they can potentially reveal: (1) ways
> in which living social groups interpret such products, (2) how members of
> such groups "work media products into their everyday lives" (Pauly, 1991, p.
> 11), (3) "the shared systems of meaning that render [particular media] mes-
> sages intelligible" to the group or groups studied (p. 3), [and, inter alia,] (4)
> the means through which interpretations of media texts are diffused within
> the group or groups studied. (Wolfe, 1995, p. 73)

Each item in this list is plausibly a part of what could be called the complex of "symbolic practices" (Pauly, 1991, p. 3) that can be activated by
the release of a music recording or other media text. Such communicative practices, Pauly (1991) insists, are best studied by qualitative methods: "The study of . . . symbolic practices constitutes the distinctive domain of qualitative research" (p. 3).

The project under discussion is designed to directly address one part
of this complex, the interpretations of lastingly popular song–recordings
of the 1960s offered by members of three social groups other than published popular music critics, that is, members of the generation that
propelled those "tracks" to their initial popularity (that is, the generation
that was approximately college age in the mid- to late '60s), program directors and music directors of radio stations that include such songs in
their playlists, and current college students. To attempt to explain such a
mass-mediated phenomenon in this way is to democratize what once
would have been presumed to have been a critical task wholly and solely
responsive to humanities disciplinary approaches: To "explain" the en-

during appeal of a text, one analyzes the text (by using theoretic tools recognized in such humanities disciplines as literary criticism and musicology). But to clear a space for living social groups other than critics to account for consumption of a media text in group members' "own words" (MacGregor & Morrison, 1995, p. 142) and to investigate what specific media audiences understand of a specific, lastingly popular media text "is not only useful but necessary" (Dyer, 1982, pp. 86–7). To clear such a space is especially necessary for researchers who are committed, as we are, to democracy—to "developing," in Giroux's words, "the critical and practical conditions through which [students] can locate themselves in their own histories and in doing so make themselves present as actors in the struggle to expand the possibilities of human life and freedom" (quoted in Semali & Watts Pailliotet, 1995, pp. 4–5).

Defense of Social Groups Selected.   "One of the prominent features of young people's current musical activities is their interest in old music" (Willis, 1991, p. 61). Even more recently, a staffer at Peoria's '60s-heavy "Big Hits" WMBD-FM, said her employer formats his station "for the baby boomers, but we have many listeners in their teens and twenties" (Angela Maglio, personal communication, March 19, 1997). Such reasons are but two that justify the selection of current college students as a living social group appropriate for this study. More locally, I teach mass communication majors, who tend to think too little about the multiple social groups communication organizations seek to reach, even groups to which these majors can claim membership, such as the group I call "current college students."

I chose to probe members of the generation that propelled '60s songs to initial popularity under the assumption that their responses might tend to be at least potentially culturally and historically significant. I chose to probe radio station program directors (PDs) and music directors (MDs) rather than, say, practicing popular musicians according to three other "social, rather than mathematical . . . conception[s]" of significance (Pauly, 1991, p. 11). First, practicing popular musicians play a smaller role in maintaining the continuing popularity of this universe of musical texts than do PDs and MDs. Second, the responses of PDs and MDs to such texts would be potentially more (qualitatively) significant to *communication* scholars than the responses of practicing popular musicians. Unlike all practicing popular musicians, *all* PDs and MDs are mass communicators, responsible for deciding what stations will communicate over the air (O'Donnell, Hausman, & Benoit, 1989).

Last, I chose to probe radio station PDs and MDs because of their possible contribution to those "institutional relations that work to determine [the] decoding practices" of radio and other audiences (Allor, 1989,

p. 455). The meanings such audiences make of media texts are influenced not only by the texts themselves but also by the industries that supply those texts (see also Bennett & Woollacott, 1987). PDs and MDs are important role occupants in the radio and music industries (Hirsch, 1969; O'Donnell et al., 1989). The overriding aim of the collaborative learning project, then, is to clarify what meanings the selected social groups have made of the selected songs and to determine if such meanings, as revealed, shed light on the issue of the enduring popularity of the selected media texts.

Final Two Source List Assignments

For large-enough CLGs, and particularly for those students interested in radio and aspiring to positions in larger markets, there is Assignment vi: Develop a list of five to eight PDs and MDs at major-market Midwestern radio stations. Each CLG must have someone do Assignments i, ii, iii, v, and vii, which requires the group member to produce a printout of his or her CLG's song's lyrics; the names of main personnel on the recording (artist's group name, e.g., the Beatles, not being acceptable); and the names of backup musicians, the chief engineer, and the recording's producer. Songbooks, such as Lennon and McCartney (1986); album covers; and, recently, several web sites have proven helpful to students choosing Assignment vii. (For songs of the Doors, for example, check out http://www.vis.colostate.edu/~user/1209/doors/lyrics/doors/ [accessed May 29, 1997]). I require this assignment from each CLG, so each group can benefit from one "official" version of the chosen song's lyrics, a version to which all CLG members can refer, and from one close textual analysis (CTA) of the chosen song. Similar reasons motivate the Week 4 CLG assignment, "[a] 3000-word reading," specific to each group, that all members of each individual CLG share. In a culture as individualistic as the United States, educators must structure in such shared experiences and incentives to collaborate (see Barry, 1989; Rau & Heyl, 1990).

After Pauly (1991) and numerous popular music studies (see, e.g., Bloodworth, 1975; Chambers, 1985; Hibbard & Kaleialoha, 1983; Mellers, 1973; Wolfe, 1995), some theory-driven analysis of each recording's "textual structures" (Jensen, 1987, p. 27) is desirable in any effort aimed at understanding such media texts. As Pauly (1991) insists, "The purpose of qualitative research [in mass communication] is not to control others' behavior or attitude, but simply to know our cultural habitat" (p. 23). That habitat is suffused with electronic and other popular media messages that circulate within such older sign systems as speech and mathematics. If Semali and Watts Pailliotet's (1995) construct of intermediality directs us to invite students to "construct . . . connections among varying concepts," message forms, "and sign systems," then teaching students to appreciate and produce theory-driven CTAs of communications encoded in a variety of media would seem to be mandatory. An intermedial media literacy that excludes such knowledges and skills is not conceivable. For, as Semali and Watts Pailliotet (1995) remind us, "Underlying this notion of 'intermedial' is the idea that electronic and other popular media are 'texts' that require comprehensive understanding" (p. 4). I shall have more to say on the topic of the CTA below.

I require students who choose Assignment vii to supply the names of the individual musicians, recording engineers, and producers for two purposes: information sharing and as a way of encouraging students to contact the message makers themselves. In five years, only one student has attempted such contact; alas, he could not get the message maker to cooperate. Then, too, I sent Wolfe (1995) to Paul McCartney with the same result. No guts, no glory.

As might be expected, students who choose to do Assignment vii tend to do the CTA; similarly, students who choose Assignment i write the literature review of books. Assignments i through iii represent a rather minimal literature review; in my experience, a reading list of five books has proven to generate reasonably adequate four- to six-page papers. (In my more than 20 years of teaching at state-supported institutions, I have found approximately only one student in four capable of processing even that amount of information or 10 popular periodical articles into an original composition of 1200 words that presents [1] an organized exposition of matter that [2] successfully constructs even a *generally* sound argument.) The dearth of scholarly outlets publishing research in popular music makes papers based on five scholarly articles a stretch for any song not recorded by the Beatles or the Doors. Some material in books, such as Empson's (1947) canonical study of ambiguous expression, and in broadly theoretical articles, such as Grossberg (1984), can round out a bibliography for Assignment ii.

Faculty can modify the reading and paper length requirements set forth above, as well as the requirement that all CLGs turn in a list of radio personnel (Assignment v). A class composed of education majors eager to transform the masses into the media literate might be better advised to have each CLG conduct a focus group of college or secondary school students rather than do Assignment v. My mass communication majors are more often more eager to "network" with other media professionals than do fieldwork with, say, former '60s students.

Week 7: "Close Textual Analysis of [the] Song (due 10/6)"

Again, after Pauly (1991) and numerous popular music studies (see, e.g., Bloodworth, 1975; Chambers, 1985; Hibbard & Kaleialoha, 1983; Mellers, 1973; Wolfe, 1995), I require some theory-driven analysis of the "textual structures" (Jensen, 1987, p. 27) of each group's song. As a matter of personal preference, I agree with Frith's (1981) observation that far too often popular music critics, both within and without academe, "have . . . fallen for the easy terms of lyrical analysis" (p. 14). Unfortunately, very few students in my department possess any musicological knowledge, including, I'm sad to say, those interested in radio. (With Howard Stern as their dominant model, however, such ignorance is understandable even if lamentable.) As a result, the overwhelming majority of students who have chosen the CTA analyze lyrics—atheoretically at first. But a multitude of theoretical perspectives are available. Hibbard and Kaleialoha (1983), for example, offer several theoretical perspectives with which they view rock and roll. The results are inconsistent, particularly when compared to Chambers (1985). Both works, however, offer comprehensive discographies, but, particularly for educators not steeped in popular music literature, Hibbard and Kaleialoha do provide a now dated but still useful annotated bibliography.

Once, while teaching a media criticism course, I asked a class, "How would you define media criticism?" One student offered, "Media criticism is an explanation of a mass media text that could have many explanations." I like that definition, and I use it to describe what role a CTA can play in the project. As Vande Berg, Wenner, and Gronbeck (1998) write in words that ring with a clarity distilled from decades of pedagogical experience, "criticism is *not* everyday, unsupported opinions— whether by ordinary [listeners], paid journalists, Hollywood [music] executives, or university students or professors" (p. 31). The question of what scholarly criticism is could occupy this book and libraries beyond. I assign a piece of criticism, the CTA, as the first paper due to signal each class that even though their chosen texts may be taken as "only" rock and roll, they deserve to be taken seriously. Consider this recommendation from distinguished media psychologist Percy Tannenbaum (1985): In a state-of-the-field article written after years of serious empirical work focused on the measurable responses of individuals to measurable and "serious" media presentations, such as news, Tannenbaum opined: "If serious scholars of communication . . . wish to come to grips with the nature of the media and their role in contemporary society," they must give entertainment "*serious* consideration" and ask, "What are the consequences of [entertainment consumption] in the life of an individual audience member, and by extension, in [the lives of] the *social groups* to which [individuals] belong?" (p. 44; emphasis added). The project under discussion asks this question. Like all the individual papers that make up the project, the CTA is meant to be shared with other group members and prompt (ideally) similarly serious scholarly regard for the song, the performer(s) who recorded it, and so on.

"Reports of Work Based on ... Assignments i), ii), iii) (Due 10/13)"

Reports of work based on the assignments are due after the CTA to optimize the possibilities of coordination among (1) the group member writing the CTA and those writing the literature reviews and (2) those four group members and the Editor. Though the Editors in smaller-sized groups often take first crack at the close textual analysis, in groups composed of six or more (i.e., groups in which at least one student will undertake a field study), a group member other than the Editor inaugurates each group's attempts to discover those meanings, or, in qualitative social science terms, those "categories and assumptions" (McCracken, 1988, p. 17) that may help the group account for the lasting popularity of the group's chosen media text. As sociologist Grant McCracken reminds us, the purpose of qualitative data collection "is not to discover how many, and what kinds of, people share a certain characteristic. It is to gain *access* to the cultural categories and assumptions according to which one culture construes the world" (p. 17). Put alternately, it is to gain access to the meanings one culture makes of and uses to construct its world. For qualitative researchers, "how many and what kinds of people hold these categories and assumptions is not, in fact, the compelling issue. It is the categories and assumptions, not those who hold them, that matter" (p. 17).

Perhaps because the approach to media literacy the project concretizes is so novel—but also consistent with the epistemology of qualitative methods—such meanings, categories, or assumptions "should not be presupposed." Rather, according to media researcher Jenny Nelson (1989), such meanings should be "discovered when determining emergent significance in ... audience ... experience" with media (p. 388; order inverted for the sake of quotation; see also McCracken, 1988). To cite an example, the close textual analyst in the "All You Need Is Love" CLG discovered that the song was *designed* by the Beatles to be enormously popular, an anthem for their generation (Russell, 1989, p. 94; see also Pirmantgen, 1975, p. 22). It was composed by Lennon and McCartney with full knowledge of its manner of initial release: "All You Need Is Love" (AYN) was to debut not as an audio recording but as a television short; on June 25, 1967—less than a month after the release of the Beatles' masterwork, *Sgt. Pepper's Lonely Hearts Club Band* (see Mellers, 1973)—AYN was performed before an estimated 400 million people in 24 nations on the first live, worldwide telecast (Dowlding, 1989, p. 185).

In contrast, Lennon and McCartney's "Strawberry Fields Forever" was the product of experiments with, inter alia, recording technology, free verse lyric composition, and sound mixing (Martin, 1994). When students discover such meanings or categories themselves, they swiftly reject what I call the *American Bandstand* hypothesis, to wit, that a lastingly popular song–recording has remained popular because *it's got a good beat and you can dance to it*. Students come to understand that rock and roll recordings seldom present inconsistent rhythm patterns, although AYN does (see Wolfe, 1995), or undanceable tempi. Student discovery of such information enhances their musical—and media—literacy and ignites further brainstorming that can produce higher-quality projects. Some time ago, a student researching the lasting popularity of the Doors' "Break On Through (to the Other Side)" found out that the last song sung at the last Doors' concert was not "Break On Through . . ." (Riordan & Prochnicky, 1991, p. 304), as director Oliver Stone renders that concert in his 1991 film, *The Doors*. The discovery generated a corresponding fieldwork question students could ask any member of any social group who had screened or even had knowledge of the film. Other discoveries spawned other questions.

Week 7: "Discuss, Modify Field Research Protocols I've Handed Back"

The process that produces the protocols accommodates such discovery (see Haefner, 1992). In their initial iteration, students' fieldwork questions express little more than off-the-top-of-the-head responses to the Week 4 assignment: "Write five questions to ask current students, five to ask former '60s students, and five to ask radio PDs and MDs for purposes of our field work later this term." To prepare for the Week 4 assignment, students may also read the model protocols they buy as part of their course packets. The intention of the assignment, however, is to invite each student to contribute to the group effort some question he or she wants the project to answer. I review all contributions and word-process an abbreviated version of each prospective protocol.

After the experience of nine protocol-building cycles, the versions that I ask student fieldworkers to compile combine questions from the course packet with ones from fellow group members. The printouts I give fieldworkers look something like this one prepared for the student who eventually group-interviewed current college students as part of an effort to account for the lasting popularity of "Break On Through . . . ": (All student names noted below are pseudonyms.)

Protocol Draft: Current College Students' Focus Group for "Break On Through . . . " (Partial)

1. When you think of this song, what comes to your mind?
2. Course packet (p. 106) (current college students Ques. #8 (abbreviated version [av]): "What aspect of this song makes it stand out?"

3. What's your interpretation of the song?
4. Joan's current college students Ques. #1 (av: "Where were you and what were you doing when you first heard 'Break On Through?'")
5. Mitchell's current college students Ques. #2 ("Has 'Break On Through' influenced your generation? If so, how?")
6. Cole's current college students Ques. #5 ("Have you seen the movie, *The Doors*?")
7. What was your response to the use of the song in the film?

After each group member's questions are returned with comments, fieldworkers then word-process a revised draft of their protocols consistent with the applicable printout. The protocol draft can be revised again after the CTAs and literature reviews are completed. In the case of the "Break On Through" CLG, after one of the literature reviewers discovered that the final song performed at the final Doors concert was "Light My Fire," we added what for present purposes I'll call protocol question #8:

> Did you know before this moment that, contrary to what the movie presents, 'Break On Through . . . ' was not the last song the Doors performed at their last concert? Assume the movie's director, Oliver Stone, knew that. (We know he did extensive research for his film.) Of all the Doors songs he could have used at that moment in that film, he chose "Break On Through . . . " What do you think is gained or lost by having Stone's Doors perform that song, as opposed to the one the real Doors played, at that moment in the film?

If the respondent permits the fieldworker use of his or her VCR, the worker can even screen the sequence, so the respondent can reexperience it as well. (As a rule, fieldworkers play an *audiotaped* copy of the CLG's chosen song to respondents prior to asking any question of them.)

Week 8: "Editor to Compose Edited CTA/ Literature Review, Due 11/10"

Again, Editors craft a coherent scholarly essay that integrates the best of the CTA with the best of the literature reviews. Editors do not integrate into the CTA/literature review any papers based on fieldwork, because the fieldworkers must have (1) knowledge of the literature reviews, (2) knowledge of sound field methods, and (3) a well-written protocol before they even start interviewing. Copies of the literature reviews with my responses to them are seldom available to fieldworkers until Week 10. Having no prior experience with qualitative interviewing, each fieldworker must then (1) arrange for and conduct interviews or focus groups, (2) transcribe the interview recordings, (3) print out presentable transcriptions (in addition to their reports), and (4) write a 1200–1500 word report on the field work—all in 21–24 days. Fieldwork reports must enunciate a thesis that specifies what the report will attempt to show or demonstrate, must identify any recurring or intensely expressed themes that resound across respondents' accounts (Pauly, 1991), and must evaluate whether and to what extent such frequent or intensely expressed responses plausibly clarify and illuminate some constituents of the chosen song's lasting popularity (see Wolfe, 1995). During the same time period, Editors assemble the CTA/literature review.

Conclusion

The theoretical roots of the collaborative learning experience called "A Cultural History of a Popular Song from the 1960s" penetrate most deeply into the field of cultural studies. But the learning experience described differs from much cultural studies audience research, which, until recently, has tended to theorize about but failed to "examine . . . empirical audiences" (Jensen & Rosengren, 1990, p. 217; see also Lull, 1988; O'Connor, 1989). The CLG experience has built class morale, provided students with a task-oriented, team-building group exercise of a scholarly stripe, offered a worthy alternative to lecturing as a means of transmitting course material, and effectively demonstrated qualitative methods of researching media audiences. Such methods have proven useful to mass communication practitioners as well as scholars. Moreover, the experience is quintessentially intermedial; it "encourage[s] renewed interest in learning about the ways in which individuals construct meaning from messages—that is about the processes of selecting, interpreting and acting upon messages in various contexts" (Semali & Watts Pailliotet, 1995, p. 6).

CLG Project Outcomes: Cognitive

Consistent with Course Objective 1 (see Excerpts from Syllabus), the project helps students identify more than one way in which the term *mass media effects* can be conceptualized. Again, the tradition of effects research has typically conceptualized media effects as behavioral or attitudinal in character (see e.g., DeFleur & Ball-Rokeach, 1989; cf. Pietila, 1994). By enacting the projects, however, students come to better understand the effects of certain song recordings on not so much the behaviors or attitudes of members of living social groups as on their "*consciousness*" (Carey, 1985, p. 30; emphasis added.). The CLG experience called "A Cultural History of a Popular Song from the 1960s" therefore qualifies as "a critical media literacy project," in part because it "expands the notion of school literacy, which is principally the ability to read the printed text, to include a critical reading of [both a broader range of] media texts" (Semali & Watts Pailliotet, 1995, p. 9) and their effects.

According to a typology devised by Scandinavian mass communication scholars Klaus Bruhn Jensen and Karl Erik Rosengren (1990), the project may be best classified as a form of what they call "reception analysis" (which is *not*, as they take pains to note, the same as the *Rezeptionaesthetik* school of literary criticism identified with Iser, 1970). Rather, "what characterizes reception analysis is, above all, an insistence that studies include a comparative empirical analysis of media discourses with audience discourses" (p. 218). In other words, reception analysis aims to identify meanings plausibly encoded in, here, one media text *and* meanings members of one or more living social groups say they decode from, again here, the text under study. Reception analysis then directs the researcher to compare the two sets of responses.

The project enables students to not merely read about but to experience the multiple meanings listeners from different social groups have made of the songs students choose as worthy of investigation. Over the five-year period I have worked on these projects, however, no student exposed to such plural meanings has come close to concluding, to quote one British cultural studies scholar, that this multiplicity warrants the inference that media texts are "meaningless" clusters of "narrative forms/devices that engender particular kinds of purchase within [audience members'] cultural parameters" (Wren-Lewis, 1983, p. 196). In all candor, the dearth of such student arguments may stem at least in part from a pedagogical tactic I use that is grounded in literary theory. Among such theorists, perhaps Culler (1975) is most comprehensible: Texts "support a variety of . . . meanings but do not permit [themselves] to be given just any meaning." If all interpretations of any given media text were valid,

> if the distinction between understanding and misunderstanding [it] were irrelevant, if neither party to [any] discussion of [any differing interpretations of the text] believed in the distinction, there would be little point to discussing and arguing about [its meaning]. But to reject the notion [that a text may be *mis*understood] is to leave unexplained the common experience of being shown where one went wrong [in an attempt to interpret a text], of grasping [one's] mistake and seeing why it was a mistake. (119–21; order inverted for the sake of quotation; emphasis added; see also Barthes, 1977)

With this theoretic warrant (among others; see Pauly, 1991), I encourage students to look for the meanings that members both within and across social groups share. As I wrote elsewhere, "the very term 'mass communication' implies broadly shared meanings" (Wolfe, 1992, p. 271). Thus, if both critics and respondents call a track such as "Break On

Through . . . " a "classic," or a "signature" Doors recording or express anything like, "It's the Doors at their best," I encourage students to look for any unity beneath the diversity of expression of, plausibly, one idea. One CLG cohered these observations into an empirically grounded explanation for the continuing presence in our culture of a song recording that when launched as a single never made the Top 10 (Riordan & Prochnicky, 1991). Significantly, ironically, "Break On Through . . . " has remained popular for a span of time that exceeds the one its composer-singer, Jim Morrison, actually lived.

Another reason "A Cultural History of a Popular Song from the 1960s" qualifies as "a critical media literacy project" is that it answers Semali and Watts Pailliotet's (1995) question, "What counts as text?" (p. 7) with an invitation to students to examine the wide variety of texts—print, electronic, cinematic, digital, and analog—that not only "form the meaning-making processes of the looming information age" (p. 5) but have constituted—and continue to constitute—students' experience (see p. 1).

The project also helps students fulfill Course Objective 2: It helps students deepen their grasp of some mass media effects that researchers have been able to verify (see Excerpts from Syllabus). In contrast to the wealth of research their textbook references on the behavioral and attitudinal effects of mass communication (see DeFleur & Ball-Rokeach, 1989), student group members discover for themselves what two trail-blazing communication researchers discovered after doing more than 30 years of mainstream media effects research, to wit, that "the sociological and cultural effects of mass communication . . . have been short-changed, if not altogether overlooked, given [the field's] research concentration of studies that take as their only measure of effect the responses of individuals," as opposed to groups or cultures (Lang & Lang, 1985, p. 58).

Concomitantly, student group members come to question the relations between research methods and the varying views of the world different methods mold (see Carey, 1985; Fry & Fry, 1985; Hall, 1977). Students come to learn the following:

1. To rely on an operational definition of a media effect that seeks to demonstrate the effect's existence by aggregating quantified responses of humans stripped by method of every indicator of their individualities but their age and gender "overlook[s] the sociological and cultural effects of mass communication" (Lang & Lang, 1985, p. 58) and radically oversimplifies the complexities, the genuine individualities, of real message receivers, because quantitative methods ignore, inter alia, the connections any sin-

gle receiver may share with any other receiver or with any larger social collective.

2. Any prior faith they may have had in the prowess, the "magic wand"ness, of demographic thinking is misplaced. Students may externalize their doubts, as Sal did, when in a skit performed as part of his CLG's final presentation, he played an overbearing, hand-held-calculator-waving social "scientist," who, while wearing a sign reading "Quantitative Researcher: A.K.A. Wolfe's Worst Nightmare," repeatedly interrupted his colleagues' field reports with shouts of "Unmethodological!" "Invalid!" and "Where are your numbers! I must see numbers!" Project work shows students how little demographic approaches truly explain.

3. Such approaches explain neither the products nor the processes of either media message reception or production. Project work leads students to agree with Pauly (1991) that real social groups are not now, nor have they ever been, identical to demographic categories. Project work makes concrete his observation that "all researchers translate the . . . chaos of the world into a system of signs, available for interpretation. The quantitative researcher" translates the chaos into numbers, whereas the qualitative researcher translates the chaos into a linked network of "discourses" (Pauly, 1991, p. 10; order inverted for the sake of quotation).

Deep into her fieldwork study of radio executives' responses to her group's song, Sue, a grad student who sells air time for a television station, *experienced* such linked, even if contradictory, discourses. Through project work, Sue saw with *her* eyes and heard with *her* ears how eagerly station ad executives embraced alternate, qualitative ways of conceptualizing audiences. Through project work, she also saw and heard the flat refusal of every radio programmer she interviewed to grasp his or her actual or potential listeners in any but demographic terms. "That seems kinda duhmb," she told our class one night in her central Illinois twang. Radio is called a medium, I'd have liked to reply, because it's neither rare nor well done.

Through project work, Barbara, an Editor of both her CLG and the campus newspaper, came to question the conventional journalists' method of data collection, the venerable Interview with the Expert (for a critique, see Tuchman, 1978). When assigned to write a feature story on student sexual practices in the Age of AIDS, she asked me if there was a way she could pursue her story by grasping her fellow students as a living social group. Ultimately, Barbara conducted a focus group of current college students on the topic, as opposed to relying solely on interviews with the likes of under assistant deans and student health service spokespersons far removed from the life-and-death prospects of satisfying early post-adolescent desire. Here, Barbara acted out an alternative method of journalistic data collection that, like the project, cleared a space for the members of living social groups other than experts to tell their tales. For Barbara, "A Cultural History of a Popular Song from the 1960s" grew her intermediality because it "encourage[d in her] renewed interest in learning about the ways in which individuals construct meaning from messages—that is about the processes of selecting, interpreting and acting upon messages in various contexts" (Semali & Watts Pailliotet, 1995, p. 6). The project enabled Barbara to understand that even her fellow students' sexual conduct entailed at least in part selecting, interpreting, and acting on mass-mediated messages. She learned that, on the one hand, the culture in which she and her student peers live "helps to shape [their] consciousness" and that "on the other, through their intentional apprehension of phenomena in the shared social world," including media phenomena, they "collectively construct and constitute social phenomena"—from the popularity of '60s songs among them to the threat of death that looks them square in the eye, just beyond every attracted smile (Tuchman, 1978, p. 182).

CLG Project Outcomes: Cognitive and Affective

Did the project, to quote Giroux again, "develop . . . the critical and practical conditions through which [students such as Sal, Sue, and Barbara could] locate themselves in their own histories and in doing so make themselves present as actors in the struggle to expand the possibilities of human life and freedom" (quoted in Semali & Watts Pailliotet, 1995, pp. 4–5)? I cannot claim such influence. When students have applied themselves to these projects, however, they have been "helped" in their efforts to "navigate the sea of [mass-mediated] messages flooding into their lives . . . The complexity of relationship between what students see and hear, what they believe, and how they interact with one another" is addressed (Semali & Watts Pailliotet, 1995, pp. 3–4). Their ability to explain the relationships among individual mass media consumers, audiences considered as social collectivities, and media messages has been enhanced. Students' definition of "school literacy" has expanded to include the ability to critically read, or interpret, popular music texts. (If I had a nickel for every time a student group member told me, "I never listened to the song that closely before," I wouldn't hesitate a nanosecond to call Ticketmaster upon hearing the Stones were comin' back to town. *Jumpin'* Jack Flash.)

More important, the projects have empowered students to learn a way to bridge the abyss of postmodern despair. To illustrate: Mel, a bright, sweet intercollegiate athlete and group member, was arrested one midsemester on a drug charge. Prior to his arrest, Mel had assigned himself the task of interviewing former '60s students about the lasting popularity of a Doors' song. In his oral report of his findings, Mel stressed how paradoxically the Doors' leader Jim Morrison was perceived by members of this generation: On the one hand, former '60s students saw Morrison as a sexually reckless, hard-drinking, drug-abusing lout. On the other, he was grasped as a spiritually driven, genuinely American, beautiful, sensitive, transcendentalist poet. Narrating these contradictions to a rapt audience fully aware of Mel's troubled circumstances, Mel not only opened doors to understanding Jim Morrison but doors to understanding Mel.

Through project work, Mel "located" himself in his "own histor[y]" and declared himself an "actor," and not merely a subject of state power, "in the struggle to expand the possibilities of human life and freedom" for which the Doors at their finest stood. As Pauly (1991) insists, "The purpose of qualitative research [in mass communication] is . . . simply to know our cultural habitat. For better or worse, modern people dwell in symbolic worlds mediated by mass communication" (p. 23). By means of the collaborative learning group project described, students come to know their intermedial habitat better. Any sense of security Sal may have derived from demographic explanations he now declares false. Sue now perceives as "dumb," if not downright prejudicial, broadcast practices so resistant to change that they discount the interests even of advertisers, let alone audiences, in optimizing their experience of the pleasures music can give. All together now: "They call radio a medium, because it isn't rare and it isn't . . . "

Barbara now realizes that the most venerable tool of journalistic data collection severs respondents from their meaningful connection with others and misrepresents them and their worlds. And by reporting stories of his elders' enduring admiration for the cultural contributions of a legendary singer-songwriter, Mel not only became "wise[r] in the ways of others" (Pauly, 1991, p. 23). He broke "on through to the other side." Like other students, he became more intermedial. And by becoming "wise[r] in the ways of others" (Pauly, 1991, p. 23), by becoming more intermedial, Mel became wiser in the ways of himself and the world he shares with you and me.

Lennon and McCartney (1967) remind us, "No one you can save that can't be saved/Nothing you can do but you can learn how to be you in time. . . . " Rock on, Mel.

References

Allor, M. (1988). Relocating the site of the audience. *Critical Studies in Mass Communication, 5,* 217–233.

Allor, M. (1989). Reply: Maps of reading. *Critical Studies in Mass Communication, 6,* 454–458.

Aspinall, N., executive producer. (1995, November 22). *The Beatles anthology* [Television series]. New York: ABC Television.

Barkin, S. M., & Gurevitch, M. (1987). Out of work and on the air: Television news of unemployment. *Critical Studies in Mass Communication, 4,* 1–20.

Barry, L. (1989). *The busy professor's travel guide to writing across the curriculum.* La Grande, OR: Eastern Oregon State College.

Barthes, R. (1977). The rhetoric of the image. In S. Heath (Ed. & Trans.), *Image-music-text* (pp. 32–51). New York: Hill and Wang.

Bennett, T., & Woollacott, J. (1987). *Bond and beyond: The political career of a popular hero.* London: Methuen.

Berry, C. (1957). *School day.* ARC Music Corp.

Bloodworth, J. D.. (1975). Communication in the youth counter culture: Music as expression. *Central States Speech Journal, 26*(4), 304–309.

Carey, J. W. (1985). Overcoming resistance to cultural studies. In M. Gurevitch & M. R. Levy (Eds.), *Mass communication review yearbook* (Vol. 5, pp. 27–39). Beverly Hills, CA: Sage.

Chambers, I. (1985). *Urban rhythms: Pop music and popular culture.* New York: St. Martin's Press.

Culler, J. (1975). *Structuralist poetics.* Ithaca, NY: Cornell University Press.

DeFleur, M. L., & Ball-Rokeach, S. (1989). *Theories of mass communication* (5th ed.). New York: Longman.

Doherty, T. (1997). Seemless matching. *National Forum, 77*(3), 39.

Doors, The. (1967). *The end.* Nipper Music.

Dowlding, W. J. (1989). *Beatlesongs.* New York: Simon & Schuster.

Dyer, G. (1982). *Advertising as communication.* New York: Methuen.

Edwards, E. D., & Singletary, M. W. (1989, Winter). Life's soundtracks: Relationships between radio music subcultures and listeners' belief systems. *The Southern Communication Journal, 54,* 144–158.

Empson, W. (1947). *Seven types of ambiguity* (rev. U.S. ed.). New York: New Directions.

Fiske, J. (1982). *Introduction to communication studies.* New York and London: Methuen.

Fiske, J. (1987). British cultural studies and television. In R. Allen (Ed.), *Channels of discourse* (pp. 254–289). Chapel Hill: University of North Carolina Press.

Frith, S. (1978). *The sociology of rock.* London: Constable.

Frith, S. (1981). *Sound effects: Youth, leisure, and the politics of rock 'n' roll.* New York: Pantheon.

Fry, D. L., & Fry, V. H. (1985). A semiotic model for the study of mass communication. In M. L. McLaughlin (Ed.), *Communication yearbook* (Vol. 9, pp. 443–462). Beverly Hills, CA: Sage.

Gilmore, M. (1990, August 23). The sixties. *Rolling Stone,* pp. 61–68.

Gillett, C. (1970). *The sound of the city.* New York: Outerbridge & Dienstfrey.

Gitlin, T. (1983). *Inside prime time.* New York: Pantheon.

Grossberg, L. (1983–1984). The politics of youth culture: Some observations on rock and roll in American culture. *Social Text, 8,* 104–126.

Grossberg, L. (1984). Another boring day in paradise: Rock and roll and the empowerment of everyday life. *Popular Music, 4,* 225–258.

Grossberg, L. (1985). If rock and roll communicates, why must it be so noisy? In D. Horn (Ed.), *Popular music perspectives* (Vol. 2, pp. 451–463). Gothenburg, Sweden: International Association for the Study of Popular Music.

Grossberg, L. (1986a). Is there rock after punk? *Critical Studies in Mass Communication, 3,* 50–74.

Grossberg, L. (1986b). Reply to the critics. *Critical Studies in Mass Communication, 3,* 86–95.

Haefner, M. (1992, 9 April). *Focus group approaches in mass communication research.* Lecture Presented to Students in Communication 360, Illinois State University, Normal.

Hall, S. (1977). Culture, media, and the ideological effect. In J. Curran, M. Gurevitch, & J. Woollacott (Eds.), *Mass communication and society* (pp. 315–349). London: Arnold.

Hesse, D. (1994, August). *Writing to learn.* Workshop presented at Illinois State University Teaching Workshop, Normal.

Hibbard, D. J., & Kaleialoha, C. (1983). *The role of rock.* Englewood Cliffs, NJ: Prentice-Hall.

Hirsch, P. (1969). *The structure of the popular music industry.* Ann Arbor: Institute for Social Research, University of Michigan.

Innis, H. (1950). *The bias of communication.* Toronto: University of Toronto Press.

Iser, W. (1970). *Die Apellstruktur der Texte.* Konstanz, Germany: Konstanz University Press.

Jensen, K. B. (1987). Qualitative audience research: Toward an integrative approach to reception. *Critical Studies in Mass Communication, 4,* 21–36.

Jensen, K. B., & Rosengren, K. R. (1990, June). Five traditions in search of the audience. *European Journal of Communication, 5,* 207–238.

Kreiling, A. (1978, July). Toward a cultural studies approach for the sociology of popular culture. *Communication Research, 5,* 240–263.

Lang, K., & Lang, G. E. (1985). Method as master, or mastery over method. In M. Gurevitch & M. R. Levy (Eds.), *Mass communication review yearbook* (Vol. 5, pp. 49–63). Beverly Hills, CA: Sage.

Lennon, J., & McCartney, P. (1967). *All you need is love.* Northern Songs, Ltd.

Lennon, J., & McCartney, P. (1968). *Hey Jude.* Blackwood Music, Inc. Reprinted in *Beatlemania (1967–1970).* Vol. 2 (1986). No editor of record. Hal Leonard Publishers, NY.

Lennon, J., & McCartney, P. (1986). *Beatlemania 1967–1970* (Vol. 2). New York: Hal Leonard Publishing.

Lull, J. (1988). The audience as nuisance. *Critical Studies in Mass Communication, 5,* 239–243.

MacGregor, B., & Morrison, D. E. (1995). From focus groups to editing groups: A new method of reception analysis. *Media, Culture and Society, 17,* 141–150.

Mailer, N. (1968). *Armies of the night.* New York: St. Martin's Press.

Martin, G. (1994). *With a little help from my friends: The making of Sgt. Pepper.* Boston: Little, Brown.

McConnell, S. (1985, June). Vietnam and the sixties generation. *Commentary,* pp. 40–46.

McCracken, G. (1988). *The long interview* (Sage University Paper Series on Qualitative Research Methods, Vol. 13). Beverly Hills, CA: Sage.

Mellers, W. (1973). *Twilight of the gods: The music of the Beatles.* New York: Schirmer.

Nelson, J. (1989). Eyes out of your head: On televisual experience. *Critical Studies in Mass Communication, 6,* 387–403.

O'Connor, A. (1989). The problem of American cultural studies. *Critical Studies in Mass Communication, 6,* 405–412.

O'Donnell, L. B., Hausman, C., & Benoit, P. (1989). *Radio station operations: Management and employee perspectives.* Belmont, CA: Wadsworth.

Pauly, J. J. (1991, February). A beginner's guide to doing qualitative research in mass communication. *Journalism Monographs, 125.*

Pietila, V. (1994). Perspectives on our past: Charting the histories of mass communications studies. *Critical Studies in Mass Communication, 11,* 346–361.

Pirmantgen, P. (1975). *The Beatles.* Mankato, MN: Creative Education.

Rau, W., & Heyl, B. S. (1990, April). Humanizing the college classroom: Collaborative learning and social organization among students. *Teaching Sociology, 18,* 141–155.

Riordan, J., & Prochnicky, J. (1991). *Break on through: The life and death of Jim Morrison.* New York: William Morrow.

Russell, J. P. (1989). *The Beatles: Album file and complete discography.* London: Blandford.

Semali, L., & Watts Pailliotet, A. (1995). *Prospectus for intermediality: Teaching critical media literacy.* Unpublished manuscript.

Steeves, L. (1987). Feminist theories and media studies. *Critical Studies in Mass Communication, 4,* 95–135.

Stone, O., director. (1991). *The Doors* [film]. With Val Kilmer and Meg Ryan. Carolco.

Tannenbaum, P. H. (1985). To each his/her own: A personal research agenda for micro issues in communication. In M. Gurevitch & M. R. Levy (Eds.), *Mass communication review yearbook* (Vol. 5, pp. 40–48). Beverly Hills, CA: Sage.

Tuchman, G. (1978). *Making news: A study in the construction of reality.* New York: The Free Press.

Vande Berg, L. R., Wenner, L. A., & Gronbeck, B. E. (1998). *Critical approaches to television.* Boston: Houghton Mifflin.

Whitfield, N., & Holland, E. (1966). *Ain't too proud to beg.* Stone Agate Music.

Willis, P. (1991). *Common culture: Symbolic work at play in the everyday cultures of the young.* Boulder: Westview Press.

Wolfe, A. S. (1988, June). *Irony, ambiguity, and meaning in CBS Television network news coverage of the death of John Lennon.* Doctoral dissertation, Northwestern University.

Wolfe, A. S. (1992). Who's gotta have it? The ownership of meaning and mass media texts. *Critical Studies in Mass Communication, 9*(3), 261–276.

Wolfe, A. S. (1995). Song of the '60s: Toward a cultural history of a mass media text. *Journal of the Northwest Communication Association, 23,* 70–90.

Wolfe, A. S. (1997, Fall). *Syllabus for "Mass Communication: Theory and Effects."* Department of Communication, Illinois State University.
Wren-Lewis, J. (1983). The encoding/decoding model: Criticisms and redevelopments for research on decoding. *Media, Culture and Society, 5,* 179–197.

Appendix One:
Music Questionnaire

Type a 500-word (two typed, double-spaced pages) response to the following.

1. Choose a song that you like from the 1960s that you've heard within the past year. Write no less than four sentences on what you think the song says and means. (If you find it difficult getting started, try answering these two questions: How do you interpret the song? What's it mean to you?)
2. Describe your most memorable experience in connection with the song you've chosen.
3. Describe anything about the song that has given you pleasure.
4. Describe any pleasant memory you link with the song in any way.
5. Describe anything about the song that has given you pain.
6. Describe any painful memory you link with the song in any way.
7. How do you think other individuals or groups interpret the song?
8. Why do you think the song is still popular today?
9. If you heard the song within the past six months on the radio, speculate on why the radio station that broadcast it considers it economically advantageous to continue playing a song that was first released around 30 years ago.
10. You may also include any information you find relevant, such as the role the song played or continues to play in the reputation of the recording artist; the discourse about the song in television, film, or print media; or common knowledge.

Appendix Two:
Role Descriptions

G Leader

1. Pulls chairs into a close circle. On first meeting:

• Has each G Mbr introduce himself or herself and identify '60s song he or she chose.

- Has each G Mbr discuss one pleasant or unpleasant memory he or she has linked with the song.

At the start of each GM, Leader
2. Collects all assignments—both originals and copies.

- Writes his or her initials on the upper right-hand corner of each assignment turned in—both originals and copies.
- Passes out copies to his or her G Mbrs; gives instructor the originals.

3. Starts the agenda for the day. (After the first GM, that's the reading of the minutes.)
Helps G Mbrs react and interact. Helps G identify points of agreement. Helps with the wording of the minutes (Exchanges phone numbers with Recording Secretary [RS]).
4. Watches the time. Makes sure G completes the agenda. (Good Leaders hand out an agenda, which may contain additions to instructor's on syllabus, to members at the start of GM.)
5. Notes points of disagreement or difficulties that remain after G has discussed agenda items. Raises these points when we come back together and in the minutes.

Recording Secretary (RS)

1. Takes minutes. Although a 500-word finished report is an outside limit, the minutes should include as many specific points as possible. G Mbrs must help RS summarize G discussion.
2. Format: At top, note G title.
Mbrs attending:_____(Leader):_____(RS): _____(Next G Mbr), etc.
Substance of GM
3. Makes copies of minutes for G Mbrs. Has them read minutes at the start of next GM. Registers any additions or corrections on both copies *legibly*. Turns in original to instructor.

6 The Power and Possibilities of Video Technology and Intermediality

Victoria J. Risko

The notion of intermediality, a concept advanced by the editors of this volume, invites thinking about different representations of meaningful ideas and the influence of multimedia on learning, pedagogy, and social practices in educational communities. Such a concept has intrinsic value for advancing our thinking on the use of multiple texts, especially those represented on videos, the Internet, and CD-ROM materials, to develop dynamic learning environments. Furthermore, this concept can stimulate thinking about how multiple texts can be used to create classrooms where community is valued and developed, where students are encouraged to learn privately and collaboratively, where multiple viewpoints are heard and respected, where both the teachers and students generate issues and problems they think are important to pursue, where individual and collaborative lines of inquiry are supported, and where ideas are studied in depth and for various reasons. Unfortunately, American educators are making little progress in developing such classrooms, according to Linda Darling-Hammond (1996) and others. Instead, she suggests that efforts to develop students' independent thinking and respect for diverse viewpoints may be more of a myth than a reality. And, as Aronowitz and Giroux (1993) argue, such classrooms don't just "include" students with diverse interests and background experiences in the routine of classroom events, they build on the assumption that everyone can contribute to each other's learning and that many different voices and interpretations should be celebrated rather than silenced.

This chapter provides an analysis of intermediality from a video technology perspective. It is organized as follows. First, I discuss theoretical perspectives that influence the use of video technology to enhance learning and inquiry. Second, I refer to this reasoning to guide my reactions to the cases presented by Watts Pailliotet and Macaul and her colleagues in this volume. Next, I identify possible benefits and challenges associated with applications of video technology. Last, I suggest implications for a form of pedagogy that encourages students' critical and independent thinking and respect for diverse viewpoints.

Video Technology in Support of Socially Constructed Learning and Inquiry Opportunities

For a number of years, my colleagues and I at Vanderbilt University have been building theory about the impact of video technology on the learning environments we are creating to encourage students' active role in their own inquiry and learning. Across a number of projects located in elementary, middle, and secondary schools and our college classes, we use videodisc, CD-ROM, computer technology, and printed texts to create problem-solving environments that invite students' collaborative and generative learning (see Cognition and Technology Group [CTG] at Vanderbilt, 1993, 1996, 1997). Students explore rich sources of information to identify issues, examine content from multiple perspectives, and resolve problems by cross-referencing information across varied texts.

In several recent projects, some of us have focused on preservice teacher education. For these projects, we couple video technology with case methodology (Barron & Goldman, 1996; Risko & Kinzer, in press). We developed video cases that represent authentic classroom events to help our preservice teachers understand complexities associated with teaching. One of these projects, directed by Chuck Kinzer and I (Risko & Kinzer, 1991, 1994, in press), enabled us to develop eight video cases that are implemented in our literacy methodology courses. We use these cases to facilitate community building in our college classes and to help our students develop deep understandings of concepts embedded in the cases. Consistent with principles of case methodology (Merseth, 1991; J. H. Shulman, 1995; L. S. Shulman, 1995), our goal is to situate learning in the exploration of interesting and realistic classroom events and to encourage active, useful, and useable construction of knowledge. Our cases are explored to encourage students to become producers of knowledge rather than passive recipients of information told to them by their instructors. A goal for case discussions in our college classes is to demonstrate that every student's contributions are legitimate and important and that there are alternative ways to resolve issues embedded in the cases.

Theoretical principles guide our development and use of video cases. These include our beliefs that (1) providing rich sources of information is essential for encouraging students' generative learning, (2) video adds a particular value to an array of texts that can support learning, (3) knowledge is developed when learning is both private and collaborative, and (4) students need to learn (and value) both how to problematize content *and* how to create ideas that go beyond conventional understandings. In the following paragraphs, I elaborate on each of these.

Our goal for using multimedia to *provide rich sources of information* is influenced by our notion of anchored instruction (Bransford, Vye, Kinzer, & Risko, 1990; CTG at Vanderbilt, 1990) and ideas associated with situated learning as discussed by Brown, Collins, and Duguid (1989). We believe that learning is greatly enhanced when students are involved in sustained exploration of complex concepts that are embedded in learning activities that are viewed as relevant to students' personal experiences and goals for learning. Our video cases represent actual classroom events occurring in diverse settings. These events are presented in narratives, pressed on videodiscs or compact discs, and accessed by menu-driven computer software. Students are invited to generate issues and problems they wish to pursue in their study of the case and to construct reasonable problem resolutions.

The cases provide several problems simultaneously and invite students' analysis, reflective thinking, and generative learning. Requiring students to frame questions and solve problems encourages them to apply and modify newly acquired concepts based on situational and contextual information (Risko, Peter, & McAllister, 1996). When people learn new information in the context of meaningful activities, such as problem-solving activities, it is likely that this information is perceived as "useable tools" for resolving problems (Bransford, Vye, Kinzer, & Risko, 1990). In such contexts, people learn about conditions under which it is important to know and use information they are learning.

We believe that *video adds a particular value* to the textual presence of our cases for several reasons. First, video provides access to information that can be difficult to describe in written and verbal accounts. Second, video is dynamic and allows students to more easily form detailed mental models of problem situations (e.g., Johnson-Laird, 1983). Third, there is much to notice in video presentations. Increasing opportunities for noticing can increase the possibility of finding information that leads to problem identification and problem solving.

We use videodisc and compact disc technology, instead of videotape, because it has random access capabilities. Our software allows access to appropriate scenes and the ability to revisit relevant information easily and frequently. Being able to revisit the same information for different purposes is extremely important for helping students recognize patterns of ideas, develop personal descriptions and interpretations, and evaluate content from different perspectives.

Our cases are open-ended, different from those in which narrators explain the problems and solutions that are represented in the cases. Instead, our students identify issues and problems they wish to pursue *individually and in collaborative learning formats*. Our students are encouraged to develop their own descriptions of case content and their own interpretations of events and relevant concepts. We believe it is important for each student to develop personal understandings of case content both before and during class discussions. In small and whole-class group formats, our students are encouraged to share their interpretations and reflections and to participate in the development of shared understandings and reactions to each other's interpretations. Ideas are revisited and reanalyzed as case resolutions are studied from different viewpoints.

We believe that students should not only be engaged in problem-solving activities, they should be encouraged also to *problematize content domains*. Allowing students to frame the problems they perceive as important, instead of responding to problems that experts define for them, is essential for inquiry learning. Problematizing issues can help students personalize content and come to their own understanding of the importance of newly acquired information and the use of this information for resolving problems.

Heibert, Carpenter, Fennema, Fuson, Human, Murray, Olivier, and Wearne (1996) support problem-based curricula. They argue that if transfer of knowledge to real-world problems is going to occur, not only should students be engaged in problem-solving activities but they should be allowed to generate issues and problems embedded in content domains. Allowing students to problematize the content is viewed as essential because students need to "wonder why things are, to inquire, to search for solutions, and to resolve incongruities" (Hiebert et al., 1996, p. 12). This type of inquiry facilitates students' ability to acquire and apply knowledge simultaneously. Rather than distinguishing instruction and experiences that develop knowledge from instruction and experiences that emphasize application of that knowledge, problem-based instruction can help students understand how to use information to think about, make sense of, and respond to problems and issues while they are acquiring new knowledge of a content domain. And as students apply information to new contexts, their learning becomes both context dependent and context independent. The first, context dependent, situates the learning of novel information in familiar contexts; the second, context independent, encourages application of knowledge to new situations. Knowledge is constructed in meaningful ways, building on students' prior experiences, and applied to novel problem situations.

In summary, the four principles described above guide our development and use of video-based materials. Multimedia can be a powerful resource for supporting students' learning and study of authentic problems. In the next section, I share my reactions to two cases presented earlier in this text. I draw on the above principles to guide my reactions to these cases.

Views of Cases

The cases provided by Watts Pailliotet and Macaul et al. serve to extend my discussion of intermediality according to a video technology perspective. First, there is Chapter 2 by Ann Watts Pailliotet. She provides a description of a precise instructional methodology used to aid her preservice teachers' critique and reflection. This method stresses generative and collaborative learning. Her use of this deep viewing methodology is built on the assumption that knowledge is socially constructed. Powerful is her assertion that textual understandings involve many types of human responses, including emotions, intellect, and meta-cognitive awareness, and that the teacher is integral to the group's learning but in a guided, scaffolded way. The teacher is one who takes on many roles to support, rather than define, learning.

The deep viewing method that Watts Pailliotet describes helps me envision many possible outcomes related to building deep knowledge as students cross-reference information from multiple texts and develop flexibility of thinking. I wonder, as Watts Pailliotet notes, how students can be encouraged to understand the power of this strategy for viewing world texts.

Second, the case Sherry Macaul codeveloped with Jackie Giles and Rita Rodenberg helps us think further about the issue of how we can support students to understand world texts from different perspectives. As noted in Chapter 3 by Macaul et al. chapter, Watts Pailliotet's deep viewing method was used with elementary/middle school students to facilitate a critical analysis of an automobile advertisement. What is eminently visible in the data they describe is how difficult it is to encourage critical analysis; students may respond to surface information and have great difficulty with interpretations of deeper information. Finding methods to encourage students to adopt different stances, to develop students' awareness of conflicting information, and to facilitate reflection that provides a need for revisiting information to pursue different issues is extremely important for advancing students' learning from different texts.

In conclusion, I believe these cases and this opportunity for reflection is useful for at least four reasons. First, our work in intermediality helps us to "problematize" the way we do schooling in our own teacher education programs. It helps us point to the complexities associated with teaching, the need for developing students' critical examination of texts, the changing conditions and diversity in our classes, and the impact of technology and electronic classrooms on our pedagogy.

Second, our work raises new questions about the terrain and culture of our college classes. It helps us think more deeply about our social practices—about the role of the teacher, as mediator, and about procedures for inviting dialogic interactions. I believe that we need to examine our own social practices and how we legitimatize multiple forms of knowledge and cultural representations that are present in our classrooms.

Third, it provides a way to push the theoretical underpinnings of our profession. Engaging in discussions about concepts such as cognition, socially constructed learning, postmodernism, problem-oriented learning, recognition of multiple texts and signs, and so on helps us to push further and examine our own theories.

Fourth, it points to the increasingly powerful role of knowledge— knowledge as tools for learning and application and knowledge that informs us, but also knowledge used to transform us (Prawat, 1993). Using knowledge to transform us requires us to use our imaginations and creativity to find ways that will help us cross barriers of differences and develop new ways to communicate across multiple texts and traditions; it requires us to move beyond perceived boundaries as we link and understand our cultural and social practices.

Taken together, these cases and this focus on intermediality hold much promise and many possibilities. Specific possibilities and implications for pedagogy are discussed in the following material.

Pedagogy

My reflection on intermediality from a video technology perspective helps me to identify several implications for pedagogy. First, there is the need for developing deep viewing and deep thinking (as also discussed by Watts Pailliotet in Chapter 2 and Macaul et al. in Chapter 3) instead of cursory learning. Yet, such thinking must be cultivated within the multimedia environment. Although multimedia adds additional fibers to the fabric of textuality, its potential influence *must be attended to* in very deliberate and knowing ways if we are going to optimize its potential. Using multiple texts, especially those represented on video, CD-ROMs, and the Internet, provides many layers of messages and information. There is much to notice and examine. But as we learned from the Macaul et al. case, students may attend to superficial information and dismiss deeper meanings, viewing added information as unimportant or irrelevant. Instructors need to invite students to develop new questions for reexamining the content and to assume different stances as they revisit texts and cross-reference ideas. It is important that we do not lose the need for argumentation, the need for addressing the "how and why" of concepts (Morris, 1988) that pushes deep thinking along many paths and many choices of topics to examine.

Our pedagogical practices must focus on ways to draw out a critical stance among our students—a stance that makes explicit the need for analysis and reflection. The deep viewing guide provided by Watts Pailliotet and tested by Macaul et al. provides one good illustration of a way that teachers can invite such analysis and reflection. And as Macaul et al. suggest, we need to use such a guide multiple times to help students revisit and analyze text for different purposes and to reach different conclusions. When revisiting text ideas, the teacher needs to guide students to initiate new pathways and support their efforts when developing alternate questions and issues that are important for exploration.

Second, the use of multimedia can be an extremely effective medium for developing problem-solving abilities. As noted above, video is rich with multiple sources of information; there is much to examine, and in-depth analysis requires several viewings. As students watch videos and are encouraged to examine multiple texts from different perspectives, they can identify issues that they perceive as problematic and then look for evidence that supports their inferences. After framing the problems that they have identified, they can refer to multiple sources to develop more complete understandings of the situation to help them conclude with plausible resolutions. As this problem-solving process develops, students enhance their understandings of novel concepts and how to use information they learn for problem solving. Such growth is consistent with descriptions of how conceptual change occurs (Hynd & Guzzetti, 1993). Involving students in sustained opportunities to examine multiple aspects of concepts embedded in texts and to link concepts for building arguments that address issues and problems can help students integrate information across texts (Guzzetti, Snyder, Glass, & Gamas, 1993). Such learning is critical for successful problem analysis and problem resolution.

Third, although problem solving is important for enhancing learning, of equal importance is building "ideational knowledge" (Prawat, 1993). A call for encouraging students to be both problem solvers *and* creative thinkers seems to be relevant to our discussion of the potential impact of multimedia texts. In a problem-solving instructional frame, students are encouraged to generate issues and understandings about problems and solutions. Such a frame helps students assimilate their existing schemata with novel information needed for responding to problems. Students analyze different sets of information to help them reach *informed* conclusions.

Conversely, idea-based learning, according to Prawat (1993), adds another dimension to students' cognitive development. Students who are encouraged to think creatively and use their imagination to wonder about novel ways to represent ideas and concepts are involved in *transforming* how they think about and use text ideas. Imagination can be cultivated in the classroom by involving students in the "world of ideas" that relate to their personal experiences and their visions of what might be possible (Egan, 1989). Situating students' learning in the study of multiple texts provides a dynamic way for helping students understand the complexity and multiple uses of information they learn. Encouraging students to use ideas to both solve problems and create new "visions" can serve to develop divergent thinking and different pathways for building complex sets of knowledge (Gee, 1992).

Fourth, using multimedia to enhance learning may help students "make the unknown known and the known unknown." What has become clear to me as I experiment with multimedia to support my teaching is how complicated it is to help students learn; how even more complicated it is to develop critical thinking and creativity. I believe that I have at least two major goals for my teaching. One is to help students understand novel concepts. To do this, I provide learning activities that support their efforts to draw on their previous experiences and contextual information to analyze novel concepts from different perspectives. I encourage them to identify issues and questions they want to pursue and to apply "new" information to resolve their issues and questions. I "test" their understandings by asking them to apply newly learned concepts to solve novel problems embedded in situations or cases that are removed from their learning contexts. During this process, they are making the unknown known; my goal is to develop their deep understandings of novel information *and* the realization of the importance and usefulness of this information.

My second goal is to create creative tension, a sense of "disequilibrium" or puzzlement about known ideas, as described by Doll (1993). We revisit concepts and consider new uses of information as we make what is known apply to "unknown" situations. Students are asked to address "what-if" questions; the contexts for using the newly acquired information change greatly. Using information to respond to novel questions and situations can encourage flexible thinking about complex information and dilemmas that involve several solution paths.

Fifth, multimedia allows us to develop new ways to communicate across multiple texts and traditions. Problem-solving goals *and* idea-formulation goals are consistent with the notion that learning is both private and social—learning is supported and enhanced when students have opportunities to develop personal understandings and when these understandings are shared and reflected on by others. Therefore, it is important that students participate in learning environments that allow both types of learning to occur. I believe that students need to have time for their own inspection of ideas and for personal reflections and interpretations to develop. Students need to decide initially on their own understandings of the importance and relevance of text ideas based on their own questions and experiences. When personal interpretations are shared, instructors need to demonstrate that everyone's contribution is legitimate and valued. Personal understandings are not less important than the ideas that are jointly constructed in group discussions. All ideas that are shared are viewed as important to the inquiry in progress and the discussion serves to help students make links across the various memories, values, and intended meanings (Gee, 1992; Slattery, 1995). Shared understandings of text ideas help to unify the members of the group and contribute to the potential success of future collaborative (and inclusion) efforts.

In the classes where we use our multimedia cases, we find that rich discussions occur frequently, everyone has access to common information, and personal and collective understandings are developed and valued. Our classroom talk displays a synergy, suggesting to us that our students' involvement in learning activities can enable and enhance knowledge acquisition for themselves and their peers (Risko, 1992; Risko, Yount, & McAllister, 1992). Developing community among class members is as important for scaffolding learning (L. S. Shulman, 1995; Risko, 1996) as it is for accomplishing goals for inclusion. The interactions that occur within the inquiry community signal the value of the social nature of learning and the need for reexamining and reflecting on diverse points of view.

Sixth, interactions that occur with the study of multiple texts can create pathways to cross barriers of differences. The knowledge that is generated by communities of students becomes important for several reasons. For one, this knowledge is viewed as important by the students—it is information that helps them solve problems; it is legitimate and relevant for their purposes. Equally important is that students begin to "understand not only the assumptions embedded in its form and content, but also the processes whereby knowledge is produced" (Giroux, 1988, p. 8). As knowledge is enhanced and transformed through collaborative efforts, students realize the importance of many voices and perspectives for constructing meaning and for advancing their own thinking. In this way, education not only becomes purposeful, but it is emancipatory (Freire, 1985). Consistent with theories of critical pedagogy, students are making sense of the particular circumstances represented in the texts; analyzing the relationships between these circumstances and their own culture and understanding; and generating recommendations for what they envision, given particular intentions and conditions.

Conclusions

Many possibilities of the impact of multimedia texts on teaching and learning are described throughout this chapter. Central to the notion of intermediality, the cornerstone concept of this text, is the need for educators who are well grounded in theories of teaching and learning to reconceptualize conventional ways that we do schooling. Conventional methods that signal the importance of "single right answers," or unitary approaches to problem solving, and that restrict the participation of students in the learning process need to be replaced with environments that value multiple interpretations and understandings and the contributions of every member. Establishing dynamic learning environments that are built around rich media contexts provides an alternative to conventional views of education. Such environments provide a way to invite personal and collaborative inquiry that is valued, that is highly participatory, and that is important for students' cognitive and creative development.

References

Aronowitz, S., & Giroux, H. A. (1993). *Postmodern education.* Minneapolis: University of Minnesota Press.

Barron, L., & Goldman, E. S. (1996). *Introducing new perspectives on teaching and learning mathematics to preservice teachers.* Paper presented at the annual meeting of the American Education Research Association. New York.

Bransford, J. D., Vye, N., Kinzer, C., & Risko, V. (1990). Teaching thinking and content knowledge: Toward an integrated approach. In B. G. Jones & L. Idol (Eds.), *Dimensions of thinking and cognitive instruction* (pp. 381–413). Hillsdale, NJ: Erlbaum.

Brown, J. S., Collins, A., & Duguid, P. (1989). Situated cognition and the culture of learning. *Educational Researcher, 18*(1), 32–42.

Cognition and Technology Group at Vanderbilt. (1990). Anchored instruction and its relationship to situated cognition. *Educational Researcher, 19,* 2–10.

Cognition and Technology Group at Vanderbilt. (1993). *The Jasper series. Theoretical foundations and data on problem solving and transfer.* In L. A. Penner, G. M., Batsche, H. M. Knoff, & D. L. Nelson (Eds.), *The challenge in mathematics and science education: Psychology's response* (pp. 113–152). Washington, DC: American Psychological Association.

Cognition and Technology Group at Vanderbilt. (1996). Looking at technology in context: A framework for understanding technology and education research. In D. C. Berliner & R. Calfee (Eds.), *Handbook of education psychology* (pp. 807–840). New York: Simon & Schuster.

Cognition and Technology Group at Vanderbilt. (1997). *Building on strengths: Accelerated, integrated curriculum and its effects on children, teachers, and parents.* Year Two Report to the James S. McDonnell Foundation.

Darling-Hammond, L. (1996). The right to learn and the advancement of teaching: Research, policy, and practice for democratic education. *Educational Researcher, 25,* 5–17.

Doll, W. E., Jr. (1993). *A post-modern perspective on curriculum.* New York: Teachers College Press.

Egan, K. (1989, February). Memory, imagination, and learning. Connected by the story. *Phi Delta Kappan,* pp. 455–459.

Freire, P. (1985). *The politics of education: Culture, power, and liberation.* South Hadley, MA: Bergin & Garvey.

Gee, P. (1992). *The social mind. Language, ideology, and social practice.* New York: Bergin & Garvey.

Giroux, H. A. (1988). *Teachers as intellectuals.* New York: Bergin & Garvey.

Guzzetti, B. J., Snyder, T. E., Glass, G. V., & Gamas, W. S. (1993). Meta-analysis of instructional interventions from reading education and science education to promote conceptual change in science. *Reading Research Quarterly, 28,* 116–161.

Hiebert, J., Carpenter, T. P., Fennema, E., Fuson, K., Human, P., Murray, H., Olivier, A., & Wearne, D. (1996). Problem solving as a basis for reform in curriculum and instruction: The case of mathematics. *Educational Researcher, 25,* 12–21.

Hynd, C. R., & Guzzetti, B. J. (1993). Exploring issues in conceptual change. In D. J. Leu & C. K. Kinzer (Eds.), *Examining central issues in literacy research, theory, and practice.* (pp. 375–381). Chicago: The National Reading Conference.

Johnson-Laird, P. N. (1983). *Mental models.* Cambridge, MA: Harvard University Press.

Merseth, K. (1991). *The case for cases in teacher education.* Washington, DC: American Association of Colleges of Teacher Education and American Association of Higher Education.

Morris, M. (1988). *The pirate's fiancee: Feminism, reading, postmodernism.* London: Verso Press.

Prawat, R. S. (1993). The value of ideas: Problems versus possibilities in learning. *Educational Researcher, 22*(6), 5–15.

Risko, V. J. (1992). Developing problem-solving environments to prepare teachers to instruction of diverse learners. In B. Hayes & K. Camperell (Eds.), *Developing lifelong readers: Policies, procedures, and programs* (pp. 1–13). Logan: Utah State Press.

Risko, V. J. (1996). Creating a community of thinkers within a preservice literacy education methods course. In K. Camperell, B. L. Hayes, & R. Telfer (Eds.), *Literacy: The information highway to success* (pp. 3–15). Logan: Utah State Press.

Risko, V. J., & Kinzer, C. K. (1991). *Improving undergraduate teacher education with technology and case-based instruction.* Fund for the Improvement of Postsecondary Education.

Risko, V. J., & Kinzer, C. K. (1994). *Improving undergraduate teacher education through dissemination of videodisc-based case procedures and influencing the teaching of future college professionals.* Washington, DC: Fund for the Improvement of Postsecondary Education.

Risko, V. J., & Kinzer, C. K. (in press). *Multimedia cases for literacy education.* Boston: McGraw-Hill.

Risko, V. J., Peter, J., & McAllister, D. (1996). Conceptual changes: Preservice teacher' pathways to providing literacy transaction. In E. Sturtevant & W. Linek (Eds.), *Literacy grows* (pp. 103–119). Pittsburg, KS: College Reading Association.

Risko, V. J., Yount, D., & McAllister, D. (1992). Preparing preservice teachers for remedial instruction: Teaching problem solving and use of content and pedagogical knowledge. In N. Padak, T. V. Rasinski, & J. Logan (Eds.), *Inquiries in literacy learning and instruction* (pp. 179–189). Pittsburg, KS: College Reading Association.

Shulman, J. H. (1995). Tender feeling, hidden thoughts: Confronting bias, innocence, and racism through case discussion. In J. A. Colbert, P. Desberg, & K. Trimble (Eds.), *The case of education* (pp. 137–158). Boston: Allyn & Bacon.

Shulman, L. S. (1995). Just in case: Reflections on learning from experience. In J. A. Colbert, P. Desberg, & K. Trimble (Eds.), *The case of education* (pp. 197–217). Boston: Allyn & Bacon.

Slattery, P. (1995). *Curriculum development in the postmodern era.* New York: Garland.

7

A Feminist Critique of Media Representation

Donna E. Alvermann

Technology, whether we're talking cars or computers, is often regarded with suspicion in popular feminist debate. Machines are seen as a form of mechanised masculinity. They're boys' toys, designed by men to do men's work—going global, going fast and going to war. They're a tool of the patriarchy.

—Catherine Lumby (1997, p. 139)

Contemporary feminist debate is fueled by antimale rhetoric such as this, according to Catherine Lumby, who argues in her newly published book, *Bad Girls: The Media, Sex & Feminism in the 90s*, that charges of sexism leveled against the media are often outdated and too simplistic. She also takes issue with the notion that the media's representation of women is inherently harmful and discriminates against them. Claiming that each of us (male or female) interprets media images and information on the basis of what we know and want to know, Lumby argues that "there is no single, 'true' reading of any image or representation; there are only points of view" (p. xxv).

Feminists on the other side of the debate assert that media representation remains an important site of contestation over who should have the right to speak for women as a whole. Procensorship feminists such as Catharine MacKinnon (1992) and Andrea Dworkin (1992), for example, argue that sexist ads and certain media images of women in popular culture invoke a public discourse that carries important messages—many of which work against women's best interests economically and socially.

The purpose of this chapter is twofold: (1) to provide a feminist critique of both sides of the debate and, in particular, the part that media representation plays in the ongoing construction of gender; and (2) to apply what is known about media representation from a feminist perspective to a sample textual analysis that teachers might do for themselves, using materials from their own classrooms. Although there is no

141

single feminist perspective (feminist theory is fragmented and rarely referred to in the singular), there is unswerving attention among feminists of all persuasions to analyzing gender as a category that structures most of our experiences of the material and symbolic worlds in which we live.

The position I take in this chapter is that gender is not a fixed property but rather an ongoing process through which femininity and masculinity are constructed in everyday practices (West & Zimmerman, 1987). This position carries with it the assumption that such practices are part of the larger context in which popular culture is "read" through and into the media's representation of the male and female subject.

The chapter begins with a definition of media and media representation. From there, a brief look at the flaws in feminist transmission models of communication leads to a consideration of cultural studies as a framework for studying how gendered images are constructed and "read" through media representation. After that, there is a section on the implications of a feminist critique of media representation for literacy education. The chapter ends with an example of a textual analysis that incorporates activities for critiquing media representation from a feminist perspective.

Media and Media Representation

The media, as in "mass" media, are often referred to as an amorphous lump labeled popular culture that includes "television, radio, videos, newspapers, alternative 'zines, Hollywood cinema, billboards, web sites, video games," and so on, according to Lumby (1997, pp. xxii–xxiii). She opposes this conception of the media for the very reason that it implies a homogeneous and passive audience. In Lumby's words,

> The "mass" in media refers to audience reach rather than inherent homogeneity. . . . The idea that the media is a monolithic institution which somehow speaks in the voice of mainstream patriarchy (with a capitalist accent) is ultimately unhelpful for understanding the relationship between feminism and the vertiginous spiral of images and information which defines contemporary culture. To use an old postmodern metaphor, the media is like a virus. It infects everything it touches, but it is also, in turn, changed by what it comes into contact with—it mutates. (p. xxiii)

This definition of the media as stated by Lumby, a third-wave feminist (as contrasted to second-wave feminists of the early 1970s), argues for the view that the meaning of a written message, a visual image, or an auditory sound bite rests not in the thing itself but instead in us—the reader, the viewer, the listener. We are the ones who make meaning through a complex and mediated relationship with things (real or imagined objects, people, events, ideas), the concepts we hold of these things, and the language we use to communicate such concepts.

This meaning-making process, composed of a system of signs the relationships of which are fixed by shared cultural and linguistic codes, is the social constructionist view of language and representation.

It is a view that owes a great deal to Saussure's (1960) work in linguistics and those semioticians who came after him and applied his theories of language and representation to a wide range of cultural practices, including media representation and the "reading" of popular culture (e.g., Barthes, 1972).

A point worth bearing in mind is that from a social constructionist view of media representation, meaning does not lie in things (e.g., commercials, newspaper ads, Madonna) or events (such as Princess Di's funeral). Nor does it lie with the author, producer, sculptor, or speaker; that is, meaning cannot be reduced to the intentions of its originator for the very reason that language is a social phenomenon and requires shared understandings.

Rather, meaning is produced within language or whatever language-like system we choose to use in representing the concepts that we want to communicate. For example, clothing can function as a language-like system. The language of fashion depends on codes that match certain kinds of clothing (e.g., jeans) with certain concepts (e.g., casualness). That not everyone shares the same codes and that meanings change over periods of time are part and parcel of the social constructionist view of media representation. A certain degree of cultural relativism, in fact, is what accounts for Lumby's (1997) feminist take on the media's representation of women being different from that of pro-censorship feminists, such as MacKinnon (1992) and Dworkin (1992).

The notion that reality is brought into existence by communicating through language is "not to say that there is nothing out there except the images in our head, as a collision with a moving car will prove, but that we can only define the meaning and make sense of that experience through language" (van Zoonen, 1994, p. 39). That language constitutes us and the world in which we live is similar to what Foucault (1980) had in mind when he wrote his treatise on power and knowledge. Unlike the linguists who preceded him, however, Foucault, a philosopher/historian by training, argued that relations of power, not relations of meaning, should be one's point of reference when studying how knowledge is produced and represented in specific historical contexts. He was interested in discourse, not language, as a system of representation. By discourse, Foucault meant what one does (practice) as well as what one says (language) about a particular topic. Discursive practices, he believed, govern the way a topic (e.g., in his work, madness, insanity, and sexuality) can be talked about and used to regulate the lives of others. Thus, for Foucault, issues of power were always implicated in the production and representation of knowledge. This point will be taken up again in a later section of the chapter that looks at the role of the media in the ongoing construction of gender, but first comes a brief historical overview of the feminist transmission models leading up to a cultural studies framework for examining the current debate on feminist censorship and the media.

Feminist Transmission Models of Communication

From the publication of *The Feminine Mystique* (Friedan, 1963) and *The Female Eunuch* (Greer, 1971) to the much discussed 1998 "Feminism: It's All About Me" issue of *Time* magazine (Bellafante, 1998), the media have remained at the center of feminist critique in the United States. In other countries, as well, impassioned feminist critiques have been hurled at the media, sometimes leading to national debates on the representation of women. In general, three themes have fueled these debates, both nationally and abroad. All three share similar assumptions about the media's role in constructing gender. The first has to do with the media's portrayal of women in stereotypical situations, presumably for the purpose of socializing future generations of young girls into appropriate feminine roles. The second concerns the representation of women's bodies in pornographic magazines, movies, and videos, thus reinforcing the notion of women as available objects who are subject to male violence or harassment. The third theme speaks to the media's role in drawing individuals into the dominant ideology by making it seem the "commonsense" thing to do (e.g., teen magazines that feature fashion and beauty tips as precursors of heterosexual romance) (van Zoonen, 1994).

These three themes, which have been part of the feminist transmission models of communication since 1970, assume a rather uncomplicated role for the media. Basically, media are seen as transmitting certain messages about gender that are then taken up by the public in general. Of late, these transmission models have come under attack by feminists who see them as oversimplifications of gender and communication. For example, van Zoonen (1994) characterizes their limitations in the following way: "With regard to gender, the problem lies mainly in the observation that media distort the 'true' nature of gender, assuming a stable and easily identifiable distinction between women and men. . . . [In terms of communication,] media audiences do not simply take in or reject media messages, but use and interpret them according to the logic of their own social, cultural and individual circumstances" (p. 40).

By proposing to view gender as a discourse—that is, a set of overlapping and sometimes contradictory practices that are articulated through language in systematic ways—cultural studies proponents such as van Zoonen (1994) and Lumby (1997) seek to problematize the media's role in gender construction. Specifically, their interests lie in understanding how audiences produce meaning, not merely "receive" it, as in the transmission models discussed above.

Cultural Studies and Gendered Images

The turn to audience research, which characterizes the majority of feminist media studies currently, is seen as both empowering and potentially fraught with danger. On the one hand, taking up the vicarious pleasures that popular culture offers can be seen as a means by which contemporary women challenge the search for universal truths or institutionalized feminism's push to "centre and cement the category 'woman'" (Lumby, 1997, p. 170). On the other hand, there is the fear that such pleasures will serve to derail the feminist movement and thereby reconcile women with the patriarchy.

This "uneasy connection between the pleasures of popular culture and the political aims of feminism" (van Zoonen, 1994, p. 7) is at the heart of the debate that is presently raging between some third-wave feminists and their procensorship counterparts. It is a debate that can best be understood in terms of Foucault's (1980) power/knowledge concept discussed earlier. This concept is central, in fact, to Lumby's (1997) argument that it is, ironically, second-wave procensorship feminists who help "produce" the pornographic media images that they so actively seek to investigate and abolish. In Lumby's words,

> While it's certainly tempting to reduce the current crisis to an opposition between a modern, enlightened feminist position and a naive . . . or old-fashioned one, I'm seeking a broader context in which to unpack contemporary debates about the extent to which media images and information are inherently harmful to women or discriminate against them. I am less interested in what pornography is (or isn't) or in what it does to people than in why feminists have become so interested in those questions. To put it simply I want to know what censorship and feminism have in common. . . . The idea that pornography is manufactured by groups who oppose it is grounded in French philosopher Michel Foucault's argument that sexuality is actively produced by forms of professional knowledge and institutions dedicated to speaking its truth—from the confessional box, to the psychiatrist's couch to talk shows. (pp. xviii–xix)

That power relations are bound up in knowledge production, particularly in terms of the media audience, is a given. For example, it was the active support of prominent procensorship feminists in 1996 that facilitated the passage of legislation in the U.S. Congress aimed at severely restricting the availability of sexually explicit material on the Internet. In turn, this move was read by free speech advocates in the women's movement as being antithetical to feminist ethics. They saw it as being a clear-cut example of how established, old guard feminists are beginning to "look an awful lot like the patriarchy" (Lumby, 1997, p. 156) in terms of the power they are able to wield in the public sphere over matters related to women's private lives.

As noted earlier, the debate over whose interests will be represented (and by whom) currently focuses on pornography and its meaning for media audiences. To MacKinnon's (1992) way of thinking, gendered images of female bodies that reduce women to mere sexual objects for men's gratification produce a knowledge about womanhood that speaks of domination. In fact, she views pornographic images in the media as being the primary means of women's subordination in the public as well as the private sphere. But to Lumby's (1997) way of thinking, the debate is not about gendered images of women's bodies, but rather it is about rejecting the victim tag for women in order to get on with the reinvention of traditional forms of knowledge and power in media culture.

One way of reinventing such knowledge involves the Internet. According to Lumby (1997), the Internet is blurring the boundaries between "real" life and virtual existence: "When we boot up our laptops and connect with the World Wide Web we create a virtual extension of ourselves which reaches out beyond the physical space we inhabit. We're splitting ourselves from our bodies and sending this disembodied self off to play in a world where gender, race and sexuality cannot be read off the surface of our texts" (p. 153). This ability of the net to blur gender boundaries is of no particular interest to the Australian feminist writer Dale Spender (1995), however. Instead, like other procensorship feminists, Spender views the net as a site from which women can join together in policing the smut that has made its way from the real world into the world of cyberspace. In Spender's words, "It is to be regretted that some of the worst aspects of real life have become prominent features of the virtual world. But women have a history of admirable achievements when it comes to establishing a more egalitarian society. What we now face is a bigger task in our efforts to change the world: because now that we have cyberspace, we have a bigger world and more to change" (p. 212).

In cyberspace, where gender identities are often intentionally masked as a means of blurring boundaries between the powerful and the not so powerful, there is hope that men and women will learn important lessons about how they view others and how others view them. Yet, despite claims that such blurring of identities will lead eventually to a more democratic and socially just world, there is still plenty of evidence that the gendered politics of media representation are alive and well (Luke, 1996). What seems clear is that although the debate about feminist censorship and the media continues, another important forum for cultural studies—media literacy education—goes virtually unexplored. That forum, though seemingly quite far removed from feminist politics, is likely to benefit from the fallout of a scholarly debate that has gendered images in the media and popular culture as its focus.

Implications for Literacy Education

Reading is one of the primary means for constructing gendered identities and negotiating their meaning in Western cultures. Yet, gendered reading practices are among the least studied aspects of literacy education (A. Luke, 1994). Where such practices have been researched, the issues that usually garner attention are gender equity and stereotyping. Although these are important issues, they do not shed light on how the literacy curriculum has been engendered. Nor do they deal with the role that media representation plays in the ongoing construction of gender. With the call for an expanded view of literacy, one that includes inquiry into altered notions of reader, writer, and text in computer-mediated learning (Reinking, Labbo, & McKenna (1997), it is likely that gendered reading practices in media-rich environments will shortly receive the research attention they deserve. In the meantime, at least two things learned from critiquing the feminist politics associated with media representation appear worth discussing here.

First is a recognition of gender's unstable role in media consumption practices. This is so, Ang (1996) argues, because "gender identity . . . is both multiple and partial, ambiguous and incoherent, permanently in process of being articulated, disarticulated, and rearticulated" (p. 125). In short, essentialist views of gender cannot account for the tastes of media audiences. Critical literacy educators would no doubt be among the first to agree. Luke (1996), for example, has long argued that attributing cognitive repertoires to male and female students along essentialist lines is not good practice. Yet, as she has pointed out recently, "Gendered socialisation patterns do create different relations to highly gendered bodies of knowledge among boys/men and girls/women" (p. 202). She draws support for her thinking from Spender (1995) and her own observations about the open-ended, multimodal, and multivocal nature of cyberspace technology. For example, Luke writes, "some feminist scholars, in fact, see the new electronic social and knowledge communities as particularly amenable to women, as a place of simultaneity, self-organisation, groupness through cooperation, a horizontal network of lateral 'click' connections without an authoritative centre of (male) control" (p. 202).

A second point that can be learned from the debate involving procensorship feminists and media representation is that viewing the media as a monolithic institution—one that speaks in the voice of mainstream patriarchy—is not a particularly useful heuristic for understanding media consumption. This point resonates with feminist pedagogy's stance on teacher-student relationships and school-based media education. Briefly, it speaks to the politics of pleasure as applied to children's and adolescents' consumption of texts, in the broadest sense of the word— that is, print-based texts, electronic-based texts, texts comprising visual images, and so on. Common misperceptions of what critical media literacy should entail is at the crux of the matter. The misperceptions have to do with teachers' tendencies to associate critical media literacy with helping students learn how to liberate themselves from texts that are designed to dupe them. One sure way to fall prey to this pedagogical trap is to ask students to critique media texts that are likely to be their favorites but which they sense are looked upon with disfavor by those in positions of authority. As Carmen Luke (1994) explains it,

> Asking students for critical interpretations of mass cultural texts is likely to cue a critical response which can often be an outright lie. As with any "critical" discourse (including that of critical pedagogy, cultural studies or feminism more generally), students are quick to talk a good anti-sexist, antiracist, pro-equity game. As educators are well aware, what students write in the essay or what they tell us in classroom discussion is no measure of what goes on in their heads. (p. 43)

To avoid putting students in positions where they can only recognize pleasure as a form of deception, Luke argues for self-reflective critical practice on teachers' parts. In her words,

> Although self-reflexivity has become somewhat of a cliché in educational circles, I am convinced that self-reflexive critique of our own pedagogies and political assumptions as media educators is paramount if we wish to avoid mechanistic transmission model pedagogies in which students are made to reproduce the teacher's preferred ideological take on the subject matter. . . . Media educators need to be mindful of the politics inherent in their textual selections and the critical textual practices they advocate because some choices can easily condemn youth's cultural terrain. (p. 43)

In sum, feminist thinking on media representation has implications for literacy educators on at least two counts. One, the instability of the role of gender in media consumption suggests that thinking along essentialist lines about what male and female students are likely to take up in media literacy instruction is unproductive. Yet, the possibility exists that certain gendered patterns of socializing may give females the advantage when it comes to learning in cyberspace. Two, just as the media are not a monolithic institution, neither is media consumption. Respecting students' choices in media texts is an important step toward becoming a self-reflexive literacy educator.

Example of Textual Analysis Using a Feminist Critique

To illustrate the usefulness of critiquing media from a feminist perspective in everyday classroom activities, I propose the following exercise. It is one I have used with students in my content literacy class at the University of Georgia. The exercise consists of a set of activities constructed to engage students in a discussion of a partial text drawn from an article in the "Lifestyles" section of a recent issue of *Newsweek*. Titled "How Would Ally Do It?" the article describes the 1990s answer to Mary Tyler Moore:

> Her name is Ally McBeal, and she's rapidly becoming the woman network execs have long lusted after: the 90s answer to Mary Tyler Moore. A Harvard law graduate with a promising career, 27-year-old Ally has the ability to both inspire and repel. She claims to want to use the law for good, but almost all of her waking hours are preoccupied by her desire to snag a man. "If women really wanted to change society, they could do it," she tells her roommate. "I plan to change society. I just want to get married first." Ally is the quintessential postfeminist. She has all the professional advantages Mary never had, but unlike her more traditionally feminist sitcom sister, she doesn't want to make it on her own.
>
> Only 13 episodes into its first season, the Fox comedy-drama has already become a TV phenomenon on Monday nights. Critics seem to either love it or hate it. In *GQ*, Terrence Rafferty snipes that "TV's Ally McBeal wants to be the thinking man's sex kitten—if only she had a brain." Yet "Ally" recently won two Golden Globes: one for best comedy series (beating out such favorites as "Seinfeld" and "Mad About You") and a best-actress award for the show's star, Calista Flockhart. But the real proof that we're in an Ally moment is the show's steady rise in the ratings; about 14 million women tune in regularly, and the show recently broke into the Nielsen top 25.
>
> "Ally" has clearly struck a nerve with twentysomething women who feel both excited and confused by the choices bestowed upon them by the feminist movement. They understand Ally's big question: "If I have it all, can I be happy?" The show doesn't offer up many answers, but it does provide comic relief, commiseration and the occasional insight, just as Mary once did.

It captures the sense of anxious expectation that people feel in their 20s, when most of life's important decisions still lie ahead. Ally works hard (allegedly) and plays hard (definitely), but what she does more than anything else is dream. And lest you dismiss the show as a purely female indulgence, along the lines of a Saturday night curled up with a pint of Ben & Jerry's, an issue of *Cosmopolitan* and a bottle of Nair, think again. "Ally" has male fans—nearly 6 million, according to one estimate. Maybe they sense Ally's secret: her creator is a man, David Kelley, who has also written every episode. (Chambers, 1998, p. 58) (From *Newsweek*, © 1998, Newsweek, Inc. All rights reserved. Reprinted by permission)

Guiding Points

A point to keep in mind in this exercise is that audiences produce meaning; they do not merely "receive" it. Another point worth remembering from an earlier section of this chapter is the need to get on with the reinvention of traditional forms of knowledge and power in media culture. To do otherwise is to invite repetition of some of the very practices we seek to abolish, such as those aimed at maintaining essentialist views of gender when attempting to account for the tastes and pleasures of media audiences. As Luke (1996) has argued, attributing certain ways of believing and acting as being characteristically male or female in origin is too simplistic in outlook.

A final point has to do with the thinking that is behind this exercise. The ideas that helped to frame it have come largely from my readings of what feminist pedagogues in Australia are writing about in terms of textual literacy. Here, the descriptor *textual* refers to the printed word as well as images, icons, and the like. Drawing from Gilbert's (1989) work on deconstructing texts in the context of schooling, Morgan (1991) has outlined what she calls her four "tenets of textuality":

1. Texts are produced within the historical and cultural contexts which shape them. The discourse available at the time of writing governs what can be said and how it can be said.
2. There can be no single "author-ised" meaning of a text prior to the text, which determines how it is to be read. Instead, different often contradictory readings and meanings will be available in specific historical, cultural and textual contexts.
3. No text is unified, complete and consistent. It must encompass silences, incoherences, contradictions.
4. Any text constructs a version of reality. That version convinces those readers who find it reflects "the way things are" or "what goes without saying". (p. 153)

It is these four tenets, applied to the text on Ally McBeal above, that compose the backbone of the following activities. Although each of the activities pertains specifically to the Ally text as it was used in my class, each is easily adaptable to texts other teachers might choose to use in their own classrooms.

Activity 1: Context Matters

Drawing attention to the context in which the article on Ally McBeal was produced helped the students in my class learn to identify whose values were being foregrounded and whose were being silenced. Two of the questions that proved useful in engaging them in a discussion of the context for the popularity of the Ally McBeal comedy-drama included the following:

1. How does the *Newsweek* description of "Ally" speak of a time in our country that is open to blurring the boundaries of "reality"?
2. Why is Ally "a heroine very much of our time" (Roush, 1998a, p. 26)? Or, if you do not agree that she is "a heroine of our time," tell why you believe as you do.

Activity 2: Read from a Different Standpoint

The aim of Activity 2 is to encourage students to step into a reading position that is different from the one they customarily fill. Langer (1990) describes something similar to this in her research on envisionment. As Morgan (1991) has noted, reading from a different standpoint makes clear "how any text offers an interested version of reality" (p. 173). Students in my class role-played the following individuals as they took on what they assumed to be each person's different views on the Ally McBeal show: Mary Tyler Moore, Gloria Steinem, Saddam Hussein, and Johnny Cochran.

Activity 3: Juxtapose Reviews of the Show

In featuring "Ally McBeal" in the "Lifestyles" section of *Newsweek*, the writer Veronica Chambers (1998) spoke of some things about the show while ignoring others. Students in my class were helped to see what was and was not said by Chambers when they contrasted her review with that of Matt Roush (1998b), a portion of which follows:

> Call me snappish. (Elaine, that insufferably intrusive secretary, surely would.) But like the insistent inner voice that taunts its title character, mine won't let me simply sit back and admire *Ally McBeal* for its style and its cast. Not when so much about the show is so indulgent and irritating, you can't help but groan and scream at the TV.
>
> To borrow a recent *McBeal*-ism, think of this as the "ick" factor. Would you ever hire a counselor-at-law who's so clearly in need of counseling, who babbles so incoherently, who dresses so skimpily, who stumbles and fum-

bles like a designer rag doll? Even if you hang on her every word and thought, it's hard to believe her for a second.

And while I've been a fan of writer-producer David E. Kelley's ever since he contrived a shocking fall down an elevator shaft for *L.A. Law*'s Rosalind Shays, his absurdist penchant for preciousness hits an all-time low, straining to create a *Seinfeld*-ian lexicon (the wattle fetish, the "penguin" sexual prank) and never knowing when to say enough, whether with fantasy or whimsy. Loved the dancing baby. Hated the dancing Ally, outside in her PJs. (p. 27)

Points that started a lively discussion in my class dealt with the issue of essentialist thinking. For example, some students wanted to blame David Kelley for portraying her as a sex object. But when they read Matt Roush's (1998b) review, which panned the very things that Ally's nearly 6 million male fans were thought to admire in the show, they had to reconsider their stance. For example, they began asking questions such as these:

1. Does Matt Roush really represent the 6 million male fans of "Ally"?
2. Why would it be helpful to know more about the two reviewers, Matt Roush and Veronica Chambers?
3. What can be learned from considering where the two reviews appeared?
4. Who produces the meaning of the show? Of the reviews?

Collectively, these activities should be viewed as starting points for helping students "read" all kinds of texts, and particularly for helping them understand how different readings serve different interests. But they are only starting points. Merely teaching students how to see in texts what previously has been invisible to them is not enough. As Scholes (1985) reminds us, "Our job is not to produce 'readings' for our students but to give them the tools for producing their own" (p. 24). Textual literacy is acquired over time—and with practice given to deconstructing, or unpacking, texts so that what seems obvious and "just the way it is" takes on a less "natural" look.

References

Ang, I. (1996). *Living room wars: Rethinking media audiences for a postmodern world*. London: Routledge.
Barthes, R. (1972). *Mythologies*. London: Cape.
Bellafante, G. (1998, June 26). Feminism: It's all about me. *Time*, pp. 54–62.
Chambers, V. (1998, March 2). How would Ally do it? *Newsweek*, pp. 58–60.

Dworkin, A. (1992). Against the male flood: Censorship, pornography and equality. In C. Itzin (Ed.), *Pornography, women, violence and civil liberties: A radical new view* (pp. 515–535). Oxford, UK: Oxford University Press.

Foucault, M. (1980). *Power/knowledge*. Brighton, UK: Harvester.

Friedan, B. (1963). *The feminine mystique*. London: Penguin Books.

Gilbert, P. (1989). *Writing, schooling and deconstruction: From voice to text in the classroom*. London: Routledge.

Greer, G. (1971). *The female eunuch*. London: Paladin.

Langer, J. (1990). The process of understanding: Reading for literary and informative purposes. *Research in the Teaching of English, 24,* 229–260.

Luke, A. (1994). On reading and the sexual division of literacy. *Journal of Curriculum Studies, 26,* 361–381.

Luke, C. (1994). Feminist pedagogy and critical media literacy. *Journal of Communication Inquiry, 18*(2), 30–47.

Luke, C. (1996). ekstasis@cyberia. *Discourse: Studies in the Cultural Politics of Education, 17,* 187–207.

Lumby, C. (1997). *Bad girls: The media, sex & feminism in the 90s.* St. Leonards, Australia: Allen & Unwin.

MacKinnon, C. (1992). Pornography, civil rights and speech. In C. Itzin (Ed.), *Pornography, women, violence and civil liberties: A radical new view.* Oxford, UK: Oxford University Press.

Morgan, W. (1991). Deconstructing texts, reconstructing courses for textual literacy. In P. Cormack (Ed.), *Literacy: Making it explicit, making it possible* (pp. 151–175). Adelaide: Australian Reading Association.

Reinking, D., Labbo, L., & McKenna, M. (1997). Navigating the changing landscape of literacy: Current theory and research in computer-based reading and writing. In J. Flood, S. B. Heath, & D. Lapp (Eds.), *Handbook of research on teaching literacy through the communicative and visual arts* (pp. 77–92). New York: Macmillan.

Roush, M. (1998a, February 28). I'm crazy about it. *TV Guide, 46*(9), 26.

Roush, M. (1998b, February 28). It drives me crazy. *TV Guide, 46*(9), 27.

Saussure, F. de. (1960). *Course in general linguistics*. London: Peter Owen.

Scholes, R. (1985). *Textual power: Literary theory and the teaching of English.* New Haven: Yale University Press.

Spender, D. (1995). *Nattering on the net: Women, power, and cyberspace.* Melbourne, Australia: Spinifex.

van Zoonen, L. (1994). *Feminist media studies*. Thousand Oaks, CA: Sage.

West, C., & Zimmerman, D. H. (1987). Doing gender. *Gender & Society, 1,* 125–151.

8 Critical Media Literacy as an English Language Content Course in Japan

Carolyn Layzer
Judy Sharkey

"Disney World!" "Coca-Cola!" "Guns!" "Cowboy!" These were among the top 10 representative objects of U.S. culture that Japanese college students generated in the first week of the class "English Seminar: Media Literacy." We were not surprised by these responses. Having lived and worked overseas for more than 10 years, we had grown accustomed to (though never accepting of) people's dependence on exported images of U.S. culture. In fact, it was the anticipation of such responses that motivated us to attempt teaching a class in media literacy.

Our purpose in this chapter is to share our experience in working with students of English as a foreign language (EFL) in exploring concepts of media literacy in order to critically view cultural images. We also present some of the challenges we faced in experimenting with a new course and approach to culture teaching/learning. We hope that teachers will find in our description ideas for ways to introduce these concepts across the curriculum.

Our Japanese students, like most foreign language learners who cannot afford to travel or live abroad, have virtual experiences with the (foreign-language) target culture through mass media products from movies and MTV to glossy magazines and tacky billboards. Attraction to foreign pop culture may even spark a student's desire to learn a particular language. One student said the reason she decided to study English was to be able to write a letter to Kevin Costner.

Unfortunately, when students do not question the cultural images and messages they receive, stereotypes are easily created and perpetuated. These images can be imprinted so deeply that they override information gained from actual interactions with individuals from the target culture. Clearly, there is a need to help language students become critical consumers of this barrage of images and messages. It was our intention to use media literacy to fulfill that need by raising learners' awareness of the impact of mass media. We wanted them to see how media shape cultural values and opinions and to enable them to deconstruct messages inherent in media products while extracting relevant cultural information.

Building the critical thinking skills necessary to become media literate cannot be accomplished in a one-week unit on "the media," yet many EFL texts treat the subject in just this manner, leaving learners with a superficial understanding of mass media. We were convinced that the subject merited a semester-long course and thus decided to design one. We were also frustrated by the numerous EFL texts that claim to teach U.S. culture but really only teach the values and norms of the dominant (white, middle-class, Anglo) culture. Our idea was to design a course that would encompass critical cultural studies and media literacy. We believe that media messages and images play an important role in shaping individuals' identities, but we pitched the idea to our program coordinator as being necessary and relevant to intercultural communication, a popular topic in the language teaching world (and a less controversial topic than critical cultural studies). The EFL course we offered may have served to motivate the students in their exploration of the world around them, and it may also have given them insight into the complexities of intercultural communication as they came to see media messages in a more critical light.

Context

We taught at a small junior college specializing in foreign languages in Osaka, Japan. The course described was taught during spring 1997, the last semester in our three-year teaching contracts. It was an elective course open to second-year English language majors. A total of six classes, each averaging 20 students, were offered. More than 95% of the students were female. Language proficiency ranged from low beginners with minimal oral skills and aural/reading comprehension to advanced students who had participated in several study abroad programs and were planning to transfer to universities in English-speaking countries. The class met twice a week for 90-minute sessions. The semester was 14 weeks.

Most of the classrooms were equipped with televisions and videocassette recorders. Students had access to a fairly extensive collection of videos at the college's language lab. The library carried a range of U.S. newspapers and magazines, including *Time, Newsweek, USA Today,*

Rolling Stone, and *Backpacker.* Students did not have school access to computers, the Internet, or any audiovisual equipment that could be used to produce their own pieces. There was no student newspaper and requests to organize one were denied by the administration. Students were not allowed to post or distribute information without permission.

Young Japanese are as inundated with mass media as are their U.S. counterparts. Pop singers and television actors pervade everyday life—their images appear throughout public spaces wherever the eye might land—and the idol "industry" is fostered and exploited by commercial interests throughout the country in ways that we are just beginning to see in the United States. Japanese animation, well known outside Japan as well, is quite popular, and programming of this kind abounds on the airwaves. The 1990s have also seen a boom in *manga,* Japanese graphic fiction (comics), which composes a substantial portion of all published material in Japan. A common sight on any train is a young, well-dressed businessman, briefcase between his legs, totally engrossed in his *manga.* Owning the latest electronic gadgets from pocket pagers to "virtual pets" (such as Tamagotchi) was a sign of hipness among our students.

Although the information age is being heralded around the world, students are not necessarily better prepared to consume the wealth of information available to them. Literacy instruction in Japan tends to follow time-honored ideas about what constitutes literacy practices and what the purpose of education should be: Teachers teach to the test, students cram and learn by rote for tests, analysis beyond identification of parts is not generally learned (whether or not it is "taught"), and questioning and critical analysis are not generally encouraged (although these practices may be class based as they are in the United States—our students came mostly from working-class and lower-middle-class homes). Thus, we found that our students were a bit perplexed by the type of questions we posed and the type of analysis we modeled. For this reason, we found it more suitable to allow students the option of first analyzing Japanese media texts in order to facilitate their comprehension of the concepts and technique of analysis. Their analyses were conducted in English. We assumed that if they learned how to analyze Japanese media texts, they would be able to apply that knowledge and skill to textual analyses in other languages.

Framework

The course followed a cycle in which we first presented a concept and supplied models or examples and then asked the students to find examples of media texts to illustrate the concepts and bring them to class to explain them. After sharing those examples, the students created their own media products incorporating the key concept. Finally, the students shared and analyzed each other's products. Each succeeding concept always built on the previous one(s).

Our instructional objectives sprang from four principles of media literacy (Davis, 1992, pp. 28–9):

Media construct reality
Media use identifiable techniques
Media are businesses with commercial interests
Media present ideology and value messages

The first three weeks of the course covered the following topics: media and media literacy, cultural symbols and values in Japan and the United States and how they are transmitted, stereotypes, issues involved in television viewing, and starting a media log. The bulk of activities consisted of building vocabulary and identifying and sharing personal media consumption habits and preferences. For example, in the icebreaker activity on the first day of class, the students compared notes on favorite television programs and radio stations and newspaper reading habits.

The remainder of the course was dedicated to covering the four principles mentioned above. In addition to creating media products such as the front page of a newspaper and a storyboard for an advertisement, the students also did two poster presentations in which they were required to synthesize what they had learned up to that point in the course. Once a week, the students discussed their media logs in pairs and small groups. At the end of the semester, the students completed a simple questionnaire, the last item asking whether individuals should learn media literacy and, if so, how they should learn it and at what age. (All the students wrote that people should learn media literacy. Most— all but 3 students out of 120—thought that it should be taught at school, but they were almost evenly divided about at what age, from elementary school through college.)

The Course

During the first week, we introduced the topic of the course and generated definitions of media, literacy, mass media, and media literacy. By sheer good fortune, Japanese public television (NHK) had recently aired a 30-minute program on media literacy in Canada. We taped the program, which was completely in Japanese, and made copies available for students to view in the language lab. As mentioned above, the students also shared personal preferences regarding their media consumption and habits. We ended the first day by asking the students to brainstorm representative objects of Japanese and U.S. culture. The Statue of Liberty, the White House, Hollywood, and the NBA (National Basketball Association) were among the most popular, in addition to those items mentioned in the opening of this chapter. The most common Japanese objects were Mount Fuji, kimono, sushi, chopsticks, and sumo. Interestingly, no corporate names or name products were among the Japanese items (whereas Coca-Cola, McDonald's, Nike, and Disney were common among the U.S. items). In the succeeding class, we distributed the tallied results and asked the students to provide the source of their knowledge of each object or image. The immediate result was that the students could see that they had received almost all of the U.S. images through mass media, whereas many of the Japanese objects came from school or family experiences as well as the mass media.

According to Gillian Swanson (1991), representation "refers to the way images and language actively construct meanings according to sets of conventions shared by and familiar to makers and audiences" (p. 123). By generating lists of representations that were familiar to the students, we hoped to create a reference that would facilitate identification of those representations in media artifacts, which would lead to analysis of the ways in which makers (media organs) use conventions and students (the audience) make meaning from them. We began with the identification of concrete objects that the students could literally point to in order to ease the transition to identifying representations of more abstract concepts of values and attitudes.

Thus, once the students had identified representative objects, we proceeded to consider cultural values. We provided the students with a list of more than 35 words such as family, self-reliance, conformity, and so on. We tried to offer a range but made sure to include stereotypical values of each culture. We also included several Japanese terms, such as *gaman*, that do not have adequate English translations. The students were encouraged to add their own words to the list as well. Next, we introduced the idea of storytelling as a traditional way of transmitting cultural values. We asked our classes to generate a list of their favorite children's stories, which we wrote on the board. In small groups, the students discussed their memories of the stories, including characters and plot. Next, we asked why parents tell their children stories. Each class was able to come up with the idea that parents tell stories "to teach us something." We followed up on this by introducing the word *fable*, defining it as a type of short story with a lesson. We used Aesop's fable "The Wolf and the Dog" as an example. The dog, who is well fed but kept on a chain, invites the wolf, who is hungry but free, to come live with him and his master, but the wolf declines. After discussing the cultural values of the dog and wolf, the students had to say which of the values, security or freedom, was more important to them, why, and how they had learned this about this value. This proved to be a very difficult question to answer.

In trying to understand why this question was difficult for our students to discuss, we wondered whether the source of difficulty lay in their lack of experience in considering this kind of issue, lack of experience in critically examining their own lives and values, or inability to express their ideas on this kind of topic in English. Nevertheless, we felt it was necessary for them to begin this process of identifying representative elements of culture that they knew in order to proceed to search for those elements in various codes (i.e., explicitly or implicitly embedded in media messages).

For homework, the students selected the 10 values that were most important to them and 10 that they believed were most important to Japanese people. They then ranked the values they had selected from most to least important. In the following class, they compared and discussed their lists and identified examples of mass media portrayals of those values. After we gave a couple of examples from popular television dramas to illustrate this, they quickly generated numerous examples of their own. One example that we gave was from the drama *Kanojo-tachi no Kekkon* and involved the lead male character's giving up his dream of working as a doctor in Papua New Guinea and instead remaining in Japan to take over his father's position as head of the hospital (when his father became seriously ill). We offered this as an illustration of the importance of filial obligation in Japanese culture (i.e., the network was promoting this cultural value). This series of activities helped our students to begin to see connections between their beliefs and the representation of those beliefs in popular cultural texts.

Once the students had understood this process, they were able to work in groups to generate a list of values they thought were most important to Americans and to cite examples from mass media (e.g., U.S. movies and television shows) that illustrated those values. Some examples included *Mrs. Doubtfire* for family and *Working Girl* for career. From this point, it was a small step for the students to find cultural symbols and values in advertisements. We provided an example of an advertisement from a U.S. magazine showing a young, healthy man and woman cycling together. A small child was riding in a trailer attached to the man's bicycle. The text read "alternate routes." We interpreted the ad as appealing to the U.S. values of individuality, family, and health. For the next class, the students brought in print advertisements with Japanese cultural values and symbols and explained them for classmates. One example was an ad for a samurai doll, which is associated with Children's Day (a Japanese holiday). The student read the cultural values to be tradition and family. Finally, they created their own advertisements, using symbols to convey cultural values (from their list of the 10 values most important to them). One pair of students created an ad for soy sauce. The print read, "a taste of Japan," and images included Mount Fuji, cherry blossoms, and a set of chopsticks. The process of creating media products is crucial in strengthening learners' understanding of the key concepts. In addition to framing the learners as producers of knowledge, this type of activity helps learners to identify areas in which their understanding of key concepts is not satisfactorily developed, providing the opportunity for self-assessment and further inquiry to understand the concepts.

After the students had begun to consider the role of media in transmitting cultural images and values, we moved into stereotypes. We started by introducing stereotypes about Japanese people and culture. A Japanese colleague provided us with a wonderful example from her experience in teaching in Malaysia: "How many *ninja* live in your neighborhood? Are any of your friends *ninja?*" were typical questions she was asked by her Malaysian students. Our students laughed at what they perceived as ridiculous questions, wondering how anyone could believe that *ninja* were running around the streets of Japan. Once they thought about the low-budget action movies, they realized how people could get such misleading views of Japan. For homework, the students had to find examples of images that broke stereotypes. An example we provided was a newspaper photograph and caption showing the new all-woman flight crew at Northwest Airlines.

Although most students seemed to get the idea, a significant portion seemed confused by the concept of stereotypes. For example, one student wrote, "This breaks the stereotype that cameras use film"; another wrote, "This breaks the stereotype that Prague is in Poland." These students seem to have confused mistaken ideas about the world with stereotypes, and it took many of them a long time to gain a clear understanding of the difference. We faced a dilemma in explaining through giving further examples fearing that at some point, presentation of stereotypes might contribute to their perpetuation (especially when presented by the teacher or textbook, both of which are culturally above questioning). One way we did address this issue was to "talk back" to the media. Occasionally, we would begin a class session by expressing exasperation over a stereotype (or message manipulation) that we had encountered since the previous class. "Did anyone see *Futari* [a drama] last night? Can you believe how stupid Mika is? Do you believe high school girls are that stupid? No way! What would you have done?" We hoped that modeling "talking back" to media would encourage the students to start doing the same.

In spite of some students having difficulty grasping the concept, many others were able to find stereotype-breaking examples. This prepared them for seeking out further examples in the media, which they then noted in a media log (see Appendix One). The media log began as a place for students to keep track of examples they found during the week, noting connections to concepts we had discussed in class up to that point and also noting their opinions about what they observed. It was crucial to our effectiveness in this course that we keep ourselves current on mass media texts by viewing television dramas and the news, reading the local papers, checking print ads, and so on. Our use of modeling with examples from these familiar sources greatly facilitated explanation. Of course, it also helped us to better understand the culture around us and to have genuine questions that we could ask students about aspects of their culture.

In presenting the four principles of media literacy (see above), we adapted commercially available materials from the Center for Media Literacy, modifying and supplementing them to fit our students' interests, linguistic level, and understanding (Center for Media Literacy, 1995; Center for Media and Values, 1992, 1994).

During the fourth week of the semester, we finally introduced the four principles of media literacy (mentioned above) and began exploring the first one: Media construct reality. Most of the activities centered on comparison of news coverage; use and implications of language, photographs, and placement; and length of stories (see Appendix Two). The students brought articles to class and analyzed their similarities and differences. One example that helped raise awareness was supplied by a student who brought in two different newspapers' articles on a soccer match. One story stated "Sixty thousand tickets were sold" whereas the other stated "Thirty thousand people attended the soccer match."

We did several activities with framing and cropping photographs (see Appendix Three). In "Frame It!" (Davis, 1992, p. 9), students have a sheet of paper with a picture frame drawn on it (approximately 1.5 x 2 inches). After cutting out the paper inside of it, the students used the frame to understand camera angles and techniques. They chose an object or person in the room to focus on and looked at it through the frame. They held the frame close to their face, then pulled it away from them, keeping the object of focus in the frame at all times. Next, the students used the frames with photographs from newspapers and magazines. By choosing where to place the frame, they could change the entire focus and thus meaning of a photograph. Before giving the homework assignment, we did one more activity. We distributed a photograph of a man and a woman in an embrace. The man appears to be at least a foot taller than the woman, reinforcing the idea that men are superior to women. He is gazing down into her eyes; she, with her head craned back, is looking up into his eyes. The photograph was cropped at the couple's elbows.

The students had to draw what was missing from the photo; in other words, complete the picture. This was a fun activity that allowed the students to be creative while learning the concept of cropping. Some students showed the man to be wearing a skirt; others gave the woman a fishtail. We shared our example of the man standing on a box so that he appears to be taller than the woman when in reality he is not. We explained how Hollywood often does this so that the plethora of short male actors will not be seen as inferior to statuesque female actors such as Meryl Streep, Sigourney Weaver, and Nicole Kidman. For homework, the students had to find and manipulate two images: one that had been cropped, which they were to expand by "completing" it; and one that they cropped. They had to explain how their manipulations changed the meaning of the photograph.

After these activities with framing, the students worked in small groups to produce the front page of a newspaper. We supplied the skeleton content of seven stories (see Appendix Four). The students had to decide which stories to include and exclude. They had to write headlines for the stories, and they were allowed to edit the contents. The finished products were displayed around the room. Groups made comparisons between their front pages and then discussed their editorial decisions.

In Week 6, we introduced the second principle: Media use identifiable techniques. Activities consisted of exploring different camera angles in film and photography and their effects on meaning making. The students learned terms such as zoom in/out, high/low angle, and pan from experimenting with their frames from the "frame it" activity. We discussed how the camera techniques affected meaning. For example, close-ups are used to show emotion; low-angle shots can portray a subject as weak or inferior. The students recorded examples in their media logs. They were encouraged to combine the two principles, that is, talk about how specific techniques are used to construct reality. For their media product, the students used storyboards to convey an important message, experience, or cultural experience. They were free to create an original story or to recreate a scene from a movie or television program. In making choices about theme, images to include, and techniques to employ, the students were actually grappling with what kind of language to use to convey the meanings they intended (i.e., making choices based on the understanding that language reflects particular attitudes and values). This kind of firsthand experience in making reasoned choices helped the students come to grips with the constructed nature of media messages.

As a way to review and demonstrate their understanding of the ideas presented up to that point, each student made a poster filled with examples and analysis of images and text from the media. The posters were displayed around the room, and class time was divided so that each student had opportunities to present his or her poster to small groups and attend classmates' presentations. Again, sharing their interpretations framed learners as producers of knowledge.

We introduced Principle 3, media are businesses with commercial interests, with several readings and activities on advertising. After covering concepts and terms such as "misinformation," "target market," "self-image," and effects of packaging, the students explored their own consumer habits, listing the names of products they bought and their reasons for choosing one brand over another. In the next step, they analyzed and deconstructed print ads that they brought to class. Again, they were encouraged to apply the other principles and concepts, such as cultural values and images, to their analyses.

From the basics of advertising, we led into how advertising (media sponsors) and the business interests of companies that own media influence content (see Appendix Five). The students grasped this fairly easily, most being able to infer, for example, why Television Station X would not do an investigative report on a company accused of dumping toxic chemicals. "Maybe that company is a sponsor of that television station."

In taking up the fourth principle, media present ideologies and value messages, we tried to pull together all of the concepts previously covered. We used materials and ideas from *Living in the Image Culture* (Center for Media and Values, 1992) to examine attitudes conveyed through "soft sell" and "hard sell" techniques in advertising, supplementing the commercial materials with newspaper articles dealing with images of women and girls in ads and movies. We also presented research conducted by a professor at a prestigious local university that dealt specifically with gender stereotyping in Japanese mass media. The students used their media logs to document evidence that would confirm or disconfirm the notions presented in these materials. Class discussions included consideration of whether the deployment of stereotypical cultural images and values was intentional and, if so, what the nature of those intentions was (e.g., attention getting, cultivating markets, creating ideology). To participate in discussions of this fourth principle, the students needed to call on understandings built during the entire semester. For example, in deconstructing a beer advertisement, a student wrote how the positioning and clothing of the subjects (Principles 1 and 2) reinforced the stereotypes that men are superior mentally and physically and women are mere decorative objects.

The final presentation took the form of a gallery-style poster display and included analysis of a print ad, a collage of media images communicating the student's own attitude toward men or women, and a student-created advertisement (print or storyboard of video) conveying his or her own ideology. Each piece was accompanied by a short explanatory narrative, and each student gave an oral presentation to small groups during the display. The small groups also critiqued their classmates presentations. The atmosphere was electrified as the students took in the wealth of knowledge they were sharing with each other.

Reflection on the Experience

As a course in English as a foreign language, this course was very successful: By midway through the semester, the students were producing English for authentic communicative purposes almost without being aware that they were using English. The media logs were densely packed handwritten pages filled with information about and analysis of television drama portrayals; commercial messages in audio, video, and print media; and news coverage. The students seemed oblivious to the fact that they were using English in their classroom discussions, group work, and presentations. We attributed this lack of self-consciousness to the motivating effect of using real-world texts in the classroom.

But beneath this superficial accomplishment lie more troubling issues that have given us important insights into the complexity of media literacy education. Not all of the issues discussed below are unique to Japanese students, and many are common among their U.S. counterparts.

Given the low English-language proficiency of many of the students and unfamiliar analytical orientation of the class, incidents of miscommunication and lack of comprehension always raised the question: Is it a first- or second-language (L1 or L2) problem? Some students did not seem able to comprehend the literal meanings of Japanese print ads. For example, one student brought in an ad that she claimed was for a kimono, but the ad was actually for a style book. In an activity centered around the purposes and effects of cropping images, one of the pictures we used was of a man with a backpack. We intentionally cropped the image so that only the man (with the backpack) was visible. When asked to say what was in the picture, many students said "a mountain."

We were also surprised by the extent to which our students seemed to be completely uncritical of the content of advertisements, even to the point of complete gullibility in some cases. For example, ads for Calorie-Mate, a popular diet food, claimed that since it contained vitamins and minerals, consuming it was good for one's health. Innumerable students repeatedly insisted to us that the plethora of ads for CalorieMate™ was evidence of how much the Japanese valued good health. Another example was the widespread belief in the claims of ads for "fat creams" that supposedly cause fat to disappear from the body.

Even when evidence was presented directly and clearly, some students still resisted drawing conclusions about the texts. For example, the students were given the concept that if Newspaper A prints a longer article on a particular topic than Newspaper B, then Newspaper A is giving greater importance to that topic than Newspaper B is. Then, they were asked to find articles on the same news story in two different papers and tell which newspaper placed greater importance on the story. Many students resisted drawing a conclusion about the editors' intentions.

Existing cultural stereotypes also sometimes obscured students' perception of events, images, and attitudes. For example, a student wrote in her media log about the character Tokiko in an episode of one television drama *(Kagayaku Tsuki no Kara)* that we happened to have seen. In the episode, Tokiko was pursued by a strange man. She became flustered in attempts to avoid him and finally ran to the door of her house and threw herself clumsily on the floor of the entranceway, where she knelt, gasping, with her hair and clothes in uncharacteristic disarray. When she later recounted the incident to her father and younger sister, they laughed at her foolishness in being frightened. One student wrote in her log that Tokiko was strong because she is the older sister. Apparently, the Japanese cultural image of the older sister as being strong superseded the images presented in the episode in our student's assessment of Tokiko's character.

Another problematic aspect of the course arose when we did a brief study of gender representation/underrepresentation in newspapers. The purpose of this activity was to raise the students' awareness of systematic underrepresentation of women in the news (a pattern that effectively makes women's participation in society invisible), but the activity backfired when the students' reaction was, "We know!" Unsaid but communicated was, "And we accept it. That's right: Men are more important than women." (In this case, we had not even begun to interrogate the nature of the scant representation of women that does exist in the mass media—the kind of images of women that are constructed in the media and meanings that readers/viewers make from those representations. We did broach this topic when considering soft sell/hard sell techniques in advertising.)

The risk of seeming to uphold or perpetuating attitudes about women in society is always present in a study of media messages. As Judith Williamson (1981–1982) points out, by questioning the ideology on which young women have constructed their identities, we are calling into question their personal identities. Joining in the condemnation of the ideology behind images of women in popular cultural texts is threatening until the young women have enough self-confidence to see those images as distinct from their own identities. In contrast with the mainstream students in our classes, some students (particularly those who were members of one of the college's varsity sport teams) seemed to have formed self-concepts that were not congruent with the dominant cultural standards of femininity. As the following excerpts from captions on some of these students' collages show, some students seemed better able to resist the notions promoted by mass media images of femininity:

Student 1—collage message:
All men in these pictures are behind the women and hold her shoulder. Stereotypes [stereotypical attitudes]: The men control women. Men are strong, and women are weak. So men protect women, women depend on men. My opinion: Men must be strong, but women aren't weak. If women depend on men, they don't live. I don't think so. Some of women are strong now women will be taller and stronger than men in the future.

Student 2—collage message:
Media show that women should be childish. They say attitude that lady should keep childish. Media say that woman had better been looked cute. *I disagree.* Because I think we should be naturally. When we look these ad, we think we also had better do like this. But it is wrong.

These students were certain enough of their own identities to exercise what Gee (1992) would call "powerful literacy" (p. 26), that is, to begin to critique dominant notions of gender. We concur with Williamson's (1981–1982) assertion that it is necessary to teach about images of gender before generating concepts of ideology.

Teaching about ideology was in fact our greatest challenge. Without addressing ideological concepts, we could not be said to be teaching critical literacy; rather, we would simply be teaching a literal level of textual comprehension. Many of the contradictions we encountered in this course could be attributed to the stage of identity formation in which our students found themselves. On the verge of entering the workforce, it behooved them to embrace conformity, since, as the Japanese saying goes, "The nail that sticks up gets hammered down." Employers do not seek out iconoclasts. On the other hand, college is the first (and for many, the only) opportunity for young women to publicly express their individuality. Most of our students, however, lived with their parents, who tended to be quite conservative, and as a practical matter, this meant they had to toe the line to some extent.

Thus, we found students giving opinions such as the following media log entries on soft sell/hard sell on the ways advertisements portray women and men:

Student 3—media log entry:
I think women should be soft and feminine. . . . Clowning shows that we are not to be taken seriously. I agree! We should not be too serious; otherwise it will be difficult to get a husband.

Student 4—media log entry:
Submissiveness is sexy. Makes me feel good.

But they also gave contradictory opinions, often even on the same page of a media log. For example, Student 4 also reported:

Student 4—media log entry:
Man is controlling woman in this way. Why? It makes me angry. I want them to be equal.

Is it this student's sense of the futility of the wish for equal status that pushes her to opt for adopting the dominant attitude, playing it safe? Is she genuinely questioning, or is she expressing the wish for equal status because she thinks it's what the teacher wants to hear? Another student expressed the difficulty of making issues black and white:

Student 5—collage message:
"Women should be thin"—I agree half. Actually, I want to be slim because thin people match cute and slim clothes. However, too thin people don't look nice, they look like only skin and bone, and unnatural diet is bad for health.

Although it was frustrating to see students mimicking dominant attitudes about gender order, we believe that the opinions expressed in the classroom did not always accurately reflect a comprehensive picture of the students' points of view on an issue. In addition to the kind of statements shown above (Students 4 and 5), informal conversations we had with students outside of class sometimes revealed positions of negotiation and resistance to dominant attitudes.

Gauging learning outcomes from performance is always problematic, but the difficulty is compounded in situations such as ours in which we were not just teachers, with all the complication of the power hierarchy involved in the teacher-student dynamic, but also foreigners. How do students perceive or value the notions about ideology and culture that we foreign women espouse? At what point does our instruction become a form of cultural imperialism? Are students justified in wondering how expressing their honest opinions or uncertainties might affect their grades in the course or, worse, their chances of getting a scholarship or offer of employment? These are among the questions that haunted us throughout the course.

Conclusions

Our experience invites more questions than conclusions, but a few insights emerge. A course such as the one described above, that seeks to facilitate a critical examination of language production and use, has at its core our assumption that language instruction can never be neutral, it is always ideologically loaded. The experience described above makes it clear that language users do not share an equal level of awareness of the ideological power of language, and insofar as media literacy instruction entails techniques of critical deconstruction of texts, we must be aware of the differential levels of awareness our students bring with them.

The degree of sophistication and maturity of each student determines the extent to which he or she is able to analyze a text. The students, who are participating in the construction of their identities, still ultimately make the choice of what to accept and what to reject. Even the decision of whether to be analytical or not is up for grabs, and the dominant culture in Japan (as in the United States) does not promote analytical behavior in the general public. Accepting dominant cultural values has its pragmatic, albeit short-term, advantages. What Lankshear and Lawler (1987) refer to as "improper literacy"—that is, the kind of literacy that "either fails to promote, or else actively impedes [understanding and action that transforms] social relations and practices in which power is structured unequally" (p.74)—is the kind of literacy that would give our students a chance at the jobs they were applying for; questioning the status quo is not the kind of literate practice that our students' potential employers were seeking.

The process of linguistic/textual analysis may contribute to strengthening analytic skills in other contexts, so students who come to the class with relatively little experience in questioning and analysis may find themselves applying their newly acquired skills outside the classroom. At the end of the semester, many of our students seemed wistful at their own loss of innocence—wanting to return to uncritical consumption of media products for enjoyment but no longer able to look at texts in the same way as before the course. We observed that the students had gone from a state of indifference to a sense of being armed to face commercial interests and make their own choices. None indicated that they would cease to be consumers, but they conveyed that they believed their newly acquired media literacy skills would help them to be more critical consumers and more discerning parents (in the future) when it came to their children's activities (such as television viewing and electronic game consumption).

In spite of the fact that this course was an English course, most of the meta-level learning ("learning about") that the students did concerned

170 / Carolyn Layzer, Judy Sharkey

Japanese texts. Perhaps because the course fell within the discipline of foreign language instruction, however, critique of Japanese texts was possible: The context provided a sort of pretext on which critical reading, normally discouraged or even prohibited, could occur. In making available a relatively safe site for ideological contestation, this course provided an opportunity for students to explore the making of meaning.

If we were to offer this course again to a similar group, however, we would begin with a more in-depth exploration of notions of culture and identity formation (including issues of gender, cultural values, etc.) and proceed to build students' understanding of their own ideologies and of dominant cultural ideologies. With a stronger foundation in ideological awareness, they would then be able to identify themes and trends, techniques, and intentions. Students come to the classroom with a vast storehouse of cultural information to be mined for insights. Through a course in media literacy, the process of excavation and analysis can be initiated.

References

Center for Media and Values. (1992). *Living in the image culture* [instructional kit]. Los Angeles: Center for Media Literacy, 4727 Wilshire Blvd., Suite 403, Los Angeles, CA 90010; (213) 931-4474, (800) 226-9494.

Center for Media and Values. (1994). *Break the lies that bind: Sexism in the media* [instructional kit]. Los Angeles: Center for Media Literacy, 4727 Wilshire Blvd., Suite 403, Los Angeles, CA 90010; (213) 931-4474, (800) 226-9494.

Center for Media Literacy. (1995). *Beyond blame: Challenging violence in the media* [instructional kit]. Los Angeles: Center for Media Literacy, 4727 Wilshire Blvd., Suite 403, Los Angeles, CA 90010; (213) 931-4474, (800) 226-9494.

Davis, J. F. (1992). *Living in the image culture: An introductory primer for media literacy education.* Los Angeles, CA: Center for Media and Values.

Gee, J. P. (1992). What is literacy? In P. Shannon (Ed.), *Becoming political* (pp. 21–28). Portsmouth, NH: Heinemann.

Lankshear, C., & Lawler, M. (1987). *Literacy, schooling, and revolution.* New York: Falmer Press.

Swanson, G. (1991). Representation. In D. Lusted (Ed.), *The media studies book: A guide for teachers* (pp. 123–145). London and New York: Routledge.

Williamson, J. (1981–1982, Autumn-Winter). How does girl number twenty understand ideology? *Screen Education, 40,* 80–87.

Appendix One
Table A.1a

Date/Time	Media	Opinion/feelings	Cultural symbols, values, stereotypes, nonstereotypes (watching for things we've discussed in seminar class)
4/24 8 p.m. (54 min.)	TV: "Futari" (drama)	*Futari*: It's interesting to see how strong the family bond is. I don't understand why the sister had to die, but I guess it was the only way to get past the problem/issue of junban. I'm surprised that the younger sister is 16 years old. She seems childish.	Japanese cultural values: (1) *Family is important* - The family eats together; they seem close and concerned about each other. (Futari) (2) *Loyalty is important* - The older sister is still loyal to her younger sister—even after death! (Futari) (3) *Junban is important* - The younger sister can't take her sister's position. It's hard for people to see her as an individual because of her birth order. (Futari)
4/25 9 p.m. (30 min.)	TV: Tunnels (variety)	*Tunnels*: I really hate the stupid violence on this show. I don't like the way female characters are often (always!) humiliated or made to look foolish. Isn't there another way to be funny?	Japanese stereotypes: Non-stereotypes: 1. *Housewife* (Futari) 1. *Caring father* (Futari) 2. *School girls* (Futari) 3. *"Stupid women"* (Tunnels)

Table A.1b

Name _____ Class _____ English Seminar 1: Media Literacy Media Log

Week: 4/24/97—4/30/97

Date/Time	Media	Opinion/feelings	Cultural symbols, values, stereotypes, nonstereotypes (watching for things we've discussed in seminar class)
4/28 8 p.m. (54 min.)	TV: "Futari" (drama)	I thought it was really hard to keep up good relationship even family. Because this family lost their balance by Chizuko (older sister)'s death. But Mika (younger sister) joined a drama club. I thought it was not good idea. Because Mika is not Chizuko. So Mika can't replace Chizuko. I thought Mika should live her life, and her mother should have a strong heart.	Japanese cultural values: (1) *Job is important* - Father cancelled their family plan. (Go to a hot spring) Because he had to do his work. (Futari) (2) *Gaman is important*- Mika joined a drama club. The practice was very hard. But if she don't want to quit, she must do gaman. (Futari) (3) *Loyalty is important* - Yuji bunted as his boss told him to. So, he continued to clean their room. (Iihito) (4) *Individuality is not important* - Most people think Yuji is an odd fellow. So most people ignored him. (Iihito)
4/29 9 p.m.	TV: Utaban	I like this program. Because I can know about a new song, new fashion, new singer.	

Table A.1b (continued)

Name _____ Class _____ English Seminar 1: Media Literacy Media Log
Week: 4/24/97—4/30/97

Date/Time	Media	Opinion/feelings	Cultural symbols, values, stereotypes, nonstereotypes (watching for things we've discussed in seminar class)
10 p.m. (54 min.)	TV: Iihito	I really like this program. I thought there was no person like him in Japan (maybe). Because I think Japanese are cold in general. For example, to old people, to physically handicapped people, etc. But he was kind of every people. I don't think kind is best. But I think we need a person like him in present society. And good fortune is brought by good behavior. I thought a good example is him.	Japanese stereotypes: 1. Hard work (Futari) 2. Japanese are cool (Iihito)

Appendix Two:
English Seminar 1: Media Literacy
Week 4: *Media Construct Reality*

There are four main principles in media literacy.

1. Media Construct Reality
2. Media Use Identifiable Techniques
3. Media Are Businesses with Commercial Interests
4. Media Present Ideology and Value Messages

For the next two classes we are going to discuss the first principle:

Media Construct Reality

Construct means to build or create. You can construct a house or construct an idea.

Reality means things that are true, not things that are imagined or thought about.

• Ask a partner the following questions. In your answers, think only about NEWS, or real events, **NOT** dramas, animation, or movies.

Do you believe everything that you read in the newspapers or watch on TV? Why/why not?

Give examples.

Do you think all TV stations are the same? (Is Asahi-TV the same as TBS? the same as NHK?) Why/why not? Give examples.

Do you think there is a difference between the Yomiuri and the Mainichi newspapers? What are some differences?

***Many people think that the news we read and hear is just reporting and it does not have any opinions or viewpoints. WRONG!!!!!

The media make decisions about what information to include and not to include in a news story. Think about this: There was a terrible accident at Keihan Sanjo in Kyoto. A news reporter from NHK was there for 2 hours. Her report on the news was only 1 minute. She had to decide which information was the most important. A reporter from TV-Osaka was also there. He also only had time for a 1-minute report. Do you think both these reporters said exactly the same thing? _____yes _____no EXPLAIN YOUR ANSWER.

When we watch the news and read it in the newspapers we must ask ourselves "What information is NOT here?"

What other things do media do to affect reporting?

•Pictures •Body language (in TV reporting) •Choice of words
•Placement of the story (most important news is usually first)

Look at some of the examples on the back of these pages and discuss them with a partner. [NOTE: The back of Paper A and Paper B showed headlines and photos from different newspapers reporting on the same stories. For example, Paper B showed the following: a headline from the *Mainichi Daily News* for April 27, 1997, "Peruvian president denies rebel executions"; a headline from the *Asahi Daily News* for April 27, 1997, "FUJIMORI DECIDED REBELS HAD TO DIE"; a photo from the *Mainichi Daily News* for April 27, 1997, showing President Fujimori stooping over almost in a crouch as he makes his way through a tunnel under Lima; and a photo from the *Japan Times* for April 28, 1997, showing the president standing erect as he walks through a different tunnel.]
QUESTIONS FOR PAPER A:

1. In which photo does Prime Minister Hashimoto look the best (the most respectable?) _____
Why?_____
2. Which photo(s) shows 2 men who seem to be equal?
_____
Why?_____
3. Which photo(s) show one man in a superior position?_____
Why?_____
QUESTIONS FOR PAPER B:

1. Explain the differences between the two headlines.
The Mainichi headline
_____,
but the Asahi headline
_____

2. Which headline do you prefer? _____
Why?_____
_____

3. How does Fujimori look in photo A?
_____

How does he look in photo B?
_____

Appendix Three:
English Seminar 1: Media Literacy
Week 4: Media construct reality: Frame it!

•A technique called cropping is used in newspapers and magazines to cut away the surroundings of photographs in order to give greater impact to the central person or main idea.

As you look at the photos you and your classmates brought, consider the following questions:

1. Does the photo seem to have been "cropped"? What might have been left out of the picture? Why was it left out?
2. If you were going to cut something out of the picture, what would you select? Why? (And how would you decide what to include and what to leave out?)
3. Does "cropping" the photograph give it a different meaning?

Using the pictures you brought, make one example of each of the below. Clearly label each example:
A. Make an example of cropping the picture to **exclude** information. [Write a brief explanation of what the new meaning of the picture is.]
B. Make an example of cropping the picture to **include** information. [Write a brief explanation of what the new meaning of the picture is.]
*After you have created these examples, you will share them with your classmates. Be ready to explain your examples!
—*—*—
Note about News Reports:
• Reporters and news editors make choices about what to include or exclude in their reporting. Their choices depend on what point of view they want to present in their article. In a way, they are also "cropping"! As you found in activities you did with newspapers, the same story can be presented very differently (or not at all!), according to what the reporter or news editor decides to include or exclude.

Homework Assignments:

1. Newspaper: Find an article in the newspaper about a topic you are interested in. After reading the article, write at least three information questions (Who, what, when, where, how, why) about information you would like to know about that story (that is **not** included in the article).

2. Media Log: Think about the activity, "Frame it!" Remember how some things were left out of the picture depending on how you framed it?
• Television and all media "frame" the world by choosing which images or elements to include and which to exclude. Some things get left outside the "frame" of a movie or TV show. Consider the following questions as you write in your media log this week:

1. *(Watch and imagine . . .)* What are the things that are often just outside the "frame" when you watch a TV drama? TV commercial (CM)? the TV news?

2. *(Watch, record, and react . . .)* How do mass media images reinforce cultural stereotypes? List cultural stereotypes that you see in the media this week. Then explain how these images are or are not representative of your experience (write in the "opinions" area).
3. *(Think about . . .)* How do other forms of media (such as radio) "frame" the world?

Appendix Four:
English Seminar 1: Media Literacy:
Skeleton Content of Stories

Story A

• President of Zaire Mobutu Sese Seko met with rebel leader Laurent Kabila yesterday.
• The two men met on board a ship on the Congo River.
• Mobutu has prostrate cancer.
• South African President Nelson Mandela mediated the talks.
• Kabila wants Mobutu to resign.
• Mobutu may resign because of his poor health and pressure from international leaders.
• If Mobutu resigns, he does not want Kabila to become president. He wants there to be elections.
• Kabila may insist that he be the next president of Zaire.

Story B

• The number of Japanese travelers who were victims of crimes last year increased 20%.
• The number of Japanese travelers who were victims of crimes last year was 15,261.
• The most commonly reported crime was theft.
• Thailand was the place where the most crimes were reported.
• Los Angeles and France followed Thailand in number of crimes reported.
• There were seven cases of terrorism last year, compared with none in 1994 and one in 1995.
• One of the terrorist incidents in 1996 was the seizure of the Japanese ambassador's residence in Peru.
• The number of Japanese who died overseas in 1996 was a record-high 444.

- 47% died from illness. 65 died in traffic accidents, and 37 committed suicide.

Story C

- Three of Japan's airlines are fighting over their frequent flier programs.
- The fight started at a funeral in Tokyo on Feb. 20 when All Nippon Airways president Seiji Fukatsu told JAL vice-president Akio Kono, "We are starting a mileage program."
- JAL and JAS felt that Fukatsu's words were a declaration of war.
- ANA has 100 domestic routes.
- JAL has 52 domestic routes.
- JAS has 99 domestic routes.
- JAS has half as many passengers as ANA.
- On March 24, ANA announced a program that would give customers free round-trip tickets after they have flown at least 32,000 kilometers.
- Shortly after the ANA announcement, JAL and JAS announced that they would also start a similar program.
- JAL and JAS are working together.
- Customers on JAL can use their miles for JAS tickets.

Story D

- Protesters threw tomatoes, eggs, and insults Sunday in the second demonstration against a right-wing Australian politician, Pauline Hanson, who has angered many Australians with her views denigrating Asians and Aborigines.
- This attack was the most angry since she gained attention with a provocative speech in September calling for an end to Asian immigration.
- Although Australian newspapers have called her a racist, opinion polls last week showed her gaining support.
- Hanson and her supporters blame Asian immigrants and Australia's Aborigines for unemployment, crime, and social division in the country.
- She wants welfare programs for Aborigines to be stopped.

Story E

- The mayor of Kitakata, Fukushima Prefecture, said Friday he will take a 50% salary cut for six months for peeping into a women's bath while at a local spa last month.

- Yoichiro Iino, 72, also apologized to the city assembly.
- He said he will also resign as head of the organization that runs the spa.
- During an official inspection of the spa on April 18, he went into the women's dressing room and looked into the bath through a glass door.
- About 20 women were taking a bath at the time.

Story F

- A Japanese adventurer completed a 780-kilometer solo trek to the North Pole on foot Saturday morning.
- He was the first Japanese to do so.
- Hyoichi Kono, 39, of Ehime Prefecture, is only the third person in history to complete the extremely difficult trip.
- Kono reached the North Pole at 6:40 A.M. Saturday Japan time, nearly two months after departing from Canada's Ward Hunt Island on March 4.
- During the trip, he encountered blizzards and temperatures as low as 50 C below zero.
- He pulled a sled loaded with about 70 kilograms of food and fuel.
- When he reached his destination, he sent a radio message to his colleagues at a base camp in Canada's Northwest Territories.
- "The weather is great and the sky is blue," he said.
- Kono was first recognized for a successful solo trek in 1991, in which he crossed the Sahara in five months using an unpowered cargo carrier.

Story G

- The Health and Welfare Ministry says that one in four middle and high school students drink alcoholic drinks once or twice a month.
- This suggests that drinking is becoming a common teenage habit, the ministry said Friday.
- A ministry survey showed that about 80% of middle and high school students have drunk alcoholic drinks.
- Although the survey is the first of its kind to be conducted nationally, the ministry said that the results show that teen drinking is on the increase.
- As a result, the ministry is considering a ban on the sale of alcoholic drinks from vending machines.
- The survey was conducted last year at 125 middle schools and 100 high schools across the nation.

- About 117,000 students responded.
- About 36% said they drink once or twice a year.
- About one in three male high school students and one in four female high school students drink once or twice a month, the survey said.
- 14% of the boys and 6.7% of the girls were weekly drinkers (high school).
- In the middle school group, 6.7% of the boys and 4% of the girls were weekly drinkers.
- Almost one in five third-year high school boys said they drink weekly.
- 0.3% said they drink daily.

Appendix Five: English Seminar 1: Media Literacy: Week 10

Principle #3: Media are businesses with commercial interests
(THEY WANT TO MAKE A LOT OF MONEY!)
In the last 2 weeks we have been discussing advertising. You should be asking yourself "What is the connection between advertising and principle #3?"

Advertising pays for TV shows.

In the United States, a 30-second commercial on a 30-minute TV news program may cost $58,000 (¥6,670,000). With 8 minutes of commercials a night, the TV network earns $928,000 a night. With 5 nights of news, the network earns $4,640,000 a week.
****STOP AND THINK*******
What do you think of this information?
$4.6 million is (a lot of money/not a lot of money) for one TV program.
I am (surprised/not surprised) that one TV program can earn this much money because_____
_____
_____

Advertising pays for newspapers and magazines.

Last month we did an activity where you made a newspaper. **Do you remember? Yes No**
In that activity you had to make decisions about which news stories to include and where to put the news stories on the page. In some magazines, the advertisements are placed BEFORE the news stories. In other words, the editors must think about the advertisements BEFORE they

think about the news stories. Advertisements in good positions cost more than ads in difficult-to-see positions.

****STOP AND THINK*******

What do you think of this information?

I (knew / didn't know) that newspaper editors think about advertisements first.

I am (surprised / not surprised) by this information because

_____

_____

_____

In the United States, you can buy a newspaper for about ¥65. (What do you think of that?)

However, it costs the company ¥100 to make the newspaper. The newspaper company NEEDS the money that advertisers pay them so that they can make and not lose money on their newspaper. (MEDIA ARE BUSINESSES.)

Advertising affects what we see and hear in the media.

A TV reporter wanted to do a story about the environment. She wanted to investigate what was causing the pollution in local rivers. She discovered that Company X had a factory that was dumping poisonous chemicals in the river. WOW! This was a big story! She told her boss about the story and he was also excited, but told her they couldn't use the story. "WHAT? You're crazy." she said.

Why do you think her boss said no to the story?

Other examples of Principle #3: Media are businesses with commercial interests.

The business interests of the companies that own the newspapers, TV/radio stations, and magazines influence what we see and hear in the media.

Walt Disney Company is making a movie about Tibet. Brad Pitt is one of the stars. Of course, Disney wants the movie to be popular so it can make a lot of money. Disney owns ABC-TV. How can it use the "news" to help it sell the movie? One way is to start doing "news" reports about the situation in Tibet. This will make people more interested in Tibet and when the movie comes out, people might say "Oh, I've been learning about Tibet in the news. It's a really interesting situation. Let's go see that new movie about it." Disney also owns part of *Time* magazine. Recently, the magazine did an article about making the Disney movie in Tibet. Most people thought it was a "news" story, but it was really an advertisement.

****STOP AND THINK*****

What is your opinion of this information?
I am (surprised/not surprised) by this information because

_____

_____

_____

General Electric (GE) is a company in the United States. It makes household electrical items such as light bulbs and air conditioners. It also makes and promotes nuclear weapons. For this reason, people who are against nuclear weapons will not buy any GE products. The word for this in English is *boycott*. Several years ago, a TV reporter for NBC-TV wanted to do a report on successful boycotts. She called an expert and asked him which boycott was the biggest and most successful. "GE has lost $60 million from hospitals who refuse to buy their medical products. So, the boycott against GE is the biggest boycott going on right now."
"Oh, I'm sorry to hear that" said the reporter.
*****STOP AND CHECK YOUR UNDERSTANDING*****
Ask a classmate: Can you explain this situation to me?
Why did the reporter say that she was sorry to hear that?
That's right! GE owns NBC-TV, so the reporter could not mention the GE boycott on TV. Instead she talked about small boycotts against tobacco and beer companies.
STOP AND THINK****
What do you think about this situation?
I am (surprised/not surprised) about the reporter's decision because

_____

_____

If you were the reporter, what would you have done? Explain your choice.

- Do what the company told me to do
- Not do a story on boycotts
- Quit my job
- Something else?

If you are interested in the complete story about GE and the NBC-TV story, you can read the article in the media literacy binder in the library.

9 Critical Viewing as Response to Intermediality: Implications for Media Literacy

Ladislaus M. Semali

Teaching critical viewing skills bolsters students' skills in traditional disciplines, combats problems of youth apathy, violence, and substance abuse, and improves students', parents', and teachers' attitudes toward school.

—**Edward Palmer (1995, p. 9)**

As intellectuals, [teachers] will combine reflection and action in the interest of empowering students with the skills and knowledge needed to address injustices and to be critical actors committed to developing a world free of oppression and exploitation.

—**Henry Giroux (1988, p. xxxiv)**

Media literacy is the ability to analyze, augment, and influence active reading (i.e., viewing) of media in order to be more effective citizen.

—**Francis Davis (1992, p. 13)**

This chapter introduces the concept of critical viewing and illustrates what it means to take a critical stance in one's teaching practice. Critical viewing is a concept built around what has become known as the discourse (language) of "criticism." A discourse of criticism is simply a critical analysis of social practice. Stuart Hall (1996) describes discourses as ways of referring to or constructing knowledge about a particular topic of practice: a cluster of ideas, images and practices that provide ways of talking about and forms of knowledge and conduct associated with a particular topic, social activity, or institutional site in society. Most of the ideas of critical viewing are drawn from media theory, critical pedagogy of representation, discourse analysis, cultural studies, and postmodernist thought. Critical viewing provides teachers and students ways of thinking about the production of knowledge and negotiating through praxis the relationship among classroom teaching and the larger institutional structures of the school and nation-state.

Through this language of criticism, innovative teachers struggle to find analytical strategies that illuminate their understandings and interpretations of textual references and social contexts found in school structures, literature, and the modern mass media—all of which tend to perpetuate inequalities on the basis of social class, race, gender, disability, and sexual orientation. When these teachers talk about critical viewing as a form of social critique in their classrooms, they are talking about actively extending students' understanding of the ways meanings are constructed by developing strategies to analyze, evaluate, critique, and interpret belief systems and communicative practices embedded in printed texts, television programs, and other popular media. As evident from the divergent quotes cited above from Palmer (1995), Giroux (1988), and Davis (1992), the education establishment does not have a coherent strategy or methodology to examine the relationship with media, particularly strategies that enable students to develop a critical stance against the manipulation, overt bias, discrimination, and seductions of media spectacles.

The main purpose of this chapter will be, first, to discuss the possibilities of criticism in classroom practice as defined by progressive educators. By defining critical viewing as a critical pedagogy of representation, I expose the misconceptions associated with response-centered approaches that have assumed the central position of critical reader/viewing practices. The main task is to show how a teacher can use critical viewing as a language of criticism to sift through multiple layers of intermedial texts and go beyond surface impression, traditional myths, and routine clichés, applying the meaning to one's own social context. The second task is to explain the interrelationship between critical literacy and the pedagogy of representation, and the third is to explore critical viewing as a response to intermediality.

Possibilities of Language Criticism

In the past, discourse analysis and reader-response criticism have been used in classrooms as analytical schemes (Karolides, 1992). These response-centered transactional approaches, which insist on the reader's role in conjunction with the text, the reader's individuality affecting and being affected by the text, have influenced many teachers in how they teach the interpretation of meaning in literature. In spite of considerable disagreement among theorists as to what these analytical approaches can do for students as they learn how language works and struggle with interpreting meaning in literature (see, e.g., Mailloux, 1982; Suleiman & Crosman, 1980; Tompkins, 1980), for many teachers discourse analysis has become a significant and viable tool for (1) deciphering and clarifying the reading process, (2) determining the role of the reader in relation to the text, (3) exploring how meaning is made, (4) defining the nature of the interpretative act, and (5) assessing the influence of reading communities and literature conventions (Karolides, 1992, p. xi).

In more recent years, this preoccupation with meaning has taken a different turn, being more concerned not with detail of how language works but with the broader role of discourse in culture. Although critics of language of criticism and educational approaches often decry their idealist multiculturalism, advocates, including Aronowitz and Giroux (1991), Freire (1970), Kincheloe and Steinberg (1997), and McLaren (1986), have complained that critical pedagogy has often been domesticated and reduced to student-directed learning devoid of social critique. By this, critical theorists insist that for students unaware of a language of criticism that is rooted in practice pedagogy can easily become irrelevant, and even dogmatic or prescriptive in certain circumstances. For example, when the notion of critical reading/viewing is used in English/language arts classrooms, analysis of texts tends to remain at the reader-response level and does not always take a "critical stance" or include the language of criticism. This chapter challenges teachers to reevaluate these analytical schemes to gain a more contextual understanding of the mutually constitutive nature of theory and practice. With this objective, I propose critical viewing as a vision of criticism.

The underlying assumption that runs throughout this chapter is that the notion of intermediality implies taking a critical stance toward the multiple perspectives imbedded in intermedial texts. Taking a critical stance calls for analytical strategies to sift through the multiple layers of texts presented in such intermedial environments of web sites, videos, and electronic bulletin boards. As a reflective approach to teaching and learning, critical viewing bridges theory and teaching practice. Advocates of this language of criticism would have us pay attention to how our society is marked by a multiplicity of cultures, meanings, and values. If students' attention were guided to how powerful groups define their own particular meanings, values, experiences, and forms of writing and reading as the *valued* ones in society, students would better understand the inequalities and violations of social justice the mass media continue to peddle through their production of entertainment programs. Furthermore, through this reflective approach, I hope to illustrate how theory and practice of a critical pedagogy helps students to engage in the social struggle over meaning and to navigate today's classrooms, which have become inundated by diverse and multiple layers of printed and electronic texts. To implement the vision of criticism illustrated in this chapter, students will be able to (1) analyze the hierarchical positioning of individuals in the social order on the basis of race, class, gender, and sexuality; and (2) acknowledge the multiple and insidious ways in which power operates in the larger society "to reproduce the interests of the dominant culture" (Hammer, 1995, p. 79).

Extending Media Literacy Practices

In the past, textual analysis was confined to the literary scrutiny of printed words. Students analyzed stories, plays, poems, essays, and novels. Today, even though this literary analysis in classrooms has expanded to include visual images and electronic messages, analysis has remained limited to response-centered transactional approaches. Teachers using these approaches are often content to seek to see in literature what has previously been invisible and to hear what has previously been inaudible. Furthermore, by adhering to a traditional reader/viewer-response model, teachers in the English classrooms maintain that their approach fosters critical thinking and critical viewing skills. Typical response-centered teaching practices include exercises such as making students write a review of a film, testing for a good cinematic scene, or asking students to indicate or imagine what they would miss if they only heard the dialogue of a film (Teasley & Wilder, 1997, p. 47). Such activities strive to ensure that content is mastered by encouraging students to take copious notes; pause to ask questions; and keep track of elapsed time, main events, and notable literary, dramatic, or cinematic aspects (Teasley & Wilder, 1997, pp. 114–5). Within this pragmatic approach, critical reading/viewing is confined to literary or artistic analysis notably appropriate for film criticism, which for the most part provides key analysis of media for entertainment and to enhance enjoyment of the arts. The superficial transfer of analytical strategies from a response-centered approach of printed works to visual images has recently been adopted by some educators in their classrooms (as well as some Newspapers in Education [NIE] organizations throughout the country; Garrett, n.d.). Such transfer is taken up by teachers to legitimize viewing of films and television in the classroom in order to respond to the longtime criticism about these mass media of entertainment. By carrying out this acclaimed active viewer model with their students (which has been for the large part adopted from Eddie Dick of the Scottish Film Council), these educators claim that they are in fact teaching critical media literacy (Dick, 1991).

Even though the reader/viewer response approach calls for students to be active viewers—paying close attention to film details, writing down immediate responses, discussing interpretations with fellow students, and supporting opinions with evidence from the film—such analysis rarely moves beyond the content of the visual imagery or beyond the ability to simply remember and understand visual information. Unfortunately, this approach and other student-centered teaching strategies like it demand a teaching paradigm markedly different from that practiced in most U.S. classrooms today. The typical U.S. model is pragmatic and skill based, relying on rote learning and lecture (Tyner, 1993). Most often, media texts are treated like pieces of literature; students typically spot themes, do a chart, fill out a log, complete worksheets, make a list, or write a response, neglecting a critical analysis of media (See examples provided by Davies, 1996, pp. 207–8.) Perhaps what Davies and others have overlooked and is probably needed, as surmised by Barry Duncan, president and founder of the Canadian Association of Media Literacy (founded in 1978), are "more cultural approaches to literature and not more literary approaches to popular culture" (Duncan, 1993, p. 14).

Therefore, teaching critical viewing must aspire to teach the youth in our classrooms, particularly those impressionable groups or individuals in desperate search of an identity and a place in the adult world. For these groups, critical viewing will bolster skills and knowledge they need to be able to consciously reflect on their interactions with media. It will enable them to address injustices; become critical actors committed to combat problems of youth apathy, violence, substance abuse, and rampant consumerism; and generate a strong commitment to developing a world free of oppression and exploitation. Linking this vision of criticism with social concerns affirms what it means to be educated and to be media literate in a media-saturated milieu in which information gathering and distribution processes thrive on the manipulation of seductive media spectacles.

Although the language of criticism of education has, since the 1970s, proliferated in academic circles, it has received practically no attention in public schools or society at large. Critical theorists in academic institutions, particularly those who engage in debates in the emerging field of cultural studies (e.g., Aronowitz & Giroux, 1991; Freire, 1970; Giroux & McLaren, 1989; Simon, 1987), use the language of criticism to provide educators with numerous insights. As a cross-disciplinary endeavor, cultural studies is concerned with institutions, representations, systems of beliefs, and communicative practices. Cultural studies has found its motive to explore culture industries and their messages from critical theory, which in its initial stages heavily criticized the marxist analysis of political economy. Its language of criticism, and the insights gained from cultural studies, have uncovered the myth that schools in U.S. society serve as the "great equalizer" that allows children from all social and economic backgrounds to compete fairly in our market place economy (Bowles & Gintis, 1976, p. 26). It has also exposed the ways in which conventional schools in society transmit a "hidden curriculum" that undermines most of our children's sense of self-esteem, efficacy, and compassion and that also profoundly narrows whose "voices" (e.g., men over women, whites over people of color, industrialists over laborers, militarists over peace activists) dictate what epistemological and social values are expressed in classrooms (Goodman, 1992, p. 271). Since the mid-1980s, however, conservatives largely have set the agenda and tone for public mood regarding education in our society with issues like school choice, vouchers, tightening standards, emphasis on phonics, back-to-basics, and so on. Clearly, this vision of criticism illustrated in Goodman's (1992) comments represents an alternative to this conservative, dominant agenda, as well as to the common view of teachers in U.S. society as educational and classroom managers.

In Pennsylvania, for example, teachers in many school districts have until now paid little or no attention to the language of criticism, particularly with specific reference to the unexplored resources of media texts. This situation may exist more because teachers accept media information as entertainment and therefore see mass media as having little to do with literacy, learning, or schools (Witkin, 1994). This is by no means an attack on the Pennsylvania teachers for benign neglect of their teaching profession. Far from it. For many educators, critical viewing, interpreting, and "reading" television are foreign concepts. Perhaps, this stems from social attitudes about the entertainment media and the scant attention given to media and television during teacher education. In studies of visual communication and media education, critical viewing is not used widely in U.S. classrooms as a tool for deconstructing media images, particularly those images that represent people's culture, identity, or ethnicity (Semali, 1997). This may be because the media literacy movement is fairly new to many schools. Although critical reading/viewing has began to occur in other countries, it is not yet happening in most U.S. public schools.

While addressing the National Leadership Conference on Media Literacy, Francis Davis (1992) outlined the long history in the United States—a history of the electronic media—regarding the influence of mass media and how the far-reaching expansion of the media has led to strategies of protecting or empowering the public: regulation, pressure on advertisers or those responsible for creation of mass media, and media education. As Davis rightly concludes from his presentation, these three current strategies are unified by their common assumption that something about the mass media environment is problematic. The public must either be protected against media or empowered so that the negative effects of the mass media are lessened and the positive enhanced.

These protectionist and civic defense arguments have driven the movement of media literacy in the United States (Buckingham, 1991, p. 13). Not so long ago, the movement to teach media literacy in public schools, which began in Britain and spread to Canada and Australia (also known in these countries as media education) was sparked by a 1972 report by the Surgeon General's Advisory Committee on television and violence. This comprehensive research study indicated that heavy viewing is related to a decrease in creativity, and violence is linked to criminal or aggressive behavior (U.S. Department of Health, 1982). This study resulted in government funding to teach critical viewing skills in the public schools, including those strategies developed by WNET–New York (WNET, 1979, p. ii). Twenty-two years later, President Clinton signed into law the Goals 2000: Educate America Act, which described what students should be taught and how they should be tested in core subjects. Later, after months of national debate and capitalizing on the successes of passing the Children's Television Act of 1990, the arts were added to the list of core subjects, which included teaching media literacy in all primary and secondary schools (Semali, 1994). As teachers steadily continue to join the national movement of media literacy, the importance of critical literacy has increased. Overall, most teachers seem positive about its validity and its social relevance to students, particularly in the efforts to enable students to resist media manipulation and rampant consumerism (National Council of Teachers of English [NCTE], 1994, 1996).

So far, efforts, research, and debates have taken place to develop a rationale for teaching media literacy in school and to enable students to resist media manipulation. To develop such a rationale and an empowering classroom model, media education must be promoted widely beyond earlier protectionist strategies. Debates and lectures by the British media educators Len Masterman (1992) and David Buckingham (1990) have suggested that television prepares viewers to be consumers through its constant repetition of commercials and fancy bedroom suites. In addition, the mass media promote male-dominant gender roles and racist attitudes (Buckingham, 1990). These views sum up the widespread idea that the media are powerful and have negative influences. Viewed this way, the mass media are seen as contributing to the perpetuation of a number of objectionable ideologies. Over time, these arguments focusing on negative effects have been used to great advantage by media education advocates in establishing the need for media literacy. But Buckingham (1990) has warned that a distinction needs to be made between "simpler, more rhetorical arguments which may be of use in promoting media literacy, and more complex understanding which should inform classroom practice" (p. 8). In other words, Buckingham (1991) warns against pushing the "negative" media effects card to sell the idea of media literacy, because, in practice, it results in an activist stance in which certain ideologies about media literacy are pushed rather than a critical stance in which participants probe the relationship with media and raise issues and questions in response to media texts. Buckingham argues against the protectionist stance held by conservatives who view the media as corruptive, responsible for illiteracy and the reason for moral decadence looming large in society.

Theories of Media Analysis

Media experts have relied on the study of language, the study of signs (semiotic/textual analysis), and constructivist and postmodern critical theories to develop methods of analysis of media texts. Some of these analytical approaches include (1) content analysis (Gerbner, Holsti, Krippendorf, Paisley, & Stone, 1969), (2) uses and gratification analysis (Blumler & Katz, 1974, 1975), (3) Semiotic/textual analysis (Hartley & Fiske, 1977; Metz, 1974; Heath, 1977; Wollen, 1969), (4) cultural analysis (Bigsby, 1976; Hartley & Hawkes, 1977; Berger, 1972; and more recently, Rushkoff, 1996; Giroux, 1997), and (5) critical analysis (Bigsby, 1975; Schiller, 1970). Unfortunately, there is no one method capable of analyzing adequately all texts in all circumstances. Current literature offers examples of single methods or a combination of these analytical frameworks. For example, in their book *Visual Messages*, Considine and Haley (1992) summarize the growing research on critical viewing of media programs. The methods they outlined in this book do not originate from any one theory.

Viewed as a process of reading television rather than analytical tools, Considine and Haley list five constituent elements: (1) interpreting the internal content of the program (e.g., focusing on the narrative analysis of what happened and why, with reference to genre codes and conventions), (2) interpreting the internal construction of the frame (e.g., media form and style), (3) recognizing the external forces and factors shaping the program (e.g., media ownership and control), (4) comparing and contrasting media representations with reality (e.g., detecting stereotyping, bias, distortion of facts, and what happens in real life), and (5) recognizing and responding to the potential impact of television form and content (e.g., action on the information, such as expressing opinions or outrage to producers or newspaper editors).

Apparently, the main preoccupation of the authors of *Visual Messages* is the form and content of the media artifact(s) rather than the process of analysis to get at the *manipulation, distortion, overt bias,* and *stereotyping.* Such a content-based framework overlooks issues of power relations, economic inequalities, and hegemonic ideologies that tend to preserve practices of dominant forces in the existing society. The making sense or reflection and action to be taken as a response of the exposure to the media is left to the individual. Considine and Haley equate critical reading with content analysis, where students in an English classroom are urged to recognize themes and lessons that are embedded in a media program (e.g., Considine & Haley, chap. 2, p. 14 or Considine, 1995). Considine and Haley assume that being able to recognize the advertising tricks is sufficient to guard students against unconscious and unwise consumption.

Clearly, there is considerable tension between content (what teachers teach) and form (how teachers teach). So far, there does not seem to be an easy resolution of such tension in the horizon. Media educators (e.g., Barry Duncan, 1993) have complained about teaching critical viewing in terms of content. They suspect this because media education is often defined and directed by media critics and theorists, not media educators. As explained above, many critical viewing practices have been prescribed by teachers of literature, borrowing much of the analytical approaches from literary analysis. As lamented by Kellner (1995b), the analytical steps summed up by Considine and Haley (1992), as well as other media literacy advocates including the Frankfurt school, do not go far enough in the reading of media and cultural products. The majority of studies in reading television have neglected the language of criticism to the extent that it touches on social, political, and ideological domains. For instance, Kellner insists that these theorists, particularly the Frankfurt school, developed a powerful critique of the cultural industries and the ways that they manipulate individuals into conforming to the beliefs, values, and practices of the existing society, but the critical theorists "lack theories of how one can resist media manipulation, how one can come to see through the ruses and seductions, how one can read against the grain to derive critical insights into self and society through the media, and how one can produce alternative forms of media and culture" (Kellner, 1995a, p. xiv). Perhaps critical viewing, when conceptualized as "a vision of criticism" of popular media and culture industries, can provide teachers and students with a framework necessary for the critical analysis of media texts and culture. Teachers can benefit from utilizing this framework to recognize the alternative sources of information available to students in school and out of the school environment.

Critical Viewing Versus Media Criticism

The concept of critical viewing is distinguished from the kind of viewing for pleasure or entertainment so often limited to television and film criticism. As a form of social critique, critical viewing goes beyond the critique of the arts. It refers to gaining skills necessary to analyze and critically dissect all forms of culture—whether print, visual, or performance—with which individuals interact, ranging from books to film artifacts, television, radio, and the other products of the cultural industries. A critical viewing of these cultural forms extends the process of *critical literacy* that gives individuals power over their culture and thus empowers them, "enabling people to create their own meanings, identities, and to shape and transform the material and social conditions of their culture and society" (Kellner, 1995a, xv).

While reviewing recent works of Peter McLaren, Henry Giroux, Ira Shor, and Alan Luke, Colin Lankshear (1994) elaborates critical literacy as a form of alternative pedagogy that examines the politics and sociolinguistic stances. Lankshear delineates what it means to be critical. He stresses that the adjective "critical" and its correlates, "criticism," "criticize", and "critique," convey the idea of judging, comparing, or evaluating on the basis of careful analysis. With critical literacy, students learn to become critical consumers who are aware of visual manipulation and stereotyping as an important project of literacy education. Ira Shor (1993) continues to define critical literacy as "analytic habits of thinking, reading, speaking, or discussing which go beneath surface impressions, traditional myths, mere opinions, and routine clichés, understanding the social contexts and consequences of any subject matter; discovering the deep meaning of any event, text, technique, process, object, statements, image, or situation; applying the meaning to your own context" (p. 32).

For Lankshear (1994), critical literacy represents a vision of criticism. His vision does not only aim at the "text" but also focuses squarely to critique the traditions and institutions that produce it. But Giroux's critical vision reflects the analysis of individuals' contexts in so far as such context is part of our everyday life. Combining Gramsci's (1988) notion of the engaged intellectual with Foucault's (1977) notion of the specific intellectual, Giroux advances the idea of teachers as "transformative intellectuals" to replace the dominant notion of teachers as educational "technicians," "managers," or "professionals." Giroux sees teachers as individuals who connect their work to broader social concerns that deeply affect how people live, work, and survive (Giroux, 1991, p. 57). As "transformative intellectuals," Giroux (1988) believes, teachers can potentially play a significant role in creating schools as "democratic public spheres" that produce this vision of criticism, grounded in social transformation. He writes:

> Teachers need to develop a discourse and set of assumptions that allow them to function more specifically as transformative intellectuals. As intel-

lectuals, they will combine reflection and action in the interest of empowering students with the skills and knowledge needed to address injustice and to be critical actors committed to developing a world free of oppression and exploitation. Such intellectuals are not merely concerned with promoting individual achievement or advancing students along career ladders, they are concerned with empowering students so that the students can read the world critically and change it when necessary. (p. xxxiv)

Put in different terms, this vision of criticism attempts to merge theory and practice and seeks to identify interrelationships and interconnections between everyday life and knowledge learned in books. Through this vision, Giroux perceives a critical pedagogy of representation doing two things: first, providing the basis for education to be "attentive to a politics of location, one which recognizes and interrogates the strengths and limitations of those places one inherits, engages, and occupies"; and, second, articulating a pedagogy that "frame[s] the discourses through which we speak" (Giroux, 1992, p. 126).

Implementing a Vision of Criticism

In an attempt to design curricula that implement this vision of "criticism," described by Giroux and Lankshear, I established a media literacy course at the Pennsylvania State University for preservice teachers. Drawing on a range of concepts and techniques elaborated by theorists and teachers working in various critical language studies, I have developed activities around a simple media text I believe has interesting possibilities for an interdisciplinary practice of critical literacy. I bring into the course the possibilities of working with media texts in conjunction with a set of rather different but relevant texts to address questions adapted from linguists and literacy educators such as Allan Luke, Paulo Freire, Donaldo Macedo, Castell, and Egan. Offered every semester, this course calls for a context where preservice teachers across several subjects—English, social studies, early childhood education, and science—work together in an integrated way to explore texts critically through their disciplines. The assumption is made that teachers will immerse themselves in a media text or topic, take the time to explore the text in order to find questions that are significant to the learner, and then systematically investigate those questions.

One competency that students acquire in this course is the ability to apply the narrative analysis method to visual and other media representations. Preservice teachers are encouraged to use this narrative method because it shifts attention from the content of stories to the structure and process of their telling; students learn to avoid rushing hastily to the judgment of moral tales without examining the evidence or analyzing the multiplicity of forms (fictional, nonfictional, print, oral, visual or pictorial, etc.). Throughout this course, students practice to question the text, the context, and the subtext. They learn how to analyze what is in the text as well as what is omitted from the text, namely the context.

Preservice teachers learn that media literacy consists of competencies in reading, interpreting, and understanding how meaning is made and derived from print, photographs, and electronic visuals. Media literacy consists of understanding connotative messages embedded in the text of the visual messages, as well as the interaction of pictures with words, the context of the viewer, and relayed messages obtained from the maker of the image. For example, in the analysis of visuals used for advertising in various print media or textbook illustrations, students strive to uncover some of the narrative meaning by questioning (1) the order of events depicted; (2) the actual history of visual production, circulation, and consumption; and (3) who produced the visual, under what circumstances, and for what possible reasons. Therefore, media literacy expands the notion of critical literacy, which includes taking a critical stance to all media texts. For teachers and students, the classroom becomes a media literacy learning environment where the learning process is not disconnected from the institutions that create knowledge and information or from the legal, cultural, political, and economic contexts that surround texts students read, whether from books, films, or the Internet.

My experience in working with preservice teachers has been insightful. It is particularly striking to observe them at the end of each semester and notice the extent to which their critical awareness has been raised. This awareness is especially visible in the rate of adoption of critical viewing, critical reading, and critical thinking skills they tend to bring into their work and the broad definition of "literacy" these students eventually apply to a variety of projects they embark on long after completing the course. Some of their projects for graduation have also resulted in academic honors theses. For instance, in preparing a lesson plan in a high school English class one preservice teacher of media literacy wrote, "Today's lesson addresses the fact that far too often oppressive events are packaged and phrased to take away any blame or remove any hint of ill-intent. Word choice and language are two techniques used by writers to shape readers' perception. [This lesson will] examine how writers present controversial issues and analyze what is and isn't included [in their narratives]." Another student, while evaluating a teaching unit that included literature circles and reading of the text, *The Lakota Woman*, remarked,

"It is just shocking to discover how much discrimination goes on in present day America towards native Americans! What is even more shocking is the fact that I had to come all the way to college to understand discrimination. I'm glad I found media literacy, the key to this understanding."

These two examples illustrate what critical pedagogy meant for these students. Their awareness was made particularly manifest when multimedia texts were introduced into the English curriculum. By applying media literacy skills to questioning how the novel, the film, and other media texts represented Native Americans, students quickly realized the diverse layers of meanings, biases, distortion, manipulation, stereotyping, and multiple perspectives present in texts. Alternative critical pedagogy meant for students to look outside of, as well as at, the representation of Native Americans. They began to ask, "Who is the author/producer/artist?" "How was he/she placed in society?" "What are the cultural forces in the society in which the author/producer/artist was socially raised and/or is working?" "What is the message of the visual statement in terms of political and social import?" "How can this message be evaluated using the prevailing values of the culture of the artist rather than the viewer?"

At the core of the critical pedagogy movement is the need (1) to develop an awareness of the constructed nature of representation in both print and visual media; (2) to provide knowledge about the social, cultural, economic, and political contexts in which media messages are produced by a variety of different institutions with specific objectives; and (3) to encourage renewed interest in learning about the ways in which individuals construct meaning from messages—that is, about the processes of selecting, interpreting, and acting on messages in various contexts. Taken together, the process described here provides a critical stance, a method students and teachers can choose to take up to resist the overt race, class, and gender biases and manipulation in the media texts students read/view.

Explorations of Media Texts: Case Studies

In the following section, I examine some of the case studies presented in this book in response to intermediality. The case studies designed by Watts Pailliotet, Serrano and Myers, and Macaul et al. serve to extend the kind of critical literacy and vision of criticism I am talking about in this chapter. An examination of these cases should not ignore the issues of theory and practice that need to guide teachers' and students' reflection and action as suggested by Giroux, Kellner, and others. Educators ought to keep in mind also that practice and theory are complementary and interrelated. For instance, all classroom practice must be informed by specific theoretical concepts. Furthermore, theory can only be fully understood in relation to specific media practices and through practical application. But some questions persist: How can teachers' reflective and teaching practices develop a critical stance to generate the critical authoring, reading, and viewing of texts that enable students to navigate the seas of multiple texts, especially those represented in multimedia formats currently flooding students' learning environments through the Internet, video, CD-rom, and so on at a time when literacy education is no longer confined to paper-and-pencil technologies or "reading" and "writing"? How does the current climate of cultural conservatism present specific challenges to critical education? How can reader-/viewer-response analysis stimulate and help students develop critical reading, critical viewing, critical listening, and critical thinking for lifelong learning? How do the case studies outlined in this volume fit the lessons teachers will take up on Monday morning in a language arts or social studies class? How do they fit with the requirements of academic standards and assessment prerogatives?

First, in Chapter 2, Watts Pailliotet introduces a process called *deep viewing*. This critical active reader/viewer approach to media texts employs a three-level analysis to critically analyze, understand, and interact with information. This approach's design combines a heuristic framework and semiotic codes for understanding text. One outstanding feature that the deep viewing method brings to the language of criticism is the insistence of reflection and action in the classroom. Watts Pailliotet underscores that for deep viewing to work, participants must pose questions and develop ways they might act in future, based on their own assessments, those of their code group, and those within the classroom. Participants are encouraged to relate texts to their own experiences, expectations, feelings, and knowledge. In essence, deep viewing makes explicit the language of criticism discussed in this chapter. It provides a practical way of making critical inquiry, personal reflection, active learning, ethical decisionmaking, ongoing research, and analytical observation to become daily activity for teachers and students. Through constant questioning of texts and modeling to students, Watts Pailliotet successfully pilots the vision of criticism in her classroom. The results confirm that students were able to analyze, respond, think complexly, critically evaluate, and teach with many texts.

The second case study that is explicit about critical literacy features a semiotic analysis of teachers' perceptions of multicultural education. In Chapter 4, Serrano and Myers explore preservice teachers' perceptions about issues of diversity. How do these perceptions shape their definitions of multicultural education? Serrano studied students' visual collages about multicultural education from a semiotic analysis perspective. He designed a project based on a semiotic frame based on Bal and Bryson's (1991) notion that signs of human culture form the perceptual ground by which intentional meanings are signified for new signs, such as words and images, in each new experience. The project was based on developing a visual poster that represented multicultural education. In a follow-up analysis of the students' production, Serrano and Myers examined the ways in which students articulated their underlying perceptions about multiculturalism, and how these interpretations might have influenced the meanings they signified in the collage itself.

How does this project stimulate critical reading/viewing? Serrano and Myers argue that the semiotic analysis of a collage provides students with a form of critical inquiry. In this case, semiotics help to establish the principle of nontransparency by establishing the dominant concept of media literacy—that of representation. The collages deal with representations and not realities, and the media meanings could not be easily separated or stripped from the forms in which they were expressed. The interpretation of visual text is contextualized by signs that are socially and culturally produced as part of our perceptual background. For example, one of the collages emphasized how family traditions and race defined different ethnicities. These texts showed that although three collage authors perceived multiculturalism differently with respect to each person's activity, identity, and ethnicity, all of their collages and responses to each other's collages highlighted the perceptual practice of segregation and self-exclusion in thinking about "others."

Serrano and Myers's chapter brings to bear important principles that impact theory and practice. For example, one of the principles of teaching critical reading/viewing is to identify where knowledge comes from and how meanings are constructed. In other words, how does anyone come to know what he or she knows about a certain event or group? How did the Internet authors come to know and enforce the rules of the discipline? Proponents of critical pedagogy would suggest that an individual's sense of self is organized according to various *categories*, such as gender, race, class, age, sexual orientation and so on, as well as those categories encompassing different "interest groups" such as social groups, list serve user groups, or political affiliations. The characteristics and values associated with these categories include the way we look, how we behave, the lifestyle we adopt, and even the way we buy goods and services. As individuals or groups, we come to recognize how certain characteristics are considered more or less socially appropriate or acceptable.

Ideas about what people are like and how they are meant to be understood already prevail in our culture. These ideas are embedded in mass media presentations and are part of the conventions or agenda of media executives who are in the business of reproducing a social hierarchy through the stories distributed through programs from news, sitcoms, and MTV to rap music. These stories, including scientific findings or data-based information, allow a certain gender, race, or class to dominate or be dominated by another that claims superiority as scientists, experts, or technicists. These ideas give meaning to our sense of self and allow us to position ourselves in relation to others. Such *contexts of meanings* and attitudes can be recognized in all media, including the Internet. We need to acknowledge the fact that the way representations of race, gender, class, or age are constructed is as important as the ideas and meaning they project, since they offer *positions* for us, through which we recognize images as similar or different from ourselves and those around us (Swanson, 1991, p. 128).

It is also important to note that Serrano and Myers's approach departs from the dominant U.S. pragmatic, skills-based model with the objective of training individuals for industry. Instead, Serrano and Myers take on a constructivist perspective, that is, an approach in which the acquisition of knowledge is viewed as incremental, socially and culturally mediated, and individually situated. In addition, learning is understood as a self-regulated process of dealing with cognitive conflicts that become apparent through experience, interactive discourse, and reflection. In the context of intermediality, Serrano and Myers's project goes farther to show that in the "intermedial" class, groups of students may be empowered by multiple texts, giving them a far wider range of cultural references at their disposal than any single teacher could have. Serrano and Myers's project shows that the expertise that once existed in the classroom was more widely dispersed. Furthermore, teachers no longer possessed an approved body of knowledge to which they alone held keys and that they were expected to pass down to students. Students could now reflect critically on information, side by side, in a way that had been difficult in the past before the visual media and the Internet made their entry into the classroom.

This case study provides a "critical vision" in an English/language arts classroom. Although it still needs to be extended to other areas outside the English classroom, it is important to note that Serrano and Myers laid out a broad-based process through which students collaboratively and individually navigated the visual media to find meaning for themselves and discover identity.

In the third case study, in Chapter 3, Sherry Macaul, in collaboration with Jackie Giles and Rita Rodenberg, takes Watts Pailliotet's deep viewing method and applies it to viewing a video, reading a text, and browsing a web site. Working with elementary/middle level students, the Macaul team explored learners' perceptions, interpretations, critiques, and sign systems as they applied to the deep viewing to construct meaning. Their findings indicate that students showed commonalities across media and also the convergence of media that was occurring. The task given to students made evident the association and application of interactivity among various media from students' background knowledge and experience as well as in the commercial or ad (visual and auditory representations such as voice, music, graphic or digital images, animations, morphing, etc.) to construct meaning ("built on meaning by viewer").

Taking a Critical Stance

Taking a critical stance to critical viewing sounds like tautology. But it is important to caution that not all instances or projects involving critical viewing are "critical." Put simply, critical viewing means different things to different people. Traditional educators have ignored the critique of schooling, social conditions, and ideological contexts for so long that it is not natural for teachers to incorporate such contexts in readings or classroom discussions. The kinds of inquiry advocated and described in this book stand apart from the positivistic, ahistorical, and depoliticized analysis employed by both liberal and conservative educators who have adopted the viewer-response and active-viewer approaches without taking a critical stance. As shown in the case studies, the vision of criticism implied in discourse analysis, deep viewing, and reader/viewer response, attempts to merge theory and practice to coincide with Giroux's critical democratic vision of schools and society. It further seeks to identify interrelationships and interconnections between everyday life and knowledge learned in books. In practice, these analytical strategies provide teachers with concrete and viable forms of critical inquiry.

To take a critical stance, one must ask, do we want our schools to create a passive, risk-free citizenry or a politicized citizenry, capable of fighting for various forms of public life and informed concern for equality and social justice? When Peter McLaren raises these kinds questions in his writings, he intends to infuse a vision of criticism (McLaren, 1988, p. 3). In this vision, he hopes to encourage teachers to take a critical stance in their teaching practice. In taking such a critical stance, teachers would no longer define curriculum in terms of the abstract categories of various isolated disciplines (such as history, English literature, social studies, etc.) but rather would incorporate themes and issues that address the concrete conditions and problems of adult life. In this new role, teachers are guides and facilitators rather than managers and dispensers of knowledge. As a method of curriculum and instruction, therefore, critical viewing challenges teachers and students to examine visual media as objects of study by exploring their languages, codes, and conceptual frameworks and ask what sense students in classrooms today make of visual media as objects of study (Manzi & Rowe, p. 42). Through the questioning of media texts, students engage in a process of learning the "deeper" meaning and thus become empowered to form identities and worldviews that are their own, resisting the media spectacles that persuade and manipulate them to accept the interests of supposedly neutral formulations of science.

Lessons

There are several important lessons to be derived from the case studies and the critical thinking they generate. First, assumptions, "common knowledge," common sense, "general" knowledge, widespread beliefs, and popular attitudes are all part of the *context of meanings* within which cultural norms or values are enhanced and circulated. Often overlooked in this perspective, however, is the fact society is marked by a multiplicity of cultures, meanings, and values. Thus, people construct the contexts of meanings out of their experiences within specific social contexts of race, gender, and class. Rather than one abstract psychological process, contexts of meanings are historically defined social practices that are subject to political, academic, and cultural hierarchies. Such contexts and our individual ranges of knowledge, values, and attitudes are governed in turn by an asymmetry of power that enables powerful groups to define their own particular meanings, experiences, ideas, conventions, and forms of writing and reading as those valued in society (Aronowitz & Giroux, 1991). It is in this hierarchy therefore that some values or meanings come to be dominant and others marginalized.

Therefore, a critical viewing of visual and media products needs appropriate reading that acknowledges that (1) media messages are constructions; (2) media messages are representations of social reality; (3) individuals construct meaning from messages; (4) messages have economic, political, social, and aesthetic purposes; and (5) each form of communication has unique characteristics. By recognizing these basic concepts of media literacy, teachers and students gain power to engage in the social struggle over meanings. They assume a critical stance and a reflective perspective that avoids generalizing a "masculinist conception of the self" and legitimating a "Eurocentric and patriarchal" worldview dominant in the mass media, schools, and the workplace (Hammer, 1995, p. 79). Critical theorists are convinced that critical viewing is an appropriate response to media literacy. As such, it is part of a process of critical pedagogy that teaches individuals how their culture, society, and the polity are structured and work. Critical media pedagogy enables teachers to mobilize students and citizens so that they can learn to "more effectively create their own meanings, lives and society" (Kellner,

1995a, p. xiv). Since children are immersed in the television experience, everyday schooling or parenting that omits an examination of TV's curriculum also ignores the world that children experience. The challenge of U.S. education therefore is to help young people navigate consciously and actively the sea of messages flooding into their lives daily through TV, movies, radio, music, video games, magazines, newspapers, and even billboards, bumper stickers, and T-shirt logos. The complexity of the relationship between what we see and hear, what we believe, and how we interact with one another underscores the need for across-the-curriculum teaching of critical thinking and critical viewing skills, that is, media literacy.

The second lesson is that teachers and students must not see these activities of viewing media as technical skills to be acquired in isolation and limited to the classroom. Since the media themselves form a day-and-night curriculum and instruction for many youth in the United States, critical media literacy needs to counter this constant bombardment by teaching individuals how to "read" and "criticize" the media and how to "produce" alternative media and culture. Many youth in the United States today are part of a large consumer society targeted by toy industries, car manufacturers, fashion designers, and other large corporations. Media products, including the advertising of consumer articles, cultural artifacts, emotions, ideals, and values, are presented as a form of entertainment. Because of the economic imperative (i.e., media corporations are in the business of making money and advertising is a major component of the media business), media products often are packaged without any warning about intended manipulation, overt bias, and distorted perspectives imbedded in their messages in order to "make money"; to sell a product; or to persuade the public politically, socially, economically, or educationally. The ultimate message orchestrated in media products may well be an intentional device to legitimize, maintain, or peddle a "hegemonic culture or ideology" (Kellner, 1995b, p. 61). As explained by Kellner (1995b), media cultural products induce individuals to identify with dominant social and political ideologies, positions, and representations. Kellner is quick to caution that, in general, a hegemonic ideology is not a system of rigid ideological indoctrination that induces consent of existing capitalist societies but, instead, "it is the use of the pleasures of the media and sound and the spectacle to seduce audiences into identifying with certain views, attitudes, feelings, and positions" (p. 60). Thus, media and consumer cultures work hand in hand to generate thoughts and behaviors that conform to existing values, institutions, beliefs, and practices.

The third lesson is that critical viewing is a process rather than an analytical skill of decoding content. Media literacy challenges educators to extend their contributions to students by designing curricula that draw on the full range of human ways of knowing. This implies that instead of preparing students for eventual literate behavior, teachers engage them in genuine acts of literacy right from the beginning and throughout the school career. It also implies that the language arts curriculum will not be fragmented into separate components for reading, composing, and editing but rather will integrate these in meaningful ways while valuing students' experiences, particularly mass media experiences. Furthermore, it implies that skills will be taught in the context of genuine reading, writing, speaking, listening, and viewing activities, rather than as separate or prerequisite components of the program.

Therefore, the traditional practices of teaching reading as separate from writing, of isolating grammar usage, spelling, and vocabulary and teaching them as separate subjects are, in my opinion, misguided and counterproductive. This is not to suggest, however, that content is not important. Rather, I view content as an ongoing developmental process on the part of the learner. I suggest that content must be relevant to the learners' experience and that larger process-related considerations should govern the selection of content. Applying this kind of critical mindedness in tackling texts and making this stance the object of media literacy alters the central tenets of the dichotomous arguments of content perspective on curriculum. That is what media literacy provides. The goal of the language of criticism is to generate among teachers and students the habits of questioning until they question all information every time they encounter it, regardless of its source.

Conclusion

This chapter proposed the language of criticism as a reflective teaching approach to theory and classroom practice. The language of critical pedagogy then was used to situate critical viewing as an analytic method of examining media texts and the ways in which the language of media is socially and historically produced. Throughout this chapter, critical viewing was described as a process rather than an analytical tool with which to engage students to question the clarity and strength for reasoning, identify assumptions and values, recognize points of view and attitudes, and evaluate conclusions and actions provided by all narratives across the curriculum—whether they be short stories, poems, plays, picture books, film, or pieces of nonfiction. The analytical process described here moves away from the limited approach of presenting course materials in the flat monotone of objectivity or conveying the false impression that knowledge is static, monolithic, and universal. Instead, the guiding assumptions are that when students are introduced to critical viewing they will implement a critical vision grounded in multiple ways of knowing and their experiences will become part of the multiple texts they encounter every day and that these texts will make up integrated parts of instruction. Such approaches provide a solid foundation for students' sense of intermediality in the construction of knowledge.

References

Aronowitz, S., & Giroux, H. (1991). *Postmodern education: Politics, culture and social criticism.* Minneapolis: University of Minnesota.

Bal, M., & Bryson, N. (1991). Semiotics and art history. *Art Bulletin, 73*(2), 174–208.

Berger, J. (1972). *Ways of seeing.* London: BBC/Penguin.

Bigsby, C. (1975). *Superculture: American popular culture and Europe.* London: Paul Elek.

Bigsby, C. (1976). *Approaches to popular culture.* London: Edward Arnold.

Blumler, J., & Katz, E. (Eds.). (1974). *Uses of mass communications.* Beverly Hills, CA: Sage.

Blumler, J., & Katz, E. (Eds.). (1975). *The uses and gratifications approach to communications research.* Beverly Hills, CA: Sage.

Bowles, S., & Gintis, H. (1976). *Schooling in capitalist America.* New York: Basic Books.

Buckingham, D. (1990). *Watching media learning: Making sense of media education.* Bristol, PA: The Falmer Press.

Buckingham, D. (1991). Teaching about the media. In D. Lusted (Ed.), *The media studies book: A guide for teachers* (pp. 12–35). London: Routledge.

Castell, S., Luke, A., & Egan, K. (1986). (Eds.). *Literacy, society and schooling.* Cambridge, UK: Cambridge University Press.

Considine, D. M. (1995). An introduction to media literacy: The what, why and how to's. *Telemedium, 41*(2), 1–6.

Considine, D. M., & Haley, G. E. (1992). *Visual messages: Integrating imagery into instruction.* Englewood, CO: Teachers Ideas Press.

Davies, J. (1996). *Educating students in a media saturated culture.* Lancaster, PA: Technomic.

Davis, F. (1992, December 7–9). *Media literacy: From activism to exploration.* Background Paper for the National Leadership Conference on Media Literacy. Queenstown, MD: The Aspen Institute.

Dick, E. (1991). *Analysis: Active viewer model.* London: British Film Institute.

Duncan, B. (1993). Surviving education's Desert Storms: Adventures in media literacy—A retrospective and a guide for tomorrow. *Telemedium 39*(1–2), 13–17.

Fiske, J. (1987). *Television culture.* London: Methuen.

Foucault, M. (1977). *Discipline and punish: Birth of the prison.* London: Allen Lane.

Freire, P. (1970). *Pedagogy of the oppressed.* New York: Continuum.

Garrett, S. (n.d.). *Messages and meaning: A guide to understanding media.* Lancaster, PA: Newspapers in Education.

Gerbner, G., Holsti, O., Krippendorf, K., Paisley, W., & Stone, P. (Eds.). (1969). *The analysis of communication content.* New York: John Wiley.

Giroux, H. (1988). *Teachers as intellectuals: Toward a critical pedagogy of learning.* South Hadley, MA: Bergin & Garvey.

Giroux, H. (Ed.). (1991). *Postmodernism, feminism, and cultural practice* (pp. 217–256). Albany: State University of New York Press.

Giroux, H. (1992). Introduction. In F. Schwoch, M. White, & S. Reilly (Eds.), *Media knowledge: Readings in popular culture, pedagogy and citizenship* (pp. ix–xxxiv. Albany: State University of New York Press.

Giroux, H. (1997). *Channel surfing: Race talk and the destruction of today's youth.* New York: St. Martin's Press.

Giroux, H., & McLaren, P. (Eds.). (1989). *Critical pedagogy, the state, and cultural struggle.* Albany: State University of New York Press.

Goodman, J. (1992). Towards a discourse of imagery: Critical curriculum of theorizing. *The Educational Forum 56*(3), 269–289).

Gramsci, A. (1988). An Antonio Gramsci reader. New York: Schocken.

Hall, S. (Ed.). (1996). *Representation: Cultural representations and signifying practices.* London: Sage.

Hammer, R. (1995). Rethinking the dialectic: A critical semiotic meta-theoretical approach for the pedagogy of media literacy. In P. McLaren, R. Hammer, D. Sholle, & S. Reilly (Eds.), *Rethinking media literacy: A critical pedagogy of representation* (pp. 33–85). New York: Peter Lang.

Hartley, J., & Fiske, J. (1977). Myth-representation: A cultural reading of News at Ten. *Communication Studies Bulletin, 4,* 12–33.

Hartley, J., & Hawkes, T. (1977). *Popular culture and high culture.* London: The Open University.

Heath, S. (1977). *Image-music-text.* London: Fontana.

Karolides, N. (Ed.). (1992). *Reader response in the classroom. Evoking and interpreting meaning in literature.* White Plains, NJ: Longman.

Kellner, D. (1995a). Preface. In P. McLaren, R. Hammer, D. Sholle, & S. Reilly (Eds.), *Rethinking media literacy: A critical pedagogy of representation* (pp. xiii–xvii). New York: Peter Lang.

Kellner, D. (1995b). *Media culture: Cultural studies, identity and politics between the modern and the postmodern.* New York: Routledge.

Kincheloe, J., & Steinberg, S. (1997). *Changing multiculturalism.* Philadelphia: Open University Press.

Lankshear, C. (1994, May). *Critical literacy* (Occasional Paper No. 3, pp. 4–26). Australian Studies Association.

Mailloux, S. (1982). *Interpretative conventions: The reader in the study of American fiction.* Ithaca, NY: Cornell University Press.

Manzi, K., & Rowe, A. (1991). Language. In D. Lusted (Ed.), *The media studies book: A guide for teachers* (pp. 40–52). London: Routledge.

Masterman, L. (1992). *Teaching the media.* London: Routledge.

McLaren, P. (1986). *Schooling as ritual performance: Towards a political economy of educational symbols and gestures.* London: Routledge & Kegan Paul.

McLaren, P. (1988). Language, social structure, and the production of subjectivity. *Critical Pedagogy Networker 1*(2–3), 1–10.

Metz, C. (1974). *Film language.* London: Oxford University Press.

National Council of Teachers of English. (1994). *Standards for the assessment of reading and writing.* Urbana, IL: Author.

National Council of Teachers of English. (1996). *English/language arts: Reading, writing, speaking, listening, viewing, and visual representation.* Urbana, IL: Author.

Palmer, E. (1995). *Television and America's children: A crisis of neglect.* New Haven: Yale University Press.

Rushkoff, D. (1996). *Playing the Future: How kids' culture can teach us to thrive in an age of chaos.* New York: HarperCollins.

Schiller, H. (1970). *Mass communications and American empire.* Fairfield, NJ: Kelly.

Semali, L. (1994, Spring). Rethinking media literacy in schools. *Pennsylvania Educational Leadership, 13*(2), 11–18.

Semali, L. (1997). Still crazy after all these years: Teaching critical media literacy. In J. Kincheloe & S. Steinberg (Eds.), *Unauthorized methods: Strategies for critical teaching* (pp. 137–151). New York: Routledge.

Shor, I. (1993). Education is politics: Paulo Freire's critical pedagogy. In P. McLaren & P. Leonard (Eds.), *Paulo Freire: A critical encounter* (pp. 25–35). London: Routledge.

Simon, R. (1987). Empowerment as pedagogy of possibility. *Language Arts, 64*(4), 370–381.

Suleiman, S., & Crosman, I. (1980). *The reader in the text: Essays on audience and interpretation.* Princeton: Princeton University Press.

Swanson, G. (1991). Representation. In D. Lusted (Ed.), *The media studies book: A guide for teachers* (pp. 123–145). London: Routledge.

Teasley, A., & Wilder, A. (1997). *Reel conversations: Reading films with young adults.* Portsmouth, NH: Heinemann, Boynton/Cook.

Tompkins, J. (Ed.). (1980). *Reader response criticism: From formalism to post-structuralism.* Baltimore: Johns Hopkins University Press.

Tyner, K. (1993). Treading water: Media education in the United States. In R. Aparici (Ed.), *Projecto didactico queria Madrid.* Madrid, Spain: Ediciones de la Torre (extracted from Media Strategies Newsletter, San Francisco, CA).

U.S. Department of Health and Human Services. (1982). *Television and behavior: Ten years of scientific progress and implications for the eighties.* Washington, DC: Author.

Witkin, M. (1994). A defense using pop media in the middle school classroom. *English Journal 83*(1), 30–33.

WNET/Thirteen Education Department. (1972). *The television Criti-Kit: Teachers' guide.* New York: Author.

Wollen, P. (1969). *Signs and meaning in the cinema.* London: Socker & Warburg.

10 *Intermediality, Hypermedia, and Critical Media Literacy*

Roberta F. Hammett

Critical media literacy, like any form of critical literacy, aims at teaching students how to read texts critically. Students are generally challenged to examine representations, to ask whose voice is heard and whose is not, to question where power lies (who has it, who has not), to attempt to understand who loses or gains in situations and events, and to try to uncover the values and ideologies that underlie texts and discourses (Giroux & Simon, 1989; Considine & Haley, 1992; Hall, 1981, 1997; Masterman, 1985). Critical media literacy also aims at teaching students to act critically—to create oppositional and resistant readings, to intervene in and reinterpret texts, to create meaning and texts; in effect, to be empowered producers of knowledge.

Critical media literacy, informed by cultural studies, has a social justice perspective that acknowledges the constructedness of readers'/viewers' subjectivities and worldview and also education's democratic responsibility to help students to question and act against power and privilege (Buckingham, Grahame, & Sefton-Green, 1995; Luke & Bishop, 1994). In classrooms, students might accomplish critical acts through discussions and through writing and other ways of representing. Often, however, their audience is restricted to their classmates and teacher. Occasionally, students and teachers find ways to engage in "projects of possibility" (Simon, 1987) that reach an audience beyond their classroom and school. Computer and Internet technologies present such opportunities. Using hypermedia technology, students can produce and share texts that challenge dominant representations, create oppositional and resistant readings, and exercise authority over texts. Thus they, too, participate in the public pedagogy that is the media.

Hypermedia are in many ways the perfect intermedial (intertextual) tool. Links between computer windows that simultaneously present a mix of electronic texts—sounds, words, images, and movies—represent the connections the hypertext author makes between ideas, themes, patterns, and representations. The reader of the hypermedia (the term is an amalgam of "hypertext" and "multimedia") selects the links he or she will follow in the series of interlinked windows. For the purposes of this discussion, however—indeed, for the purposes of critical literacy—it is the connections between multiple texts that the authors, not the readers, make that are significant. These connections or juxtapositions reveal ideologies, question interpretations, generate meanings, expose assumptions, support or argue for beliefs, examine representations, and probe biases and stereotypes. Or rather, the authors who create the hypermedia accomplish these media-literate acts, as is illustrated by the examples described in this chapter. Also demonstrated is the importance of computer and hypermedia technology as a tool for producing knowledge and for constructing meanings, rather than as means for passively consuming prepackaged information that is often personally irrelevant and inevitably limited. It must also be noted that the empowered and critical use of this or any other technology can only be accomplished within a critical pedagogy—the tool itself does not promote critical literacy any more than a pen does.

This chapter describes the major enterprise in a media literacy course for secondary English education students, part of a three-course summer block that also included "Adolescent Literature" and "Literacy and Secondary English Teaching Methods I." Described here is the major common project or assignment of these courses. A supervising professor and two doctoral students were involved in the conception and instruction of this English/language arts education block and the hypermedia assignment. Further detailed descriptions of these and other experiences with hypermedia authoring by various groups of students in the Pennsylvania State University's English teacher education program can be found elsewhere (see Myers, Hammett, & McKillop, in press a, in press b).

The authoring of hypermedia involves a number of activities. In the hypermedia work described in this study, for example, the students learned and used various Macintosh-based software to digitize sound, images, and videos; to create original quicktime movies; and to set up the hypertext, for which they used the program *Storyspace* (Bolter, Joyce, Smith, & Bernstein, 1994).

In *Storyspace*, authors create windows or spaces that contain their texts. These texts are displayed in iconic form on a field so that the authors may organize them. Authors may decide to arrange all the spaces connected to one theme like Russian dolls, one within the next (although generally it is multiple windows or boxes within each of the windows). Thus, windows or spaces may present other spaces of hierarchically arranged text windows or may display linked text windows that contain their various digitized texts. The two very different hypermedia compositions created by two student groups who called themselves "Decisive" and "Indecisive" are described to illustrate. The group "decisive," for example, has two windows at the top level of their project: "Introduction" and "Credits." In the window "Introduction" are three more windows to represent their three main themes: "Hate and Propaganda," "Identity Formation," and "Nature versus Technology." In the "Identity Formation" window are 10 more windows, which represent all the text spaces related to that theme. Similarly, the "Nature versus Technology" window contains two windows ("Intro to Nature" and "Intro to Technology"), but each of these contains four more windows. This hierarchical arrangement is permitted though not mandated by *Storyspace*. There are multiple ways for authors to organize their text spaces and three ways for authors to view their arrangements: the chart view, which looks like a genealogy chart; the *Storyspace* view, which I have just described; and the outline view, which looks like a traditional essay outline. Generally the *reader* does not see any of these views. The authors usually decide that the project will open with a text window. Decisive's project, for example, opens with an introduction that includes a humorous quicktime movie about the group's difficulties creating its hypermedia, written instructions for viewing quicktime movies and navigating through the hypermedia, and a list of the four paths: Hate and Propaganda, Identity Formation, Nature versus Technology, and Credits. The reader can choose any of these four entries into the hypermedia. It is very important to note, however, that the authors can offer links in and out through all of these spaces and between all of these themes.

Intermediality is perhaps best realized in three features of these programs. First, *Storyspace* allows the author to set up the hypertext so that as the reader moves from space to space, the windows visited remain open unless purposely closed by the reader. The various texts are thus juxtaposed or displayed side by side. Second, each window may contain a number of "texts." Multiple windows, presented sequentially and/or simultaneously, may thus contain any combination of print text and digitized video, audio, and visual images. Windows may also be created so that sounds (voice, music, and songs) begin to play as they open and sized so that visual images and words may be displayed as well. The spaces in Indecisive's project, for example, tend to contain print text, two or three images, and two or three quicktime movies. (Other authors may choose to simplify windows with one or two kinds of digitized texts and more links between them.) Third, quicktime movies can be created and displayed, with or without other texts, in the windows. These quicktime movies present a series of images, with transitions, accompanied

210 / Roberta F. Hammett

by a sound track. Alternatively, quicktime movies may be created from digitized video to which a (different) soundtrack or commentary has been added.

The Classroom Experiences

Two groups of three students collaboratively created the hypermedia that explored the multiple texts and literacy concepts of all three courses. The students themselves were all native (White) Pennsylvanians. Most of them were in their early 20s; one was in her late 20s. Two of the young women had young children. All of them were undergraduates in their third or fourth year. Ahead of them was another "block" of education courses (nine credits) and a full semester preservice teaching experience. Some of them had discipline-specific credits (English courses) to take as well. The group Indecisive was made up of three young women, including the two young mothers; Decisive consisted of two young men and a young woman. None of them were close friends, although a couple of them, who were from the same area, knew one another before the courses began. The groups were created out of necessity and the members got to know one another as they worked together.

One of the precepts of the secondary English/language arts education program is summed up in the phrase "doing it, talking about it, teaching it"; for, as much as possible, students are given the opportunity to experience the activities that they, we hope, will incorporate in their pedagogy as teachers. The classroom experiences of the adolescent literature and secondary English methods courses thus included the reading of "text sets" (Short, 1992), the participation in reading and literature circles (Atwell, 1987; Daniels, 1994), and the use of writing workshops (Atwell, 1987; Graves, 1983). Each student selected two books from a long list of adolescent novels to read, and then as groups they explored common themes in the novels and shared the connections they could make among these multiple texts. They also read and discussed several common texts selected by the instructors: *Ceremony* by Leslie Silko (1977), and two films, *The Dollmaker* (Petrie, 1983/1990) and *Women in the Shadows* (Welsh, 1991). They also opted to see the recently released Disney film *Pocahontas* (Gabriel & Goldberg, 1995) as a group. Their discussions of the common and individual texts gave rise to many of the themes explored in their hypermedia—nature, prejudice, gender, identity, representation, and so on.

These themes and discussions reflected the interests and pedagogy of the instructors, who were influenced by both critical theory and feminism, and who thus introduced social justice issues into classes. The course texts were chosen because they explored issues of social justice, identity, class, prejudice, representation, and so on. Having decided to emphasize approaches to literature that incorporated critical literacy, reader response (Rosenblatt, 1978), interpretive communities (Fish, 1980), and intertextuality (Barthes, 1974; Morgan, 1985; Landow, 1992), the instructors selected a group of texts that facilitated such instruction. The representation of Native Americans (and Canadian First Nations through the National Film Board [NFB] films) was chosen as a focal point because of the literary quality of the Silko novel and because of the then-current media focus on Native Americans (as will be demonstrated in the descriptions of the hypermedia). *The Dollmaker* was used to raise issues relating to class.

Both of the instructors are White, middle-class women who represented North American perspectives. They were committed to a critical pedagogy that challenges learners to reevaluate ideas about self in relation to others, to rethink responsibilities as citizens in a democratic society, and to strive to bring about change. The hope was that the students would engage in critical praxis and would link theory (course readings) with practice (manipulating images, creating and recreating texts, and producing new messages and meanings) through the authoring of hypermedia. Both instructors wanted the students to assimilate concepts, extend understandings, and construct meanings during the course, but also wanted to demonstrate to these future teachers the kinds of experiences they might want to offer their students in their future classrooms.

In the media literacy classroom, the "doing it, talking about it, teaching it" approach was also being implemented. For example, as an introduction to the concept of representation, including self-representation, students brought in artifacts that they felt represented an important aspect of their identities. Favorite audio CDs (The Doors), photographs, and a china horse were among the texts selected by the students to represent aspects of themselves. As they showed these to one another and subsequently discussed them, they began to understand the nature of representations, the complexity of intersubjectivities, and the constructedness of identity. And they expanded their notions of what texts are to include audio CDs, photographs, and even stuffed animals. (Throughout this paper "reading" is broadly conceptualized to include viewing and listening and "text" similarly broadly defined to include videos, television shows, songs, people and institutions, print texts of various genres, and so on.)

Throughout the media literacy course, the students read and discussed several texts, which included: *Visual Messages* (Considine & Haley, 1992), *Television Culture* (Fiske, 1987), *Teaching the Visual Media* (Greenaway, 1991), *Rethinking Media Literacy* (McLaren, Hammer, Sholle, & Reilly, 1995), selections from the video series *Media and Society*

(Spotton, 1989), selections from the video series *Constructing Reality* (Adkin & Moscovitch, 1993), and several alternative television programs (*Torn Between Colors*, 1990; *Paper Tiger Television Looks at Alternative Media in the Bay Area*, n.d.; and *Renee Tajima Reads Asian Images in American Films*, n.d.). I asked such questions as, what is media literacy? Why teach media literacy? What do we mean by representation? Who represents whom in popular media? What signs and codes are involved in conveying representations? What do we mean by "hidden" meanings and ideologies? Are kids (and other viewers) vulnerable, innocent, enslaved, and in need of protection from media? Or are they empowered viewers who can (re)interpret, question, and disrupt media texts? How can we encourage such resistance? These class experiences, like those of the other courses in the summer block, laid the theoretical groundwork for the understandings of critical media literacy reflected in the hypermedia.

The Hypermedia Instruction

The three summer courses in this English education block were taught over a six-week period. Adolescent literature and English methods were scheduled in the morning and media literacy in the afternoon. Soon these schedules were all but abandoned for different ones. Long movies (*The Dollmaker* and *Pocahontas*) were screened in the evening. Although formal classes continued, computer lab time was arranged, and instruction in all the software involved in hypermedia authoring was provided, often on a need-to-know basis. One instructor led the way with this instruction, although both assisted the student groups as they carried out the hypermedia assignment. Students began to work all hours of the day and night on their hypermedia, reading assignments, and other course requirements. Instructors who incorporate computer technology in curricula often find that students will devote long hours to computer work. Such was the case here. Even though computer system crashes and mistakes often led to deleted files, the students persevered and recreated the projects.

For this assignment, the students were asked to collaboratively produce hypermedia to explore the themes they found important and interesting in the course texts. Some planning on paper of themes, connections, and ideas was encouraged, although computer work commenced almost immediately, with word processing and scanning images. Digitizing audio and video followed. As the students built their hypertexts, they made mental connections with other texts and were reminded of previous literacy experiences. Visits to libraries, video rental outlets, and even attics followed as students tracked down and brought in the texts they knew would help them to create experiences for readers and illustrate the concepts they wished to examine and explicate. Inestimable hours were spent by the students authoring these hypermedia.

Decisive

The group Decisive created a hypermedia project with a number of very different sections. The group scanned the book covers of the adolescent novels they read and provided brief introductions to the novels' themes, characters, and plots. They created a "Credits" space that included a hot, or linked, thumbnail version of the book cover image that, when selected, takes the reader to the introduction of that text. Other links lead the reader into the themes section of the hypermedia. To illustrate: The thumbnail picture of *Reflections of a Rock Lobster* (Fricke, 1981) in the credits window links to the introduction window of the novel. This window contains links that lead the reader back to the "List o' Texts" window or to the "Gays and Lesbians" window in the "Hate and Propaganda" section of the hypermedia. In that window, links are available to take the reader to various other sections of the hypermedia.

In addition to the section that introduces the adolescent novels the group read, there are three main themes sections: "Nature versus Technology," "Identity Formation," and "Hate and Propaganda," each with multiple windows that each display multiple texts. To continue following themes and spaces in the "Hate and Propaganda" section, the "Gays and Lesbians" space offers a link in the highlighted word "Nazis" that opens a window with a thumbnail of the book *Maus* (Spiegelman, 1973), a quicktime movie, and this print text written by the group:

> The Berlin Wall was torn down in 1989. The wall stood for twenty-eight years, separating the city of Berlin in half. It also represented the division between political ideologies: Democracy versus Communism. The wall served not only to separate the city, but also the world. The Berlin Wall was the embodiment of the Cold War.
>
> The world celebrated when the Wall was destroyed. However, the hate did not end with the demise of the Wall. In fact, a modern Nazi movement has begun. Once again, people were being chastised for their race, religion, and beliefs. Neo-Nazi propaganda has been spreading hate throughout the world.
>
> Will this rebirth lead to another Cold War: one that involves personal differences rather than politics?

Thus the destruction of the Berlin wall seems to stand for freedom, but this group dramatically suggested that it may also signify neo-Nazism by creating a quicktime movie that displays first a group of young men destroying the wall with sledge hammers and then another group of young men with fists raised in the Nazi salute. The transition adds the drama: Gradually the new picture emerges from the center of the previous one, like a hole being chipped out of the wall to reveal a new view plane. And that is the critical and transformative reinterpretation offered by these students—as they assume power over the texts and over the positions those texts offer.

What seems to be happening here is an illustration of the creation of what Fiske (1987), citing Hall (1981), calls a "negotiation." According to Fiske, the text represents a dominant or preferred reading (a dominant ideology and audience) but is open to an oppositional reading (minority position) that questions the most socially correct or accepted meaning. Discussing both reading positions may lead to a negotiated reading—an accommodation of both readings that the student creates. This, too, is a form of intermediality as defined by Semali and Watts Pailliotet (Chapter 1, this volume).

Juxtaposing texts also allows the hypermedia authors to pose questions to the reader and to shift the meanings of signs. Links between the introductions to the novel *Fahrenheit 451* (Bradbury, 1953/1993), in which book burning is condemned, lead to the Hendrix window, in which symbolic flag burning is approved. An image of the flag in the parade is shown to the background sound of Hendrix's rendition of the U.S. national anthem, introduced this way by the group:

> In August 1969, Jimi Hendrix appeared at the Woodstock Music and Art Fair in upstate New York. It was the biggest celebration of the counter culture, billed as "Three Days of Peace and Music." The high point of the set was the Star Spangled Banner, Hendrix's poignant deconstruction of the American national anthem. Delivered at the height of the Vietnam war and civil rights unrest, it was a compelling statement.

The group then goes on to shift the meaning of the flag, again by reporting:

> BOSTON APRIL 5, 1976
> America's Bicentennial: Old Glory flew from tall-ship masts and was sequined on disco queens. In Boston some 300 white protesters, mostly teenagers who didn't want blacks bused to their schools, waved flags outside City Hall. A young lawyer in a three-piece suit, ironically late to an affirmative-action meeting, dashed through the crowd. With the cry of 'There's a nigger, get him!' the protesters began to beat Ted Landsmark . . . the flag was transformed from a symbol of pride into a weapon of hate.
> —*Life*, May 1995

These images and statements, presented together in one window and in linked windows that can be then displayed simultaneously, are powerful examples of the group's use of the tool to represent their questions, explorations, and constructed meanings. In these and other windows, they reveal the underlying values and ideologies, which are presented as biases and stereotypes and, more subtly, as omissions and exclusions. As Giroux and Simon (1989) assert, the function of schools in general and media literacy in particular is to create citizens who are able to exercise power over their own lives, as well as the conditions of knowledge production and acquisition. These images suggest just such empowerment.

Another aspect of critical literacy and intermediality demonstrated in these hypermedia involves supplying the missing context (or providing a more complete context or contextualizing a representation) so that bias is revealed. Often in media, particularly advertisements, context is removed deliberately to present a bias (Fox, 1996). In their discussion of a Sony advertisement in their "Nature versus Technology" section, Decisive contextualizes the image and its promises:

> This advertisement asks you if your life is worth a Sony product. It pictures a Sony camcorder as a thrilling device [the camera is on a roller-coaster track], able to record all the exciting moments in your life. These ads target everyone, playing on the belief that a better lifestyle makes you a successful person. Has Sony's technology made your life better? Or is Sony saying that you need technology to remember your life? Either way, it is not saying much for the ability of a person to internalize and understand our precious memories.

This critical reading of the Sony ad demonstrates the group's ability to both decode the advertisement and to contextualize it, thus disrupting its effectiveness. It also conveys their perspective and publishes their voices in a way that is empowering.

Indecisive

The collaborative group Indecisive authored a hypermedia project it calls "What Shapes Us!" to explore the themes designated as "identity," "representation," and "spirituality." Several quicktime movies are focal points in their hypermedia. One of these, with the musical accompaniment of Peter Gabriel's song "Shaking the Tree," presents a series of images of Native American females and carefully chosen transitions. Beginning with the Disney animated portrait of Pocahontas, the images morph into representations of what the group called the "real" Pocahontas 1 and 2, representations of Pocahontas in Elizabethan fashions. Teacher questioning (I asked them what made these representations real) helped the students to recognize that these also were representations reflective of the culture and attitudes of their time. These images move through a carefully chosen transition to a fourth representation—really two representations, for the Pocahontas image is wiped away slowly from the upper left-hand corner to gradually reveal first a picture on the wall of two cherubic "Indian" children in feather headdresses and then finally a little Native American girl sitting on a couch. The five representations, juxtaposed as they are, question one another, as the written text points out:

> Representations are often assigned to us by the media and long held belief systems. These representations are sometimes accurate; often they're not. Dominant, mainstream representations are believed to be accurate. We want to juxtapose these long-standing portrayals with more truthful representations and explore their effects on identity.

Such oppositional or resistant readings (Trend, 1994) characterize critical literacy, and their inclusion in this hypermedia helps to create an experience for readers that may cause them to think about contradictory world views as they are "read" in lived experiences and texts. Not only do they suggest alternative points of view, but also they give expression to differing perspectives and voices.

Critical media literacy, as illustrated in this hypermedia, aims to expose ideologies that underlie texts/ideas and to present alternative ideologies:

> As we began our class sessions by talking about *Ceremony* we found that Tayo, a young Native American man, felt that he had caused a drought for his people on their reservation by praying against the rain in the jungles of Vietnam. Tayo begins a spiritual journey through pain, confusion and finally peace. Many people seem to be on spiritual journeys these days as they search for peace and meaning in a hectic and troubled world. Native Americans, like Tayo, are exploring the spiritual roots and ways of their tribal culture, wondering if what they have lost will help them find their identity.

To supplement their written text and its exploration of ideologies, the group created a quicktime movie that included a number of different religious images from a number of different religious and cultural traditions. As the images changed from shaman to child praying to drum circle to blond angel to Mary and so on, a song played:

> *Someone told me long ago*
> *There's a calm before the storm*
> *I know—It's been coming for some time. . . .*

By sequencing images in their hypermedia, Indecisive contested dominant ("traditional") and limited religious views and opened up possibilities for multiple views and representations of spirituality. The hypermedia become sites of struggle in which binarisms and dualities can be challenged and spaces for diversity can be opened up (Giroux, 1991).

Challenging the position assigned by texts or dislodging self as the object of the text's meaning and repositioning self as the subject (creator) of meanings (Freire & Macedo, 1987), thus opening up multiple possibilities for being and action, is another outcome of critical literacy supported by hypermedia authoring tools. In their representation section, the group Indecisive demonstrates this potentiality. Their introductory comment:

> The dominant culture, although we consider ourselves superior, is also affected by the representations of the media. White females have been portrayed in a negative way. Sex, violence, and superiority have been common themes among representations of women. It is difficult for women to detangle themselves from these representations and to form their own identity.

This commentary is followed by a quicktime movie that, beginning with an advertisement that shows several men looking at a woman whose skirt is hiked up by static, juxtaposes multiple images of women with the Madonna song in which the words "Express yourself, Don't repress yourself" are repeated over and over. The images are a variety of representations of position, age, ethnicity, and so on—some of which are problematic to the group (e.g., Disney's Belle [Trousdale & Wise, 1991] and Ariel [Clements & Muskert, 1989]) and some of which were not (such as the photograph the group saved as "Betty Hettler 101," the number signifying her age). This rewriting of female representation in the media created a space for the young women in the group—Jodi, Wanda, and Paula—to rewrite their identities as women (Gilbert & Taylor, 1991).

Finally, the group points out how the semiotic signs of eagle, flute music, and buffalo are used in media discourses to represent Native Americans and to construct their identity (not identities):

> The minority culture includes various groups. Some groups are merely excluded from being represented and others are badly distorted in their representations. One group that has been represented in various ways is the Native American culture. Movies such as "Dances with Wolves" and "Pocahontas" develop a certain stereotypical Native American image. This culture is no longer a group with many individual personalities. It has become a group with spiritual and environmental connections, etc. It has been said that a Native American film can not be called thus unless it has flute music, buffalo, and an eagle.

Thus the group analyzed and illustrated its sense of how media discourse (Hall, 1981) works to define Native American culture in limiting ways. But the group also attempted to describe other possibilities in its print text and digitized images and videos. The group comments:

> "The Indian in the Cupboard" is another movie portraying Native Americans. Native American consultant Jean Shenandoah was brought in during the production of the movie to assure accurate portrayal of the Iroquois nation. I am sure that other consultants were available for the other movies. Shenandoah consulted the elders of her tribe before making any decisions. Are these opinions breaking through dominant culture?

The group also include a digitized portion of a television program depicting a young Native American man and describing his vision. Although the group seems to approve this representation, it concludes this space by pointing out,

> Are these representations accurate? Perhaps we can no longer answer the question. Everyone has been so influenced by these representations that we may no longer know the truth.

These words provide an appropriate conclusion for the descriptions of the hypermedia. Using this tool, the students examined, compared, challenged, and replaced representations in such a way that any "truth" is decentered and readers, like the authors, are left with unanswered questions, debatable opinions, and beliefs still under construction.

Conclusion

These descriptions are only a few of the many spaces and the multiple texts presented in these two hypermedia, and my words and interpretations—my reading—narrow their potential meanings and readings greatly. As each different reader follows different paths through the hypermedia, bringing her or his own experiences and texts to bear on these texts, limitless readings are possible. The hypermedia authors are producers of texts and knowledge; so, too, are readers of hypermedia. I read from a White, middle-class, Canadian perspective. I read and interpreted as a critical feminist pedagogue, hopeful that my students were becoming more critical consumers and producers of texts.

Most media education programs (Ontario Ministry of Education, 1989) and media literacy critics (Buckingham et al., 1995) emphasize the importance of learning how to deconstruct media messages and representations, as well as construct them (Ferrington & Anderson-Inman, 1996). Hypermedia authoring, as illustrated in this chapter, provides opportunity for both foci. These students recognize that media messages have social and political consequences, that they have the power to shape attitudes and influence policy (Considine, 1995). They also demonstrate, however, that it is possible, as has been pointed out, to shift the power relations between text and viewer (Buckingham et al., 1995). Illustrated here and in the hypermedia is what Buckingham et al. describe as a "terrain on which young people actively construct and explore their own cultural identities, [one that] enable[s them] to investigate the relationships between who they 'are' and how they are represented" (p. 81). It is to be hoped that these young people, when they are teachers, will use computer technology and all the many other tools at their disposal to challenge their students to do the same.

Textbooks and curricula are not politically neutral any more than media are. Critical media literacy, as part of the programs for preservice and in-service teachers as well as curricula at all levels of schooling, can teach all students to work to reveal the politics of such texts, to ferret out their ideologies and underlying assumptions, and to provide additional perspectives. Asking whose voice is not heard and what representations are problematic is not enough; venues for broadcasting those different voices and alternative perspectives must be found or created and utilized. Intermediality and critical media literacy can encourage teachers, students, and all citizens to examine texts and issues related to politics and power, identity and representation, freedom and community, and justice and equality. In addition to this, critical media literacy can help students and teachers to envision and take action to achieve a more equitable society.

References

Adkin, D., & Moscovitch, A., directors. (1993). *Constructing reality: Exploring media issues in documentary* [film]. Montreal: National Film Board of Canada.

Atwell, N. (1987). *In the middle: Writing, reading, and learning with adolescents.* Portsmouth, NH: Boynton/Cook and Heinemann.

Barthes, R. (1974). *S/Z* (D. Allison, Trans.). Evanston, IL: Northwestern University Press.

Bolter, J. D., Joyce, M., Smith, J. B., & Bernstein, M. (1994). *Storyspace.* Watertown, MA: Eastgate Systems.

Bradbury, R. (1993). *Fahrenheit 451.* New York: Simon and Schuster. (Original work published 1953)

Buckingham, D., Grahame, J., & Sefton-Green, J. (1995). *Making media: Practical production and media education.* London: The English and Media Centre.

Clements, R., & Muskert, J., directors. (1989). *The little mermaid* [video]. Burbank, CA: Buena Vista Home Video.

Considine, D. (1995). An introduction to media literacy: The what, why and how to's. *Telemedium, The Journal of Media Literacy, 41*(2), i–vi.

Considine, D. M., & Haley, G. E. (1992). *Visual messages: Integrating imagery into instruction.* Englewood, CO: Teacher Ideas Press.

Daniels, H. (1994). *Literature circles: Voice and choice in the student-centered classroom.* York, MN: Stenhouse.

Ferrington, G., & Anderson-Inman, L. (1996). Media literacy: Upfront and on-line. *Journal of Adolescent and Adult Literacy, 39*(8), 666–670.

Fish, S. (1980). *Is there a text in this class? The authority of interpretive communities.* Cambridge, MA: Harvard University Press.

Fiske J. (1987). *Television culture.* London: Methuen.

Fox, R. (1996). *Harvesting minds: How TV commercials control kids.* Westport, CT: Praeger.

Freire, P., & Macedo, D. (1987). *Literacy: Reading the word and the world.* South Hadley, MA: Bergin and Garvey.

Fricke, A. (1981). *Reflections of a rock lobster.* Boston: Alyson.

Gabriel, M., & Goldberg, E., directors. (1995). *Pocahontas* [video]. Burbank, CA: Buena Vista Home Video.

Gilbert, P., & Taylor, S. (1991). *Fashioning the feminine: Girls, popular culture and schooling.* North Sydney, AU: Allen and Unwin.

Giroux, H. (1991). Postmodernism as border pedagogy: Redefining the boundaries of race and ethnicity. In H. Giroux, (Ed.). *Postmodernism, feminism, and cultural politics: Redrawing educational boundaries* (pp. 217–256). Albany: State University of New York Press.

Giroux, H., & Simon, R. (1989). *Popular culture, schooling, and everyday life.* New York: Bergin and Garvey.

Graves, D. (1983). *Writing: Teachers and children at work.* Portsmouth, NH: Heinemann Educational Books.

Greenaway, P. (1991). *Teaching the visual media.* Milton, Queensland: Jacaranda Press.

Hall, S. (1981). Notes on deconstructing "the popular." In R. Samuel, (Ed.), *People's history and socialist theory* (pp. 227–240). London: Routledge and Kegan Paul.

Hall, S., (Ed.). (1997). *Representation: Cultural representation and signifying practices.* Thousand Oaks, CA: Sage.

Landow, G. (1992). *Hypertext: The convergence of contemporary critical theory and technology.* Harcourt, Brace, Jovanovich.

Luke, C., & Bishop, G. (1994). Selling and reading gender and culture. *The Australian Journal of Language and Literacy, 17*(2), 109–119.

Masterman, L. (1985). *Teaching the media.* New York: Routledge.

McLaren, P., Hammer, R., Sholle, D., & Reilly, S. (Eds.). (1995). *Rethinking media literacy: A critical pedagogy of representation.* New York: Peter Lang.

Morgan, T. (1985). Is there an intertext in this text? Literary and interdisciplinary approaches to intertextuality. *American Journal of Semiotics, 3,* 1–40.

Myers, J., Hammett, R., & McKillop, A. M. (in press a). Connecting, exploring, and exposing self in hypermedia projects. In M. A. Gallego & S. Hollingsworth (Eds.), *Challenging a single standard: Perspectives on multiple literacies* (chapter 5).

Myers, J., Hammett, R., & McKillop, A. M. (in press b). Opportunities for critical literacy/pedagogy. In D. Reinking, M. McKenna, L. Labbo, & R. Kieffer (Eds.), *Literacy for the 21st Century: Technological Transformations in a Post-Typographic World.*

Ontario Ministry of Education. (1989). *Media literacy: Resource guide.* Toronto: Queen's Printer.

Paper Tiger Television looks at alternative media in the Bay Area. (n.d.). San Francisco: Deep Dish TV Network.

Petrie, D., director. (1990). *The dollmaker* [video]. Beverly Hills, CA: CBS/Fox. (Original production 1983)

Renee Tajima reads Asian images in American films. (n.d.). San Francisco: Deep Dish TV Network.

Rosenblatt, L. (1978). *The reader, the text, the poem: The transactional theory of the literary work.* Carbondale: Southern Illinois University Press.

Short, K. (1992). Making connections across literature and life. In K. Holland, R. Hungerford, & S. Ernst (Eds.), *Journeying: Children responding to literature* (pp. 284–301). Portsmouth, NH: Heinemann.

Silko, L. (1977). *Ceremony.* New York: Penguin Books.

Simon, R. (1987). Empowerment as a pedagogy of possibility. *Language Arts,* 64(4), 370–383.

Spiegelman, A. (1973). *Maus: A survivor's tale I: My father bleeds history.* New York: Pantheon Books.

Spotton, J., producer. (1989). *Media and society.* Montreal: National Film Board of Canada.

Torn between colors. (1990). San Francisco: Deep Dish TV Network.

Trend, D. (1994). Nationalities, pedagogy, and media. In H. Giroux & P. McLaren (Eds.), *Between borders: Pedagogy and the politics of cultural studies* (pp. 225–241). New York: Routledge.

Trousdale, G., & Wise, K., directors. (1991). *Beauty and the beast* [video]. Burbank, CA: Buena Vista Home Video.

Welsh, C., producer. (1991). *Women in the shadows.* Montreal: National Film Board of Canada.

Werner, W., & Nixon, K. (1990). *The media and public issues: A guide for teaching critical mindedness.* London, ON: Althouse Press.

11 *Afterword*

Douglas Kellner

We are in the midst of one of the most dramatic technological revolutions in history, which is changing everything from the ways that we work to the ways that we communicate with each other to how we spend our leisure time. The technological revolution centers on information technology. It is often interpreted as the beginnings of a knowledge society and therefore ascribes education a central role in every aspect of life. This Great Transformation poses tremendous challenges to educators to rethink their basic tenets, to deploy the new technologies in creative and productive ways, and to restructure schooling to respond productively and progressively to the technological and social changes that we are now experiencing.

At the same time that we are undergoing technological revolution, important demographic and sociopolitical changes are occurring in the United States and throughout the world. Emigration patterns have brought an explosion of new peoples into the United States in recent decades and the country is now more racially and ethnically diverse, more multicultural, than ever before. This creates the challenge of providing people from diverse races, classes, and backgrounds with the tools to enable them to succeed and participate in an ever more complex and changing world.

Cultural studies and critical pedagogy have begun to teach us to recognize the ubiquity of media culture in contemporary society, the growing trends toward multicultural education, and the need for media literacy that addresses the issue of multicultural and social difference.[1] There is expanding recognition that media representations help construct our images and understanding of the world and that education must meet the dual challenges of teaching media literacy in a multicultural society and sensitizing students and publics to the inequities and injustices of a society based on gender, race, and class inequalities and discrimination. A critical cultural studies sees the role of mainstream media in exacerbating or diminishing these inequalities and the ways that media education and the production of alternative media can help create a healthy multiculturalism of diversity and more robust democracy. Such critical perspectives can thus help us confront some of the most serious difficulties and problems that face us as educators and citizens as we move toward the 21st century.

In response to the challenge to develop new pedagogies for new technologies, progressive educators have been urging the creation of pedagogic practices that promote multicultural understanding, that empower students, and that reconstruct education. Postmodern theory has alerted us to the importance of perceiving and accepting differences and to the ways that hierarchies of difference are socially constructed. Since cultural differences are constructed in part at the level of meaning and signification through the mediation of media and cultural representations, students and citizens must become aware of the ways that culture constructs a system of social differences, with hierarchies, exclusions, defamations, and sometimes legitimation of the dominant social groups' power and domination. A critical multicultural education will thus make teachers and students sensitive to the politics of representation; to the way media audiences' images of race, gender, sexuality, and cultural differences are in part generated by cultural representations; to how negative stereotyping presents harmful cultural images; and to the need for a diversity of representations to capture the cultural wealth of contemporary postmodern and global societies.

The studies in *Intermediality* respond to the challenges of new technologies by offering a variety of critical pedagogies and approaches to the issue of learning to read, interpret, criticize, and evaluate a diversity of forms of media and culture. Since media culture is a form of pedagogy and socialization, we need to develop a critical pedagogy to counter media manipulation and socialization and to empower students and citizens in their interaction with powerful institutions and technologies. And since we are now entering into new forms of computer and multimedia culture, we need to develop even more complex and sophisticated literacies to participate in the new culture and society that is rapidly transforming previous forms of life.

The contributors to this volume propose developing practices of critical media literacy organized around the concept of intermediality. *Inter* refers to the need to develop pedagogy for a variety of forms of media culture ranging from television to film to the Internet and new multimedia. Inter suggests as well that we live within diverse and evolving forms of media culture and need to develop literacies to interact with types of media ranging from print media to visual media to multimedia to new virtual technologies.

Inter also refers to the interdisciplinary perspectives needed to understand new technologies and media, to teach new literacies, and to develop students and citizens able to interact in an ever more complex and changing world. New literacies must build on traditional print literacies and theories of language, but must also draw on visual literacy and forms of art education, as well as cultural studies that engage a wide range of media texts ranging from television to computer culture to develop critical media literacy. But with the explosion of computer and new technologies, we also need to develop new forms of computer and information literacy to survive the challenges of an infotainment society.

Moreover, and crucially, intermediality requires new forms of interaction between student and teacher. Following the insights of the late Paulo Freire that genuine education takes place in the interaction between students and teachers, that students can be teachers and teacher should be learners, and that thus the sphere of inter is crucial to an emancipatory and democratic pedagogy, the contributors propose new pedagogical practices that make students and teachers alike participants in new learning processes. Thus, new technologies require not only new literacies but new pedagogies to restructure education to make it more responsive to the growth of a high tech and multicultural society.

The contributors to *Intermediality* propose a variety of ways to relate theories of new literacy and pedagogy to practice, to actual hands-on classroom situations. They show how the concepts and methods of intermediality can be deployed in a variety of situations and contexts, ranging from elementary school to the university and beyond. In developing pedagogy to engage the diversity and variety of new forms of media in our always evolving media culture, it is important to note that there is no one pedagogy that can be employed as master method that will work in all contexts and situations. Rather new intermediality pedagogies are experimental and open ended, subject to revision and development as they are put to the test in the classroom and concrete pedagogical situations. The studies collected here are provisional reports from the field that sketch out some new perspectives and pedagogies, apply them in a variety of actual teaching situations, and report on their successes and limitations.

It is therefore up to teachers using these studies to develop their own pedagogies, to apply and refine the perspectives developed here, and to further contribute to generating theories and practice of new intermediality pedagogy. The conception of deep viewing, for instance, sketched out by Ann Watts Pailliotet and employed by several contributors to this volume, can be used in a variety of classroom situations and applied to a variety of different texts. For instance, Watts Pailliotet applies intermedial premises to analyses of print textbooks, the social context of classrooms, and the employment of videotapes of their own teaching; Macaul, Giles, and Rodenberg discuss their use of the method in analysis of TV/videos, newspapers, and web sites.

Intermediality thus contains a series of reports from the trenches in the battle to create new literacies, and if it is to be of use, teachers will apply its methods and concepts while developing new ones in the struggle to create education able to meet the challenges of the coming millennium. It is encouraging that a variety of progressive educators are attempting to develop new pedagogies and concepts for expanding and reconstructing education in an era of technological revolution and profound social and cultural change. The new multimedia environments require a diversity of multisemiotic and multimodal interaction, involving interfacing with words and print material and often images, graphics, and new audio and video material. The New London Group produces the concept of *multiliteracy* to describe the types of literacy required to engage new multimedia technology, and individuals involved in the University of California at Los Angeles and San Diego with the *la classa maqica* project are using new computer and multimedia technology to teach basic reading and writing skills, as well as new computer and multimedia literacy and forms of social cooperation and interaction.[2]

Finally, it is also important that students learn not only to decipher the meaning of media but to produce their own artifacts (see Hammer 1995). Genuine learning is both deconstructive and reconstructive, providing the tools both to dissect the multiple forms of our culture and to create new ones. Producing more active, participatory, and creative students will require transmission of skills and competencies needed to take part in new media and technological environments. The studies in this book contribute to the process of creating new literacies for a new era and thus make important contributions to democratizing and enhancing education for the future.

Notes

1. For my own views on critical media pedagogy and cultural studies, see Kellner, 1995a, 1995b. Other texts on media literacy and education include Masterman, 1985/1989; Schwoch, White, & Reilly, 1992; Giroux, 1994, 1996, 1997; Giroux & McLaren, 1994; Dines & Humez, 1995; Sholle & Denski, 1994; Carson & Friedman, 1995; McLaren, Hammer, Sholle, & Reilly, 1995; Luke 1997a, 1997b. See also the work of Barry Duncan and the Canadian Association for Media Literacy (web site: htUp://www.nald. ca/province/que/litcent/media.htm).

2. For other recent conceptions of multimedia literacy, see the discussions of literacies needed for reading hypertext in Burbules & Callister, 1996; the concept of multiliteracy in Luke, 1997a, 1997b; the concept of hyperreading in Bur-

bules, 1997, and the chapters in Snyder, 1997; and the conception of multiple literacies in Kellner, 1998.

References

Burbules, N. C. (1997). Rhetorics of the web: Hyperreading and critical literacy in page to screen. In I Snyder (Ed.), *Taking literacy into the electronic era* (pp. 102–122). New South Wales: Allen & Unwin.

Burbules, N. C., & Callister, T. (1996, Winter). Knowledge at the crossroads: Some alternative futures of hypertext learning environments. *Educational Theory, 46*(1), 23–50.

Carson, D., & Friedman, L. D. (1995). Shared differences. In L. D. Friedman (Ed.), *Shared differences: Multicultural media and practical pedagogy* (pp. vii–xix). Urbana and Chicago: University of Illinois Press.

Dines, G., & Humez, J. (Eds.). (1995). *Gender, race, and class in media.* Thousand Oaks, CA, and London: Sage.

Giroux, H. (1994). *Disturbing pleasures.* New York: Routledge.

Giroux, H. (1996). *Fugitive cultures: Race, violence, and youth.* New York: Routledge.

Giroux, H. (1997). *Channel surfing: Race talk and the destruction of today's youth.* New York: St. Martin's Press.

Giroux, H., & McLaren, P. (Eds.). (1994). *Between borders: Pedagogy and the politics of cultural studies.* New York: Routledge.

Hammer, R. (1995). Strategies for media literacy. In P. McLaren, R. Hammer, D. Sholle, & S. Reilly (Eds.), *Rethinking media literacy. A critical pedagogy of representation* (pp. 225–235). New York: Peter Lang.

Kellner, D. (1995a). *Media culture.* London and New York: Routledge.

Kellner, D. (1995b). Cultural studies, multiculturalism, and media culture. In G. Dines & J. Humez (Eds.), *Gender, race, and class in media* (pp. 5–17). Thousand Oaks, CA, and London: Sage.

Kellner, D. (1998). Multiple literacies and critical pedagogy in a multicultural society." *Educational Theory, 48*(1), 103–122.

Luke, C. (1997a). *Technological literacy.* Melbourne: Literacy Institute, Adult National Languages & Literacy Network.

Luke, C. (1997b). Media literacy and cultural studies. In S. Muspratt, A. Luke, & P. Freebody (Eds.), *Constructing critical literacies* (pp. 19–50). Cresskill, NY: Hampton Press.

Masterman, L. (1989) *Teaching the media.* London and New York: Routledge. (Original work published 1985)

McLaren, P., Hammer, R., Sholle, D., & Reilly, S. (1995) *Rethinking media literacy: A critical pedagogy of representation.* New York: Peter Lang.

Schwoch, J., White, M., & Reilly, S. (1992). *Media knowledge.* Albany: State University of New York Press.

Sholle, D., & Denski, S. (1994). *Media education and the (re)production of culture.* Westport, CT: Bergin & Garvey.

Snyder, I. (Ed.). (1997). *Taking literacy into the electronic era.* New South Wales: Allen & Unwin.

About the Editors and Contributors

Donna E. Alvermann is research professor of reading education at the University of Georgia, where she teaches courses in content literacy. Recently, she has begun to explore the potential of feminist pedagogy and poststructural theory for interpreting literacy practices in middle and high school classrooms through a book titled *Reconceptualizing the Literacies in Adolescents' Lives*. She is currently cochairing the International Reading Association's Adolescent Literacy Commission.

Jackie K. Giles is coordinator of Newspapers in Education (NIE) at the *Eau Claire Leader Telegram* and a former elementary classroom teacher. She coordinates and provides in-service programs to teachers and students in K–12 schools as well as undergraduates at the University of Wisconsin–Eau Claire. As a representative to the state NIE, she works with coordinators from across Wisconsin to design tabloids and materials for use in classrooms and summer NIE institutes. She works closely with the Eau Claire Area Reading Council on the annual 60 Minute Pledge to promote reading each spring. She serves as a member of the board of directors for the Literacy Volunteers of America–Chippewa Valley and assists with their annual Break for Books and Corporate Spelling Bee.

Roberta F. Hammett is assistant professor of education at Memorial University of Newfoundland, St. John's, Canada. She began research in hypermedia composing with Dr. Jamie Myers while she was a doctoral student at The Pennsylvania State University. She continues to pursue that research interest while teaching courses in literacy (in all its multiple forms) and secondary English education. Other recent publications include "Molesting Stephen King: Engaging in Alternative Reading Practices," with James Albright, in B. Powers, J. Wilhelm, and K. Chandler (Eds.), *Reading Stephen King: Student Choice, Censorship, and the Place of Popular Literature in the Canon* (National Council of Teachers of English, 1997), and "Critical Media Literacy: Content or Process?" with Ladislaus M. Semali, in *Review of Education/Pedagogy/Cultural Studies* (in press). Her World Wide Web address is http://www.ucs.mun.ca/~hammett/.

Douglas Kellner is George Kneller Chair in the Philosophy of Education at the University of California at Los Angeles and is author of many books on social theory, politics, history, and culture, including *Media Culture* and *The Postmodern Turn* (with Steven Best).

Carolyn Layzer is a doctoral candidate in the language and literacy education program at The Pennsylvania State University. She teaches methods courses in elementary language and literacy education. She has worked and traveled in Africa, Asia, and Latin America. Her research interests include critical multicultural education and media literacy.

Sherry L. Macaul is an associate professor at the University of Wisconsin–Eau Claire. She teaches undergraduate and graduate courses in literacy instruction and assessment in the Department of Curriculum and Instruction. She is a member of the Media Literacy Special Interest Group of the National Reading Conference and chair of the Wisconsin State Reading Association's Reading and Technology Committee. She served on the English Language Arts and Educational Technology Standards Task Forces for Wisconsin. She is a certified reading specialist who has taught in the elementary school and has served as a K–8 Reading Teacher. Her recent research interests are in the areas of literacy, technology, and assessment.

Jamie Myers is associate professor at The Pennsylvania State University. A literacy teacher since 1977, he has taught secondary school English and reading, university undergraduate and graduate courses in language across the curriculum, reading remediation, ethnographic research, and English education. His scholarship explores the social contexts of classroom literacy events with particular attention to the cognitive, social, and political consequences of culturally valued curricular designs.

Victoria J. Risko is professor of language and literacy and a research scientist in the Learning Technology Center at Peabody College of Vanderbilt University. She is the recipient of the 1991–1992 Association of Teacher Education's Distinguished Research Award for her research in multimedia and teacher education. She is a past president of the College Reading Association and currently serves as cochair of the Commission on Diverse Learners and Video and Literacy Special Interest Group of the International Reading Association. Her research interests focus on instructional applications of multimedia, teacher development, diverse learners, and text comprehension. Her e-mail address is Victoria.J.Risko@vanderbilt.edu

Rita K. Rodenberg is currently a Grade 4 classroom teacher and Grades 7 and 8 science teacher at Epiphany Lutheran School in Eau Claire, Wisconsin. She has taught elementary/middle school for 25 years. During many of her years in teaching, she has taught multiage classes. In addition, she has served as the principal for her school. She earned her master's degree in reading and is a certified reading teacher and reading specialist who has provided expertise and support to her school in the areas of reading/language arts. She possesses an avid interest in new technologies and promotes the integration of technology and literacy across the curriculum. She is an advocate of student directed learning.

Ladislaus M. Semali is associate professor of education at The Pennsylvania State University, where he teaches media literacy to preservice teachers. His work has been published in the *International Review of Education, Comparative Education Review,* and *Pennsylvania Educational Leadership.* Research interests explore the comparative study and analysis of media languages, contexts of cross-cultural literacy curricula, and critical media literacy across the curriculum. He authored *Postliteracy in the Age of Democracy* and coedited *What Is Indigenous Knowledge? Voices from the Academy.*

Ramón A. Serrano is associate professor at St. Cloud State University in Minnesota. He teaches courses in language and literacy, English as a second language, children in poverty, and action research. His research interests are working with children in poverty and gangs. His latest work is "Schooling for Gangs: When School Oppression Contributes to Gang Formation," a chapter he wrote for Carole Edelsky's book *Making Justice Our Project: Teachers Developing a Critical Whole Language Pedagogy.*.

Judy Sharkey is a doctoral candidate in the language and literacy education program at The Pennsylvania State University. She teaches secondary language arts methods courses and supervises preservice teachers. She taught English to speakers of other languages in Latin America, Asia, and the Middle East. Her research interests include critical media literacy and critical autobiography in teacher education.

Ann Watts Pailliotet is assistant professor of education at Whitman College in Walla Walla, Washington, where she teaches preservice literacy methods, critical reading of children's literature, and media literacy. She is a past winner of the National Reading Conference Student Outstanding Research Award and College Composition and Communication Citation for outstanding classroom practice. Her research interests include media literacy, preservice education, critical pedagogy, and values instruction with literature and popular texts.

Arnold S. Wolfe is associate professor of communication at Illinois State University. His teaching and research interests embrace mass media theory and criticism with an emphasis on feminist and semiotic approaches. He has published articles on film and television semiotics in *Critical Studies in Mass Communication,* on theories of the mass media audience in *Popular Music and Society,* and in the *Journal of Media Economics* on the effects of foreign takeovers on freedom of expression in the film industry. His deconstruction of ABC *Nightline* coverage of the space shuttle *Challenger* explosion was published by the International Visual Literacy Association in 1998. His work in this volume extends a line of research attempting to account for the enduring popularity of 1960s popular music. Referencing D. Crosby, he "almost cut [his] hair/It happened just the other day."

Index

All You Need Is Love (AYN), 115, 116
American Bandstand hypothesis, 116
Ang, Ien, 147
Arafat, Yasser, 13
Aronowitz, Stanley, 129, 185
Association of Supervision and Curriculum
   Development, 5
Australia, 150, 189
AYN. *See All You Need Is Love*

Bal, Mieke, 78, 196
Ball-Rokeach, Sandra, 101
Banks, James, 76–77
Barton, David, 55
Beach, Richard, 56
Britain, media literacy movement, 189
Broudy, Harry, 56
Brown, John, 131
Bruce, Bertram C., 55
Bryson, Norman, 78, 196
Buckingham, David, 189–190, 219

Calfee, Robert, 55
Calhoun, Craig, 17–18
Canada, media literacy movement,189
Canadian Association of Media Literacy, 187
Carey, James, 99
Carpenter, Thomas, 132
Castell, Suzanne de, 193
Center for Media Literacy, 162
Chambers, Iain, 100, 114
Chambers, Veronica, 151–152
Children's Television Act of 1990, 189
Classroom examples
   collaborative. *See* Collaborative learning
     group project
   critical media literacy. *See* Critical media
     literacy course in Japan
   critical viewing, 193–195
   deep viewing. *See* Deep viewing in the
     classroom
   hypermedia assignment. *See*
     Hypermedia assignment

   mass communication. *See* Collaborative
     learning group project
   multicultural education. *See*
     Multicultural education in the
     classroom
   textual analysis through feminist
     critique, 149–152
   video technology. *See* Video technology
Clinton, Bill, 13, 189
Close textual analysis, 108, 112–115
Collaborative learning group project
   assignments, 108–109, 112–113,
     117–118, 127–128
   close textual analysis of song, 113–115
   defense of method, 109–112
   fieldwork, 116–117
   origins, 97–101
   outcomes, 118–123
   overview, 102, 106–108
   syllabus, 101–102, 103–106
   See also Mass communication
Collins, Allan, 131
Consciousness, and the media, viii
Considine, David, 20, 38, 190–191
Cooperative learning. *See* Collaborative
   learning group project
Critical literacy
   as alternative pedagogy, 192–192
   and deep viewing, 196, 198–199
   and hypermedia, 217
   and multicultural education, 196–198
   teaching, 17–18
   See also Critical viewing
Critical media literacy
   as a bridge, 4, 7
   and hypermedia. *See* Hypermedia
   and the media, 201
   need to teach theory and practice,
     19–20
   origins, 15
   and politics of texts, 219
   and teaching, 118–119, 207, 224–226
   See also Intermediality

Critical media literacy course in Japan
  assignments and materials, 171–173,
    175–182
  background, 155–157
  description and objectives, 157–158
  initial classes, 158–162
  media are businesses theme, 164,
    180–182
  media construct reality theme, 162–163,
    174–177
  media present ideologies theme,
    164–165
  media use identifiable techniques
    theme, 163–164
  reflections on, 165–168
Critical theory, 17–18, 187–188. See also
    Critical literacy; Critical viewing
Critical viewing
  and classroom teaching, 184–185,
    187–188, 191
  critical stance on, 199–200
  overview, 183
  process rather than skill, 201–202
  and the social struggle over meaning,
    200–201
  theory and practice, 185–186, 195–196
  versus media criticism, 191–193
  See also Critical literacy
Culler, Jonathan, 119
Cultural images, and the media, 155–156,
    160–161
Cultural studies, 15, 118, 187–188, 207,
    223–224
Curricula
  and critical media literacy, 7–8
  of media literacy, 193–195
  problem–based, 132–133
  See also Classroom examples; Pedagogy;
    Teaching

Darling–Hammond, Linda, 129
Davies, John, 187
Davis, Francis, 184, 188
Deep viewing, viii–ix, 21, 31–32
  and critical literacy, 196, 198–199
  structure of analysis, 32–35
  and video technology, 133–134
Deep viewing in the classroom
  assignments for pre–service teachers,
    42–46
  future activities in middle school
    course, 71–72

overview of courses, 38–40, 53–54,
    57–58
recommended classroom procedure,
    35–38
student responses, 49–50, 58–67
results, 47–48, 67–68
teaching observation skills to
    pre–service teachers, 40–42
DeFleur, Melvin, 101
Dewey, John, 16
Dick, Eddie, 186
Discourse
  analysis, 31, 184–185
  of criticism, 183
  defined, 56
  gender as, 145
Diversity. See Multicultural education
Dobbs, Barbara, 10
Doll, William, 136
The Dollmaker, 210–212
Duguid, Paul, 131
Duncan, Barry, 19, 187
Dworkin, Andrea, 141, 143

Education
  lack of strategy for addressing
    media, 184
  media ignored in teacher, vii
  multicultural. See Multicultural
    education
  and technology, 9–10, 14–15, 223
  See also Multicultural education;
    Pedagogy; Teaching
Educational standards, and intermediality,
    68–71
Egan, Kieran, 193
Eisner, Elliot, 56
Emig, Janet, 7
Empson, William, 113
English as a foreign language, and media
    literacy, 155–156

Feminist theories
  critique of media in the classroom,
    149–152
  and literacy education, 147–149
  and media audiences, 145–147
  and media representation, 141, 142–143
  and transmission models of
    communication, 144–145
  See also Gender
Fennema, Elizabeth, 132

Firestone, Charles, 56
Fiske, John, 15, 214
Flood, James, 5, 21, 55
Foucault, Michel, 143–144, 145, 192
Frankfurt School, 15, 18, 191
Freire, Paulo, 185, 193, 225
Frith, Simon, 114
Fry, Donald L., 99
Fry, Virginia H., 99
Fuson, Karen, 132

Gee, James, 56, 167
Gender
    and the internet, 146–147
    and the media, 141–142, 144–145,
        147–149, 166–168
    See also Feminist theories
Gilbert, Pam, 150
Giles, Jackie, 133, 198, 226
Gilmore, Mikal, 100
Gilster, Paul, 56
Giroux, Henry, 15, 111, 122, 129, 184, 185,
    192, 193, 195, 199, 215
Goals 2000: Educate America Act, 189
Goodman, Jesse, 15, 188
Gore, Al, 22
Gramsci, Antonio, viii, 192
Greene, Maxine, 7
Gronbeck, Bruce, 114
Gross, Larry, 15
Grossberg, Lawrence, 113

Haley, Gail, 38, 190–191
Hall, Stuart, 183, 214
Hartley, John, 15
Heath, Shirley, 21, 55
Heyl, Barbara S., 101, 102, 106
Hibbard, Don, 114
Hiebert, James, 132
Hobbs, Renee, 56
Human, Piet, 132
Hypermedia, 207–208, 217
Hypermedia assignment
    classroom procedure, 212–213
    description of results, 213–218
    overview of hypermedia possibilities,
        208–210
    overview of students and instructors,
        210–212

Illinois State University, 98
Information literacy, 4–5

Intermedial
    classrooms, 17–18
    instruction, 9–11
    literacy, 5–6
    pedagogy, vii–viii
    state of being, 118, 123
Intermediality, 1–9, 54, 68, 224–225
    in the classroom, 2, 129, 225–226
    and critical examination of worldviews,
        13–14
    as critical stance, 185
    defined, vii, 57
    and educational standards, 68–71
    and empowerment, 198
    and hypermedia, 215
    and hypermedia assignment, 209–210
    negotiated reading, 214
    and video technology perspective,
        129–138
Internet, and gender, 146–147
Intertextuality defined, 56–57. See also
    Critical media literacy

Japan, 157. See also Critical media literacy
    course in Japan
Jensen, Klaus Bruhn, 110, 119

Kaleialoha, Carol, 114
Kelley, David, 152
Kellner, Doug, viii, 191, 195, 201
Kincheloe, Joe, 185
Kinzer, Chuck, 130

Labbo, Linda, 55
Langer, Judith, 151
Language instruction, and ideology, 169
Lankshear, Colin, 169, 192
Lapp, Diane, 5, 21, 55
Lawler, Moira, 169
Lennon, John, 100, 112, 115, 123
Leveranz, David, 7
Lewinsky, Monica, 13
Liston, Daniel, 16–17
Literacy
    changes in conception of, 22, 55–56
    club, 8
    education and feminist theories of
        media representation, 147–149
    information, 4–5
    intermedial, 5–6
    and mass media, 98, 188
    methodology courses, 130

powerful, 167
student definitions of, 50–51
See also Critical literacy; Critical media
literacy; Media literacy
Luke, Alan, 192, 193
Luke, Carmen, 147–148, 150
Lumby, Catherine, 141–143, 145, 146

Macaul, Sherry, 133, 135, 195, 198, 226
Macedo, Donaldo, 193
MacKinnon, Catherine, 141, 143, 146
Mailer, Norman, 98
Mass communication
impact on Baby Boomers, 100–101
teaching, 98–100
See also Collaborative learning group
project; Media
Masterman, Len, 189
McBeal, Ally, 149–152
McCartney, Paul, 99, 112, 113, 115, 123
McCracken, Grant, 115
McKenna, Michael, 55
McLaren, Peter, 15, 185, 192, 199
McLuhan, Marshall, 9
McMahon, Barrie, 10–11
Meaning
and media, 142–144
production of, 6, 78
social struggle over and critical viewing,
200–201
web of, 7
Media
and construction of
consciousness/worldview, viii, 12–14
and critical media literacy, 201
and cultural images, 155–156
"effects" literature, 98–99, 118–119
and gender, 141–142, 144–145, 147–152,
166–168
history in the U.S., 188
and meaning, 142–144
permeation of life, 6–7, 223–234
as public pedagogy, 207
See also Mass communication
Media criticism, definition of, 114
Mediacy, 22
Media literacy
as expansion on critical literacy, 18
and foreign language students, 155–156
and hypermedia, 214–215
key concept, 14
lack of common definition, 98

movement, 188–190
need for, vii, 200–201, 223–234
teaching in the classroom, 11, 193–195
Media representation, and feminist
theories, 141–149
Messaris, Paul, 55
Methodologies
case, 130
content analysis, 190–191
deep viewing. *See* Deep viewing
discourse analysis, 184–185
reception analysis, 119
semiotic analysis, 196–198
textual analysis. *See* Textual analysis
Morgan, Wendy, 150
Morrison, Jim, 120, 123
Multicultural education, 2, 75, 224
applications. *See* Multicultural
education in the classroom
and critical literacy, 196–198
definitions of, 76–77
need to include self and other, 91–95
student resistance to, 75–76
Multicultural education in the classroom
classmate reactions to students' work,
89–91
common perceptions among students,
80–81, 91–92
interviews with selected students, 81–89
overview of assignment, 78–79
theoretical limits and challenges,
92–95
Multimedia, 129–138
Multiple literacies (multiliteracies), 11, 21,
55, 226
Murray, Hanlie, 132
Myers, Jamie, 195–198

National Forum on Information Literacy,
5
National Leadership Conference on
Media Literacy, 188
National Reading Conference, 1, 19
Negotiation, 214
Nelson, Jenny, 115
Netanyahu, Benjamin, 13
Newman, S., 56
Newspapers in Education, 186
Nieto, Sonia, 76–77, 94

Olivier, Alwyn, 132
Olson, David, 55

Other, perception of in multicultural
        education, 91–95

Palmer, Edward, 184
Pauly, John, 99–100, 101, 110, 112, 113, 121,
        123
Pedagogy
    alternative, 192
    critical, 185, 195, 200–201, 223–226
    intermedial, vii-viii
    and video technology perspective,
        134–138
    See also Education; Teaching
Peirce, Charles, 78
Pennsylvania, absence of critical media
        viewing in classrooms, 188
Pennsylvania State University, 75, 193–195,
        208
Perception, of texts, 77–78
Pocahontas, 210, 212
Pocahontas, 215–216
Postman, Neil, 14–15
Practice, and theory, 8–9, 19–20, 185–186,
        195–196, 197
Prawat, Richard, 136

Quin, Robyn, 10–11

Rau, William, 101, 102, 106
Ravitch, Diane S., 77, 93
Reception analysis, 119
Recording industry, as vehicle of mass
        communication, 100–101
Reflective teaching, 16–17
Reinking, David, 55
Risko, Victoria, 12
Rodenberg, Rita, 133, 198, 226
Rosengren, Karl Erik, 119
Roush, Matt, 151–152

Saussure, Ferdinand de, 143
Scholes, Robert, 152
Self
    identity, viii
    need to perceive within multicultural
        context, 91–95
    and text, 217
Semali, Ladislaus, vii-ix, 99, 112–113, 120
Serrano, Ramón, 195–198
Shor, Ira, 192
Silko, Leslie, 210–211
Simon, Roger, 215

Situated learning, 131
Sleeter, Christine, 94
Smith, Frank, 8
Spender, Dale, 146, 147
Steinberg, Shirley, 185
Stereotypes, 161–162, 166
Stone, Oliver, 98, 116
Storyspace, 208–209
Surgeon General's Advisory Committee,
        report on television violence, 189
Suzuki, Bob, 77, 94
Swanson, Gillian, 159
Sweet, Anne, 56
Symbolic practices, 110

Tannenbaum, Percy, 114
Teachers
    progressive, 2, 184
    as transformative intellectuals, 15–16,
        192–193
Teaching
    anchored instruction, 131
    connecting home and school
        environment, 10–11, 14
    and critical media literacy, 192–193,
        207
    critical viewing, 183–185, 187–188
    and ideology in language instruction, 169
    and intermediality, 2, 17–18
    need for theory and practice, 19–20
    reflective, 16–17
    response–centered approaches,
        184–185, 186–187
    through collaborative learning
        experience, 118. *See also*
        Collaborative learning group
        project
    See also Classroom examples;
        Curricula; Education; Pedagogy
Technology and education, 9–10, 14–15,
        223. *See also* Video technology
Texts, 4–6
    explaining enduring popularity of,
        109–112, 115–116
    meaning in, 115–116
    perception of, 77–78
    and self, 217
    what counts as, 120
Textual analysis
    close, 108, 112–113
    deep viewing. *See* Deep viewing
    methods of critical viewing, 190–191

negotiated reading, 214
response–centered approaches, 19–20,
184–185, 186–187
Theory, and practice, 8–9, 19–20, 185–186,
195–196, 197
Tiedt, Iris, 77, 93
Tiedt, Pamela, 77, 93
Tyner, Kathleen, 7

U.S. Department of Labor, Secretary's
Commission on Achieving Necessary
Skills, 5
University of Georgia, 149
University of Wisconsin, Madison, 19

Vacca, Jo Anne, 38
Vacca, Richard, 38
Vande Berg, Leah, 114

Vanderbilt University, 130
Van Zoonen, Liesbet, 145
Video technology, 130–138. *See also*
Multimedia

Watts Pailliotet, Ann, vii-ix, 53, 57, 60, 99,
112–113, 120, 133, 135, 195–196, 198,
225
Wearne, Diane, 132
Web of meaning, 7
Weiner, Richard, 57
Wenner, Lawrence, 114
Williamson, Judith, 166–167
Willinsky, John, 55
Worldview, construction of, viii, 12–14
Worth, Sol, 15

Zeichner, Kenneth, 16–17